Functional Skills

Maths

Level 2

This pack contains course booklets for each area of the Level 2 Maths qualification. The booklets have study notes and clear examples matched to each learning objective, with lots of questions and helpful knowledge organisers.

We've also included a Mixed Practice booklet to test all the skills you'll need, with handy tips for answering trickier questions. Cracking!

Unlock your Online Edition (including Answers)

This pack includes a **free Online Edition** containing all **four Course Booklets** and **full answers**. To access these digital extras, just scan the QR code below or go to cgpbooks.co.uk/extras, then enter this code!

3646 7251 7608 6681

By the way, this code only works for one person. If somebody else has used this book before you, they might have already claimed the code.

P.S. Don't miss out on our Study & Test Practice and 10-Minute Tests!

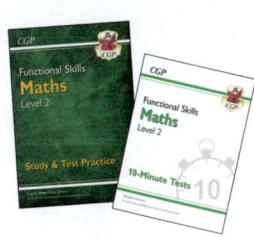

Fritz Jansen · Uta Streit · Angelika Fuchs

Schreiben lernen nach dem IntraActPlus-Konzept

auch für Förderschule und Legasthenie-Therapie

Heft 1

Fritz Jansen
IntraActPlus
Neuried, Deutschland

Uta Streit
IntraActPlus
Neuried, Deutschland

Angelika Fuchs
Jork, Deutschland

ISBN 978-3-662-71254-2

Die Deutsche Nationalbibliothek verzeichnet diese Publikation in der Deutschen Nationalbibliografie; detaillierte bibliografische Daten sind im Internet über ▶ https://portal.dnb.de abrufbar.

© Der/die Herausgeber bzw. der/die Autor(en), exklusiv lizenziert an Springer-Verlag GmbH, DE, ein Teil von Springer Nature 2025

Das Werk einschließlich aller seiner Teile ist urheberrechtlich geschützt. Jede Verwertung, die nicht ausdrücklich vom Urheberrechtsgesetz zugelassen ist, bedarf der vorherigen Zustimmung des Verlags. Das gilt insbesondere für Vervielfältigungen, Bearbeitungen, Mikroverfilmungen und die Einspeicherung und Verarbeitung in elektronischen Systemen.
Die Wiedergabe von allgemein beschreibenden Bezeichnungen, Marken, Unternehmensnamen etc. in diesem Werk bedeutet nicht, dass diese frei durch jede Person benutzt werden dürfen. Die Berechtigung zur Benutzung unterliegt, auch ohne gesonderten Hinweis hierzu, den Regeln des Markenrechts. Die Rechte des/der jeweiligen Zeicheninhaber*in sind zu beachten.
Der Verlag, die Autor*innen und die Herausgeber*innen gehen davon aus, dass die Angaben und Informationen in diesem Werk zum Zeitpunkt der Veröffentlichung vollständig und korrekt sind. Weder der Verlag noch die Autor*innen oder die Herausgeber*innen übernehmen, ausdrücklich oder implizit, Gewähr für den Inhalt des Werkes, etwaige Fehler oder Äußerungen. Der Verlag bleibt im Hinblick auf geografische Zuordnungen und Gebietsbezeichnungen in veröffentlichten Karten und Institutionsadressen neutral.

Gestaltung/Layout: Matthias Heid, Neuried

Planung/Lektorat: Joachim Coch
Springer ist ein Imprint der eingetragenen Gesellschaft Springer-Verlag GmbH, DE und ist ein Teil von Springer Nature.
Die Anschrift der Gesellschaft ist: Heidelberger Platz 3, 14197 Berlin, Germany

Wenn Sie dieses Produkt entsorgen, geben Sie das Papier bitte zum Recycling.

Einführung

Die Schablone

Dem Material liegt eine Schablone mit zwei Fenstern bei. Diese wird für alle Lernschritte benötigt, bei denen das Kind nicht abschreiben, sondern Gelerntes aus dem Gedächtnis wiedergeben soll.

Das kleinere Fenster ist für das Schreiben von Buchstaben gedacht (z. B. Seite 11), das größere Fenster für Silben (z. B. Seite 15) oder erste Wörter (z. B. Seite 79).

Die Schablone sollte immer so auf die Seite gelegt werden, dass die unbeschriftete Seite oben ist.

Beispiele für das Arbeiten mit der Schablone finden Sie auf unserer Homepage:

Videoanleitungen und Seiten zum Ausdrucken finden Sie hier:
www.intraact.plus/lesen-und-schreiben

Vorübungen zum Schreiben

Bevor erste Buchstaben geschrieben werden, gibt es einige Vorübungen (Seite 3–6). Mit diesen lernt das Kind, in Linien zu schreiben und übt sich in der Stifthaltung. Es braucht aber noch keine zusätzlichen Aufgaben wie das Wiedergeben von Buchstabenformen zu bewältigen. Für Kinder, die hier mehr Wiederholung benötigen, können diese Seiten erneut auf der oben angegebenen Internetseite heruntergeladen werden.

Die Lernschritte

Dieser Schreiblehrgang hat die gleiche Struktur wie „Lesen lernen nach dem IntraActPlus-Konzept", d. h. die Buchstaben werden in Blöcken zu je 4 Buchstaben eingeführt (AMLU, amlu, FSIN, fsin usw.).

Innerhalb jedes einzelnen Blocks werden immer die gleichen Lernschritte durchlaufen:

Lernschritt 1 Buchstaben nach Vorlage schreiben

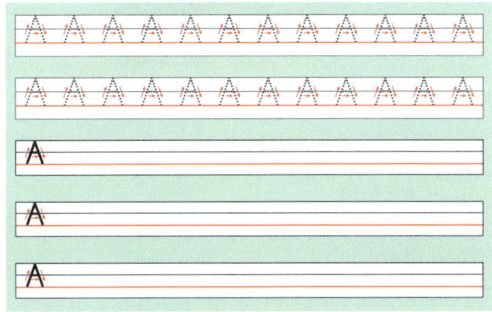

Beispiel: Seite 7

Lernschritt 2 Buchstaben aus dem Gedächtnis wiedergeben

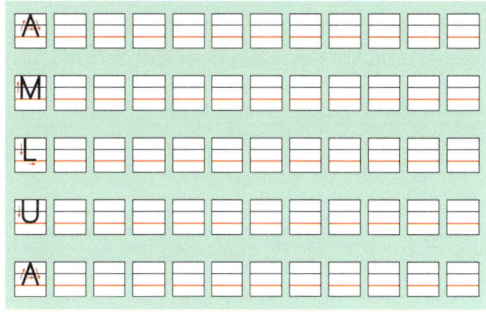

Beispiel: Seite 11

– Die Schablone wird so auf das Blatt gelegt, dass nur das erste Kästchen „A" zu sehen ist.
– Das Kind merkt sich den Buchstaben und den Schreibablauf.
– Die Schablone wird um ein Kästchen nach rechts weitergeschoben.
– Das Kind schreibt den Buchstaben in das leere Kästchen (in unserem Beispiel das „A").

Achtung
– Kinder, die sich mit der Handhabung der Schablone schwertun, arbeiten zunächst ohne diese.
– Achten Sie darauf, dass das Kind den Buchstaben mit dem richtigen Schreibablauf wiedergibt. Wenn es sich hierbei schwertut, ist es gut, wenn es noch einmal auf Lernschritt 1 zurückgeht.

Lernschritt 3 Buchstaben nach Diktat schreiben

Die Diktatübungen sind hellblau hinterlegt, damit sie schnell erkannt werden. Sie können mit der ganzen Klasse oder in der Einzelsituation durchgeführt werden. Sie sind aber auch für Partnerarbeit gut geeignet. Hier das Vorgehen in Partnerarbeit:

Kind 1 diktiert. Es hat die Seite mit der Diktatvorlage aufgeschlagen (z. B. Seite 13). Es hat die Schablone bereitgelegt. Die Schablone hilft ihm dabei, immer an der richtigen Stelle im Diktat zu sein.

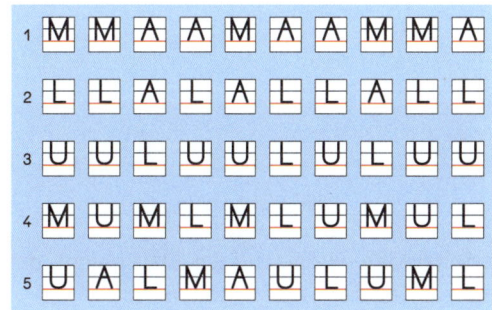

Beispiel: Diktatvorlage Seite 13

Kind 2 schreibt. Es hat die Folgeseite mit den leeren Kästchen aufgeschlagen (z. B. Seite 14). Wir empfehlen, dass auch dieses Kind mit der Schablone arbeitet, damit es die Buchstaben nicht aus dem vorangehenden Kästchen abschreibt, sondern aus dem Gedächtnis abruft.

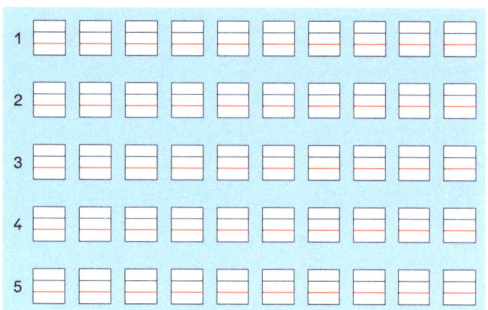

Beispiel: Diktat schreiben Seite 14

- Kind 1 legt die Schablone so auf das Blatt, dass nur das erste Kästchen zu sehen ist. Es diktiert den ersten Buchstaben.
- Kind 2 schreibt den diktierten Buchstaben in das erste Kästchen.
- Kind 1 kontrolliert, ob richtig geschrieben wurde.
- Fehler werden sofort korrigiert.
- In entsprechender Weise werden die weiteren Kästchen der jeweiligen Reihe bearbeitet.

Achtung
- Die Seite, in die das Kind schreibt, ist immer die Rückseite der Diktatseite. Dadurch wird Abschreiben verhindert.
- Wenn Sie in der Einzelsituation mit dem Kind üben, empfehlen wir, die Seite, auf die das Kind schreibt, von unserer Homepage herunterzuladen.

Lernschritt 4 Silben oder Wörter lesen und aus dem Gedächtnis schreiben

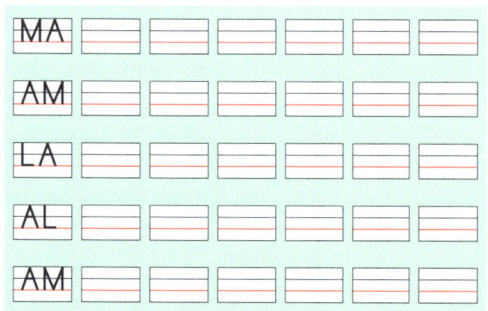

Beispiel: Seite 15

- Die Schablone wird so auf das Blatt gelegt, dass nur das erste Kästchen „MA" zu sehen ist.
- Das Kind liest die Silbe und merkt sie sich.
- Die Schablone wird weitergeschoben.
- Das Kind schreibt die Silbe aus dem Gedächtnis auf.

Lernschritt 5 Silben oder Wörter nach Diktat schreiben

Siehe Anleitung zu Lernschritt 3.

Achtung
Solange Kinder Buchstaben noch nicht mit Leichtigkeit zusammenziehen können, sollte diese Übung nicht in Partnerarbeit durchgeführt werden. Stattdessen kann die Lehrkraft der ganzen Klasse diktieren.

Stifthaltung

Achten Sie bei allen Schreibübungen auf eine „richtige" Stifthaltung. Unter „richtig" verstehen wir eine Stifthaltung, die es dem Kind ermöglicht, feine Bewegungen mit den Fingern und dem Handgelenk mit nur minimalem Kraftaufwand auszuführen. Eine „richtige" Stifthaltung braucht das Kind unbedingt, wenn es später einmal längere Texte schreiben möchte. Sie ist die Voraussetzung dafür, dass es nicht zu unnötigen Verspannungen in der Schulter und im ganzen Körper kommt.

Auch Fehler können automatisieren. Wenn ein Kind häufig mit falscher Stifthaltung schreibt, automatisiert es die falsche Haltung. Je länger mit einer fehlerhaften Haltung geübt wird, desto schwieriger ist es, sich diese später wieder abzugewöhnen. So wird der Stift richtig in die Hand genommen:

Der Stift wird auf den Mittelfinger gelegt.

Zeigefinger und Daumen halten den Stift.

Damit das Kind sich auf die Stifthaltung gut konzentrieren kann, ist wichtig,
- immer nur kurz zu üben (anfangs nicht länger als 5–10 Minuten),
- möglichst täglich zu üben.

Manche Kinder benötigen mehr Wiederholung. Es kann sein, dass für sie die Seiten in den Übungsheften nicht ausreichen. Für diese Kinder gibt es Kopiervorlagen der einzelnen Seitentypen zum Ausdrucken hier online:
www.intraact.plus/lesen-und-schreiben

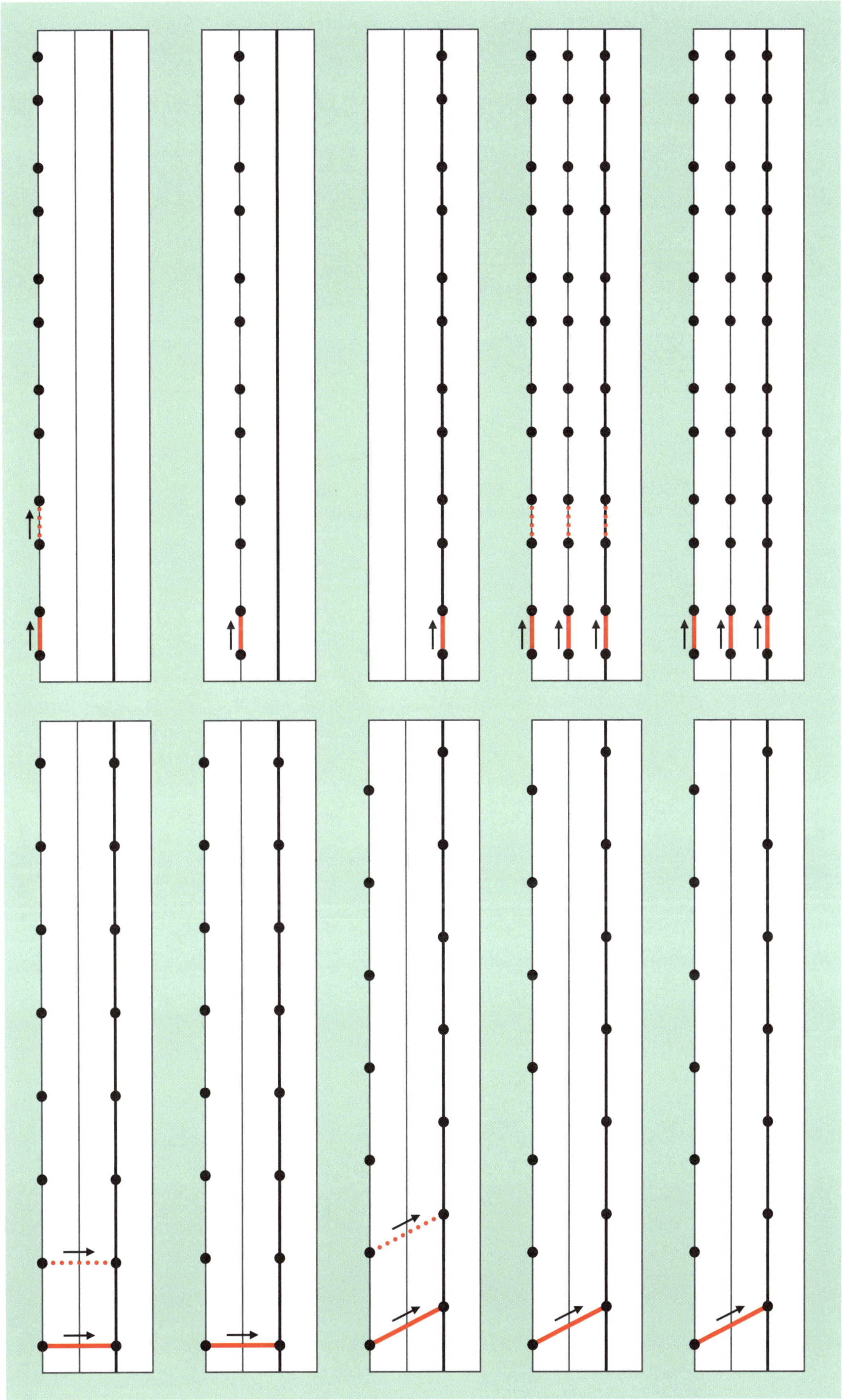

Vorübungen

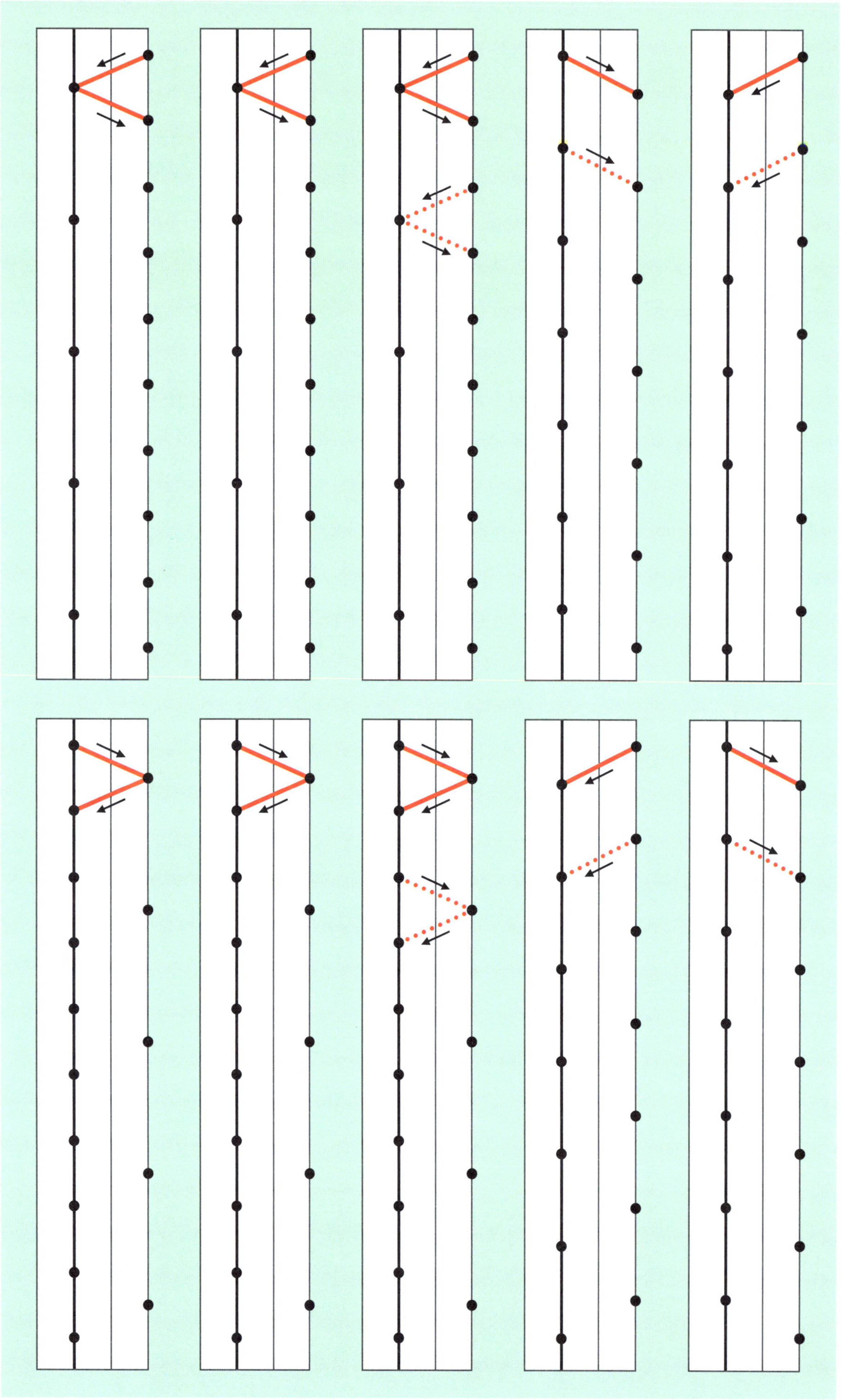

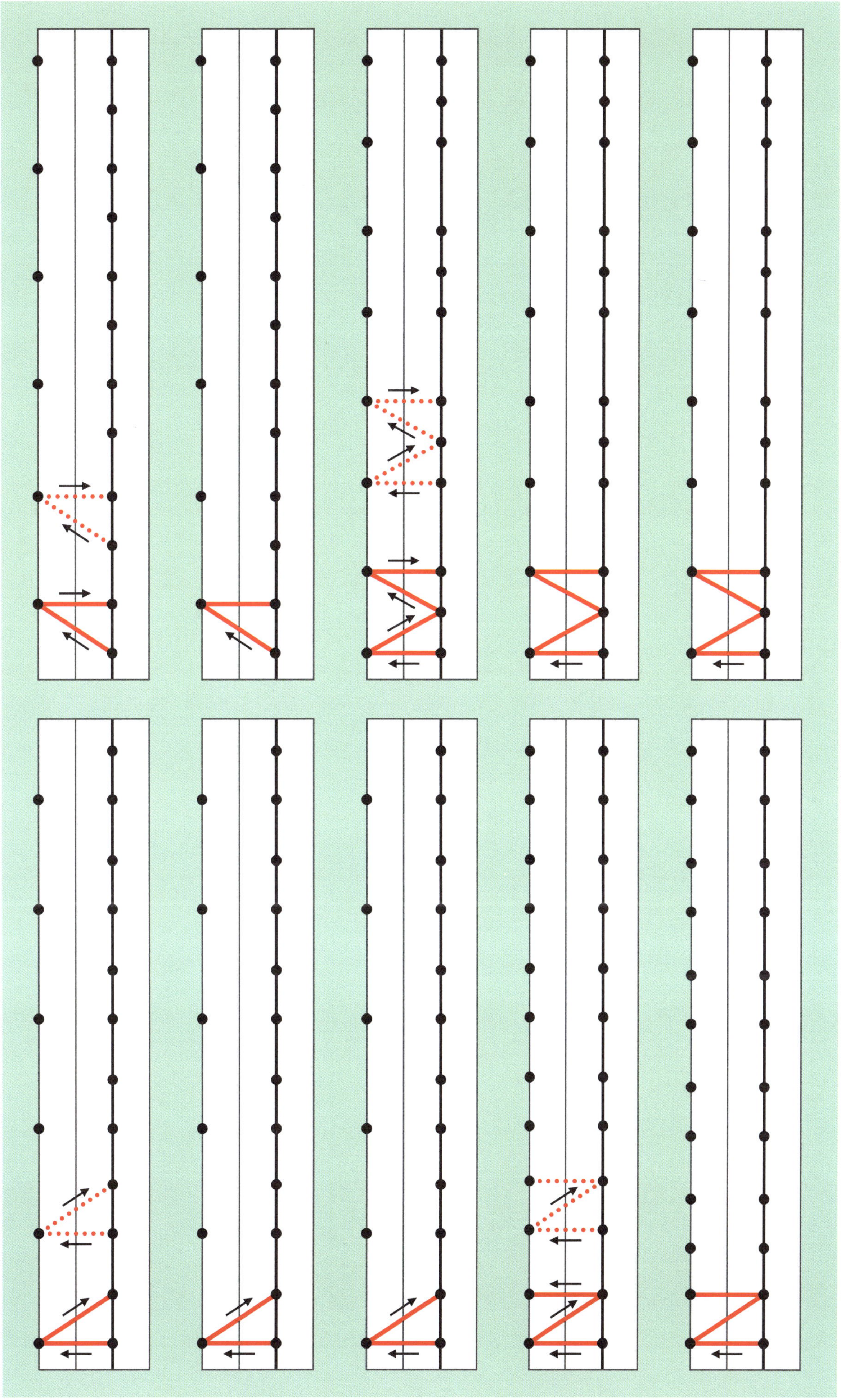

Vorübungen

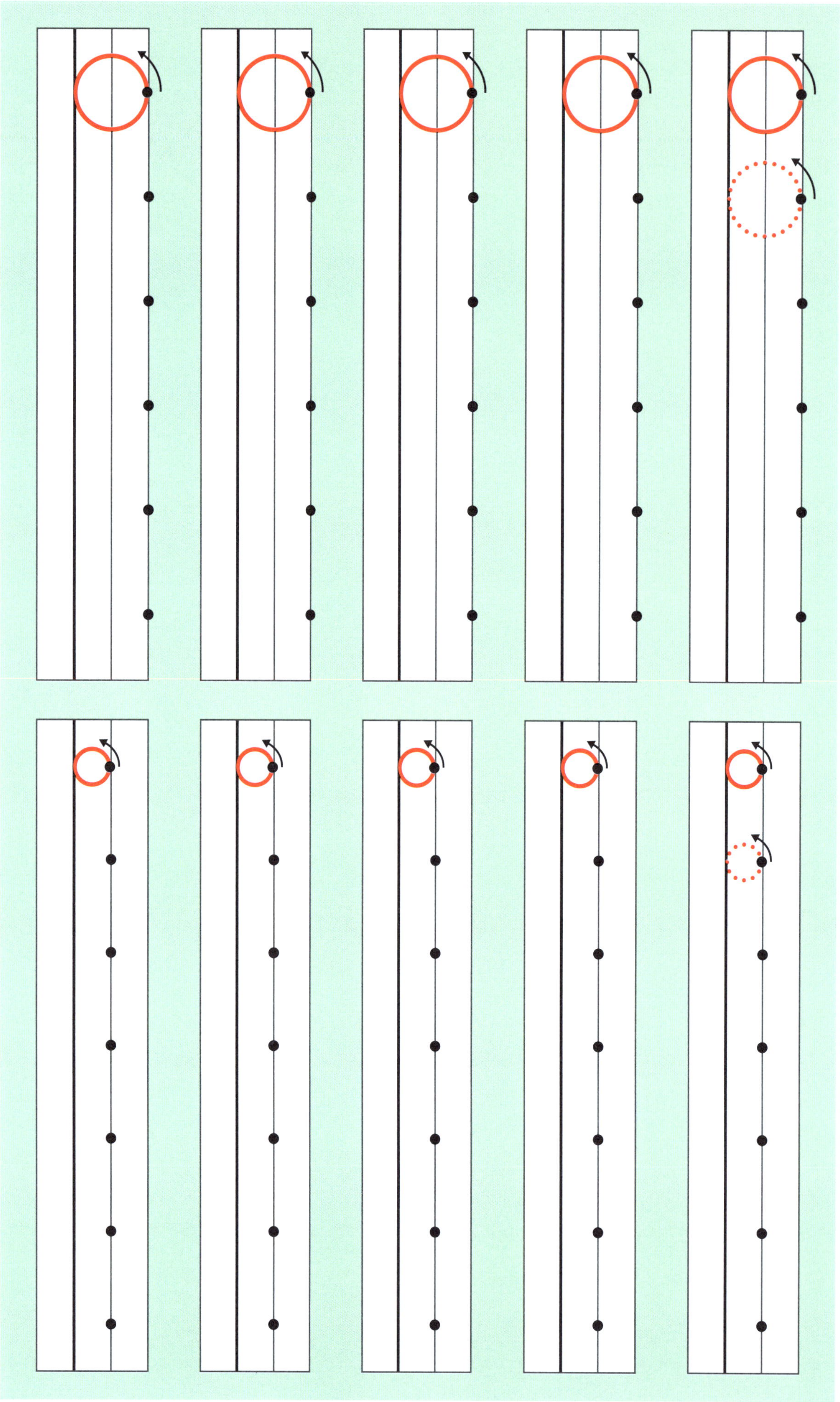

Vorübungen

Buchstaben schreiben

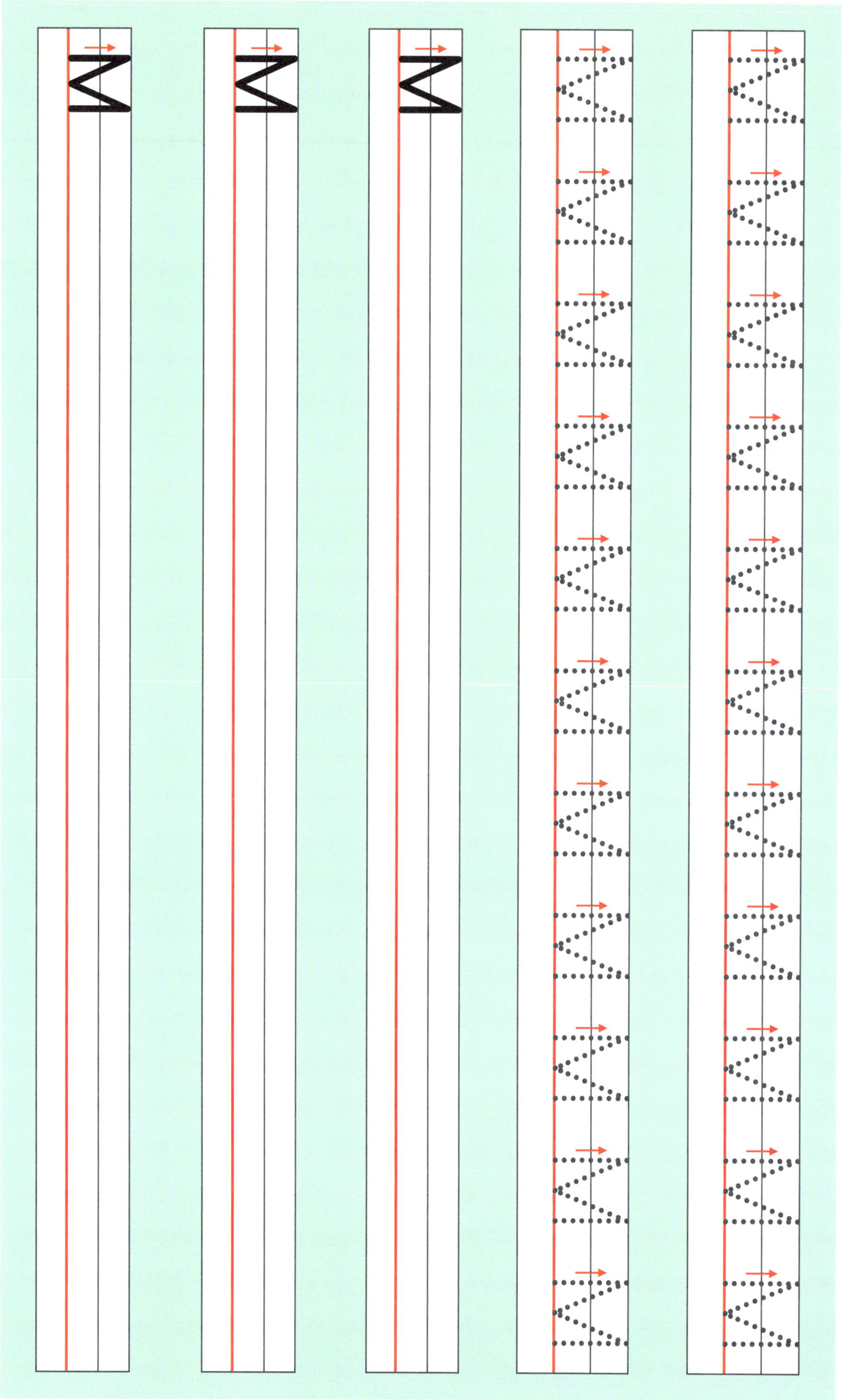

Buchstaben schreiben

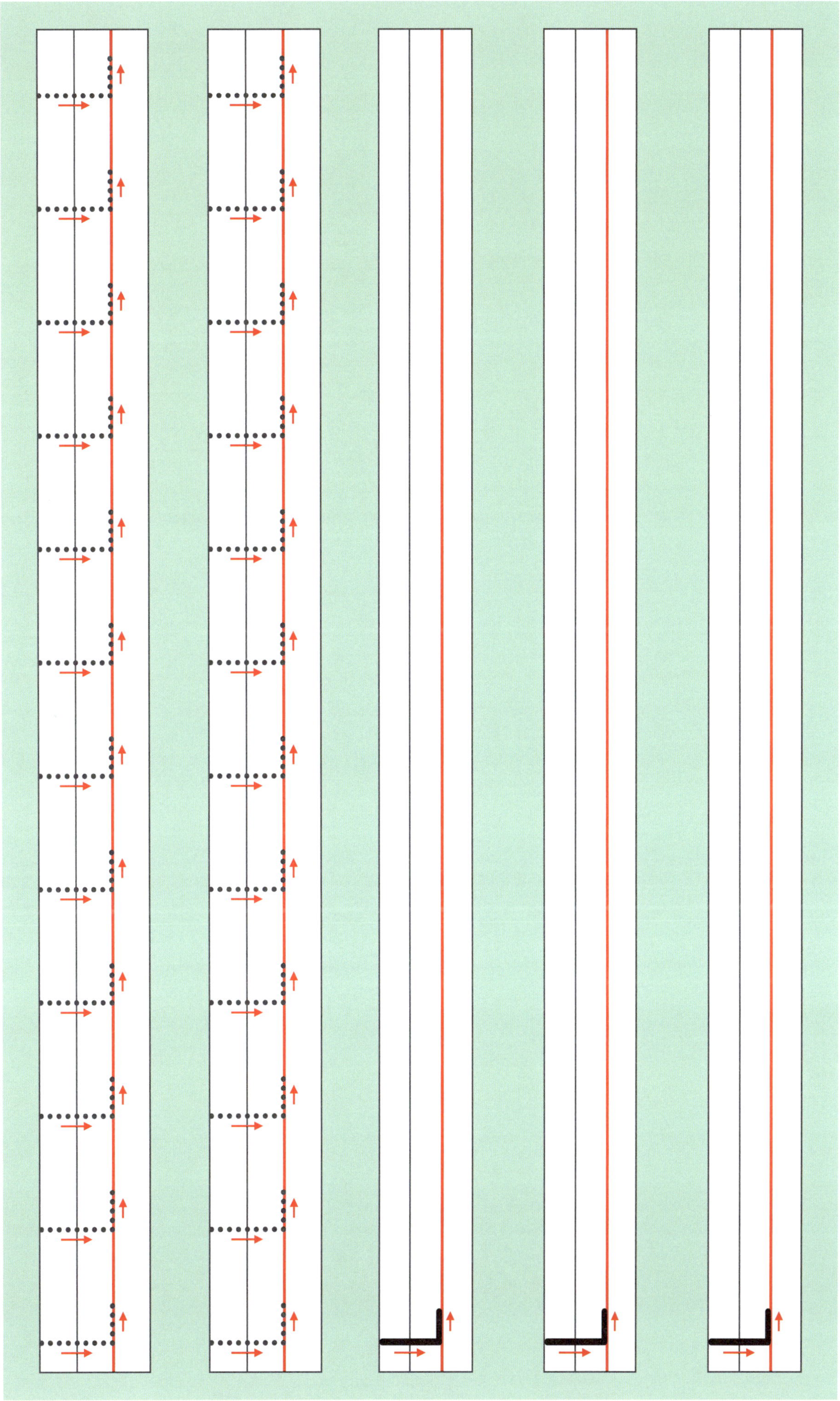

Buchstaben schreiben

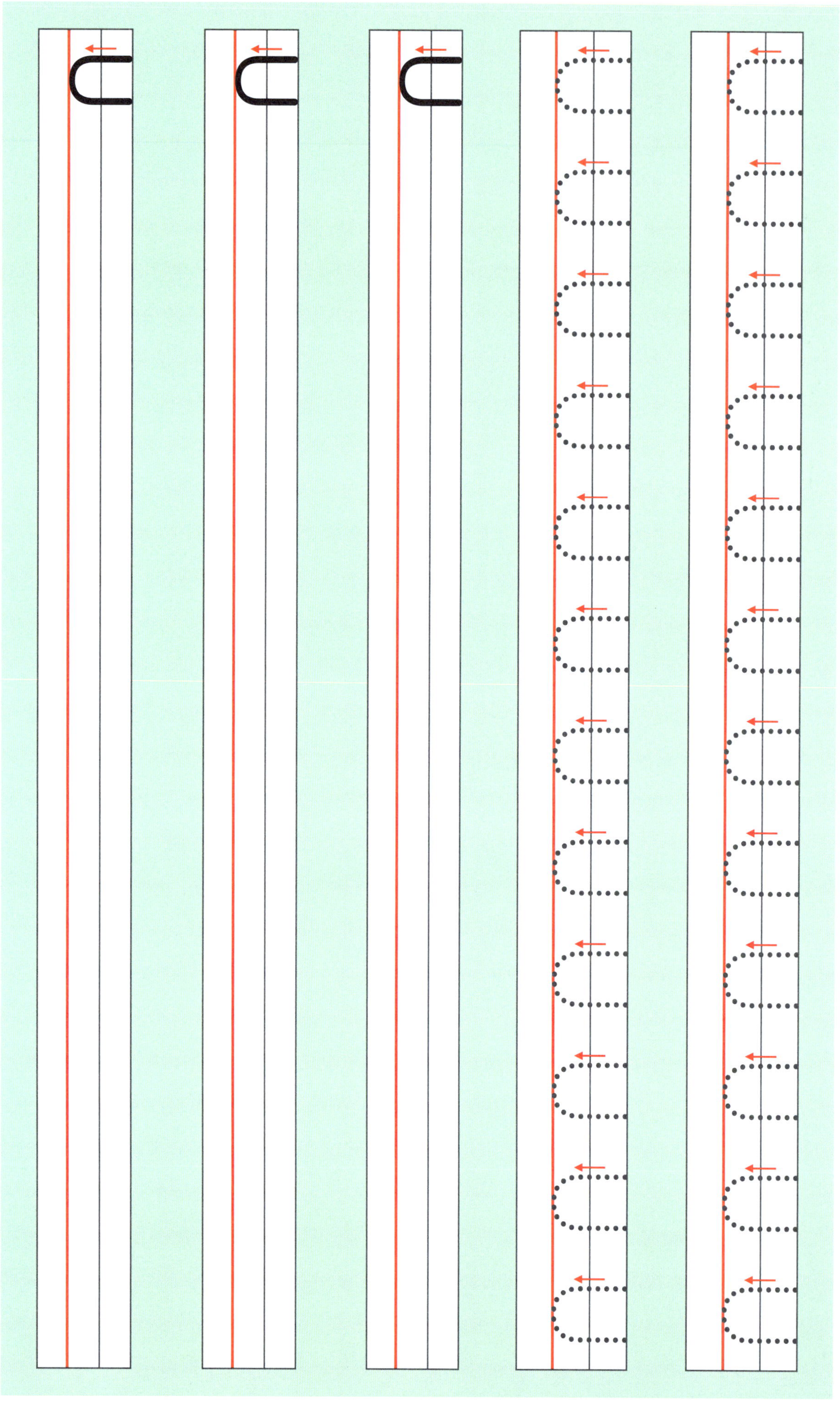

Buchstaben schreiben

lesen • abdecken • schreiben

A M L U A

M A M L U

lesen · abdecken · schreiben

Diktat vorlesen · prüfen

1	M	M	A	M	A	M	A	A	A
2	L	L	A	L	L	A	L	L	L
3	U	U	L	U	U	U	U	L	U
4	M	U	M	L	M	L	M	U	L
5	U	M	A	L	U	L	U	M	L

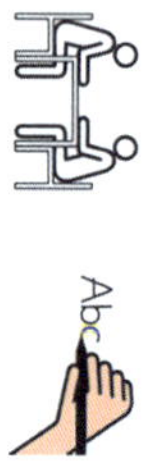

lesen · abdecken · schreiben

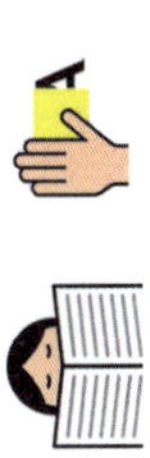

MA AM LA AL AM

| LU | UL | MU | UM | UL |

Diktat vorlesen · prüfen

1	MA	AM	AM	AM	MA
2	MU	MU	MU	MA	MU
3	LA	LA	AL	AL	LA
4	LU	MA	MU	LA	MU
5	AM	AL	UL	UM	AM

Diktat schreiben

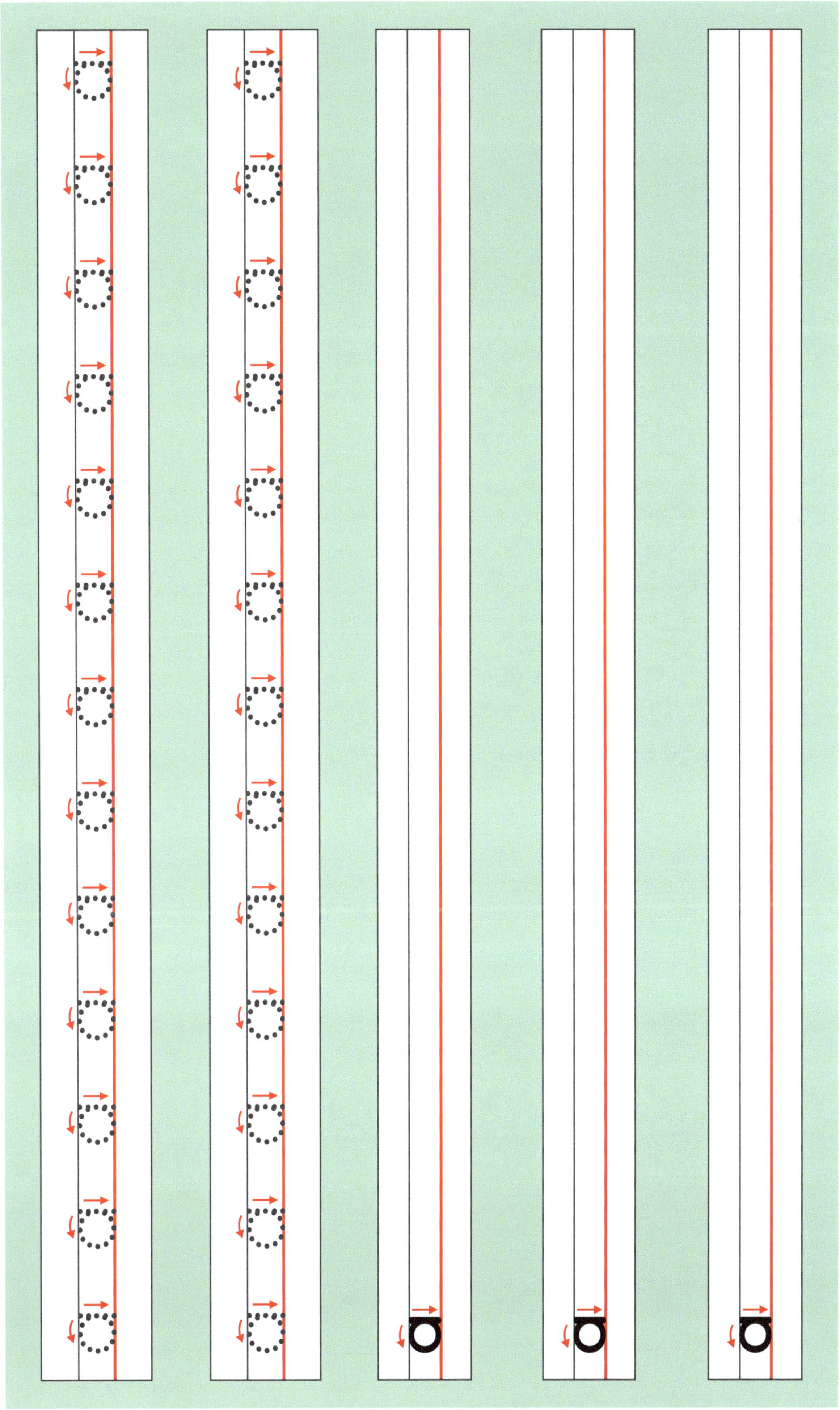

Buchstaben schreiben

Buchstaben schreiben

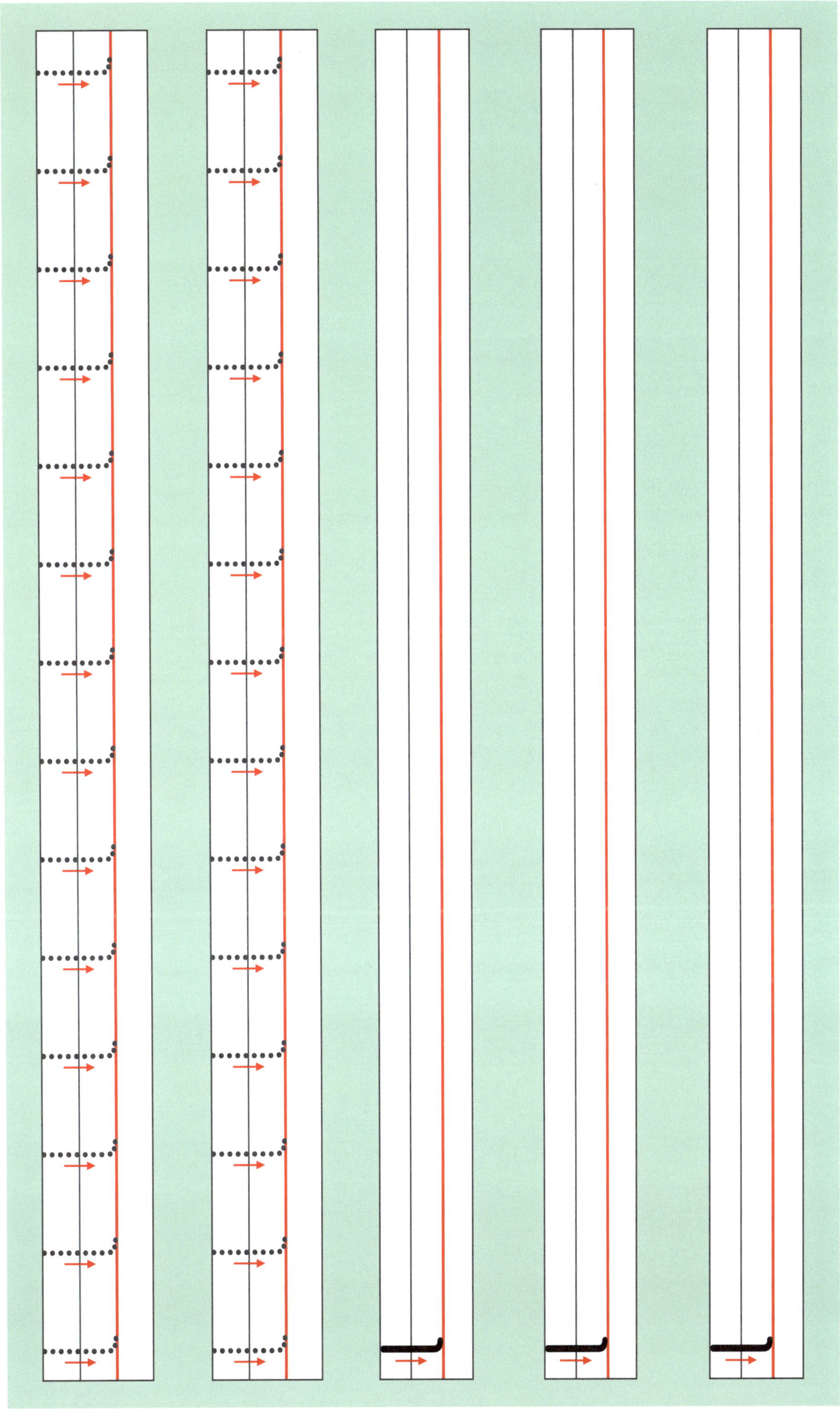

Buchstaben schreiben

21

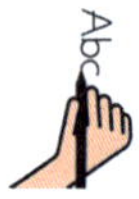

lesen · abdecken · schreiben

a w a j u

lesen · abdecken · schreiben

Diktat vorlesen • prüfen

1	a	m	m	a	a	m	a	m	m
2	t	t	a	t	t	t	a	t	t
3	u	u	t	u	t	u	t	u	u
4	t	u	m	u	t	m	m	u	m
5	t	m	u	t	u	a	m	a	u

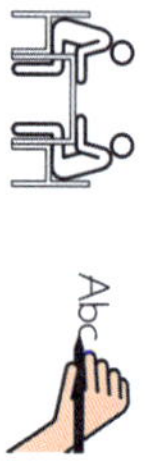

Diktat schreiben

1

2

3

4

5

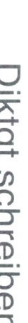

lesen • abdecken • schreiben

ma

am

la

al

am

F. Jansen, U. Streit, A. Fuchs, *Schreiben lernen nach dem IntraActPlus-Konzept*

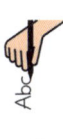

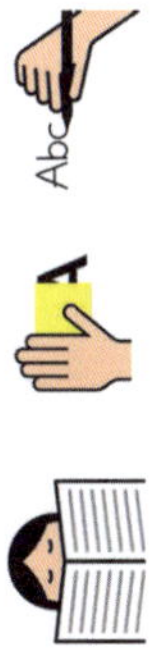

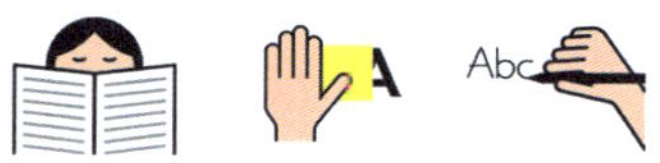

am um mu ul lu

lesen · abdecken · schreiben

Diktat vorlesen · prüfen

1	ma	ma	am	ma	am
2	mu	ma	mu	mu	ma
3	ta	ta	at	mu	at
4	lu	ma	mu	ta	lu
5	am	at	ut	um	um

Diktat schreiben

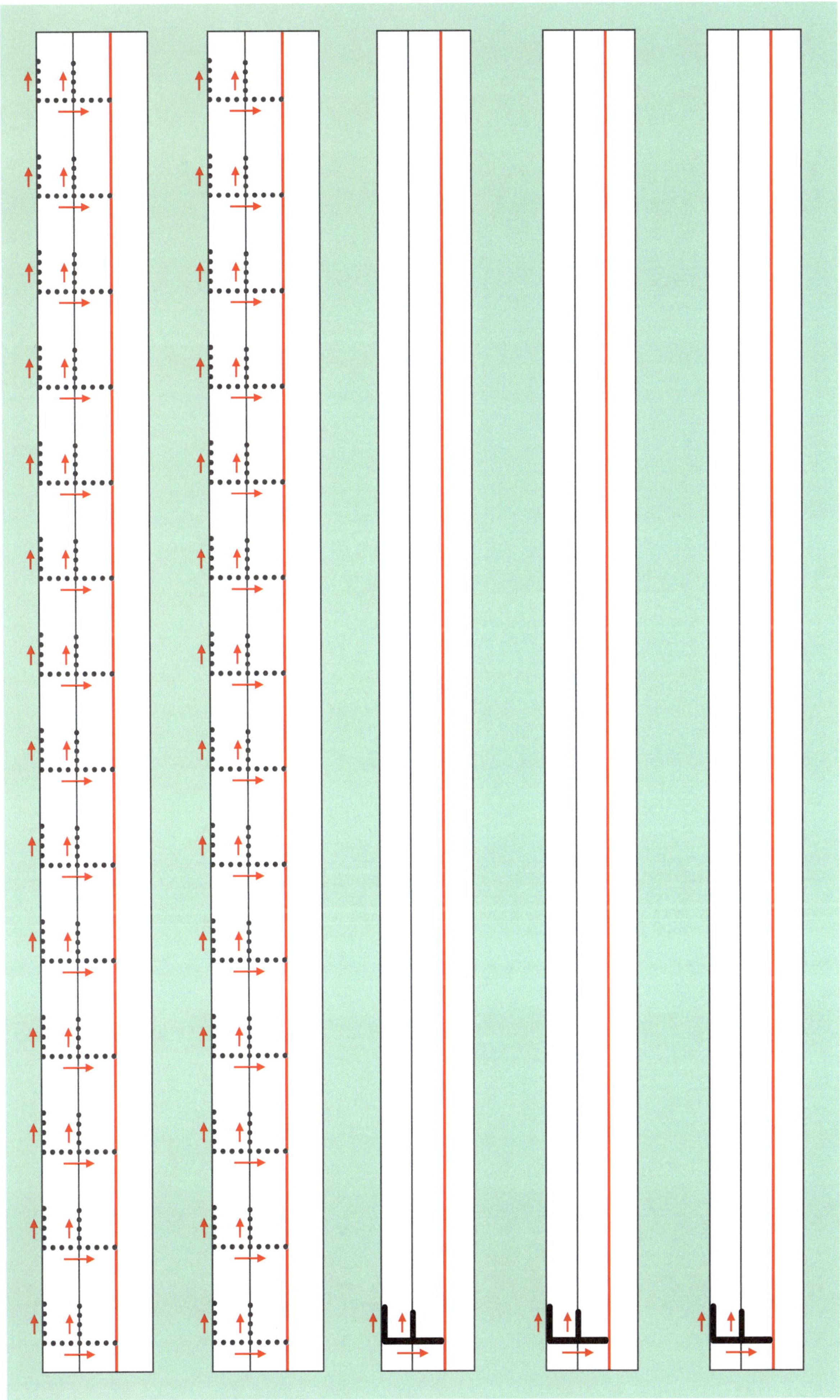

Buchstaben schreiben

Buchstaben schreiben

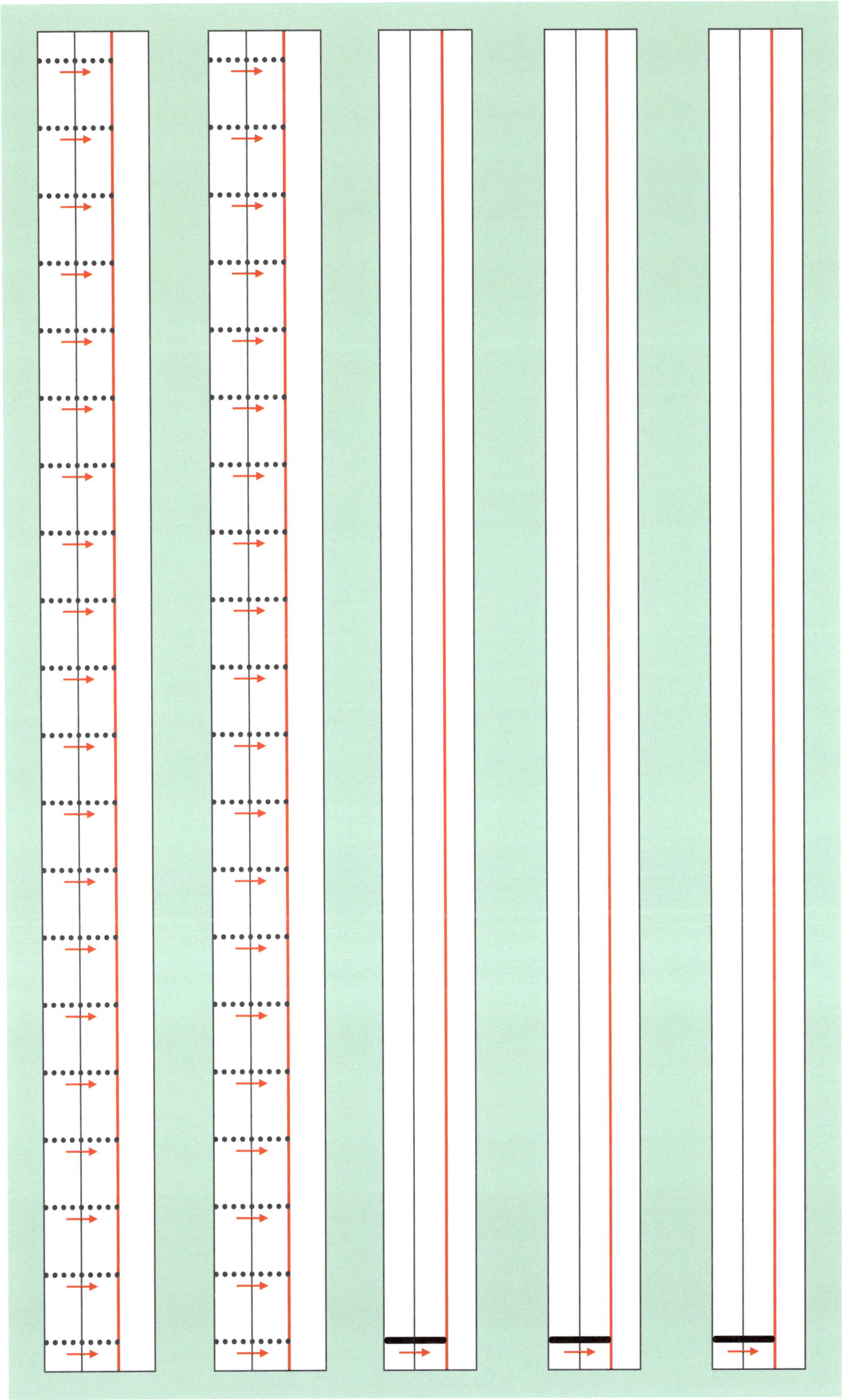

Buchstaben schreiben

33

Buchstaben schreiben

34

lesen · abdecken · schreiben

F S I N S

F N S F N

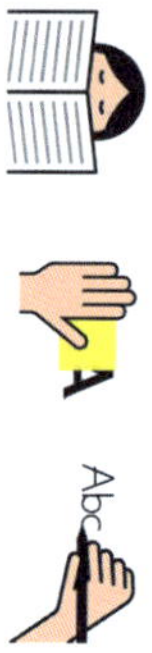

lesen · abdecken · schreiben

Diktat vorlesen · prüfen

1	F	F	S	F	S	F	S	F	S
2	I	S	S	S	S	S	I	S	S
3	N	N	N	I	N	N	I	N	N
4	F	N	F	N	F	N	F	F	I
5	S	N	S	S	N	S	S	F	S

Diktat schreiben

lesen · abdecken · schreiben

FI
IF
SU
US
AS

IN	AN	NA	UN	NU

lesen · abdecken · schreiben

Diktat vorlesen · prüfen

1	FI	FU	FA	FI	FA	FU
2	SU	US	SU	US	AS	IS
3	NA	NU	NU	NA	NU	NA
4	NA	MA	MA	NA	NA	MA
5	NI	MI	MI	NI	NI	MI

Diktat schreiben

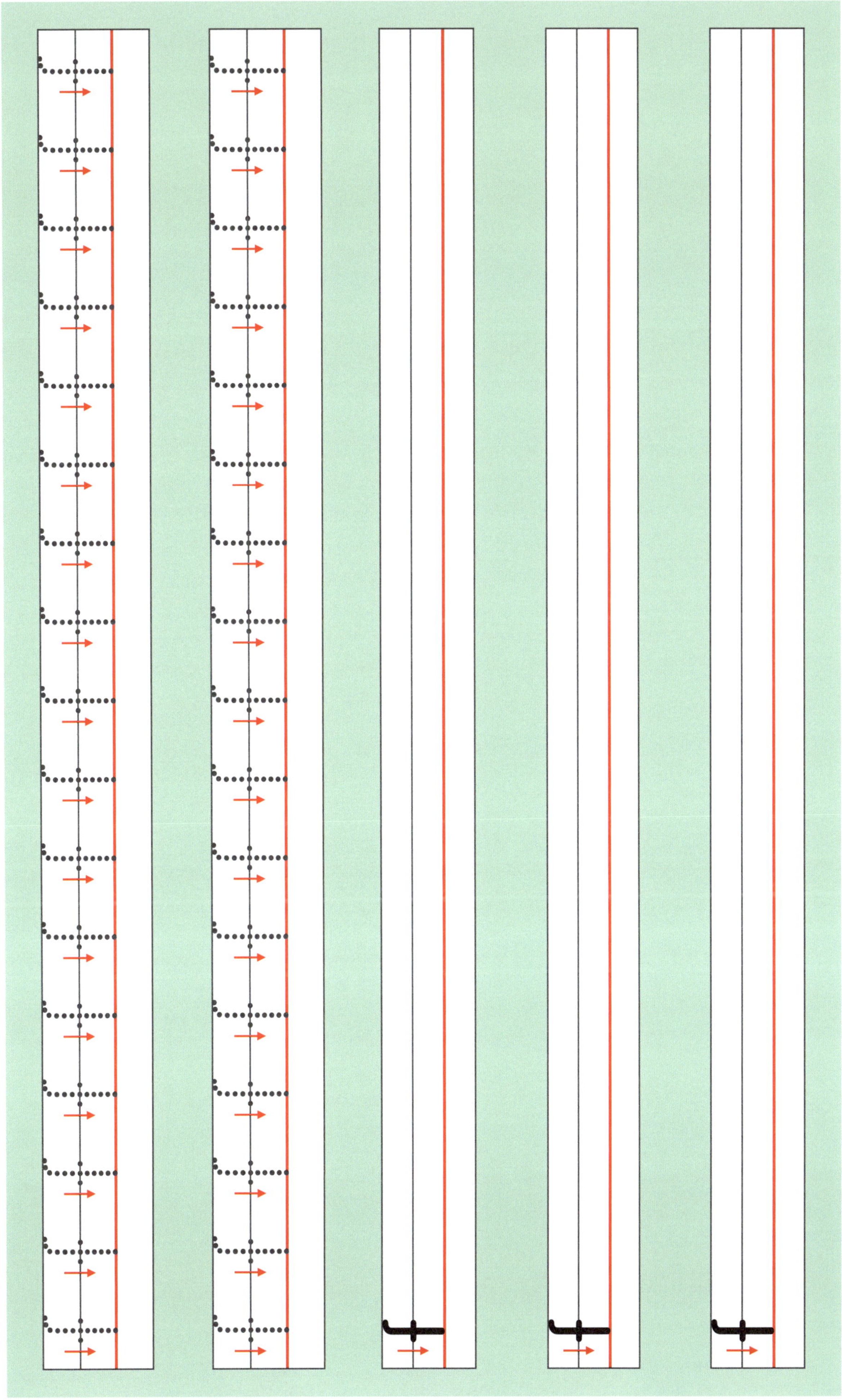

Buchstaben schreiben

Buchstaben schreiben

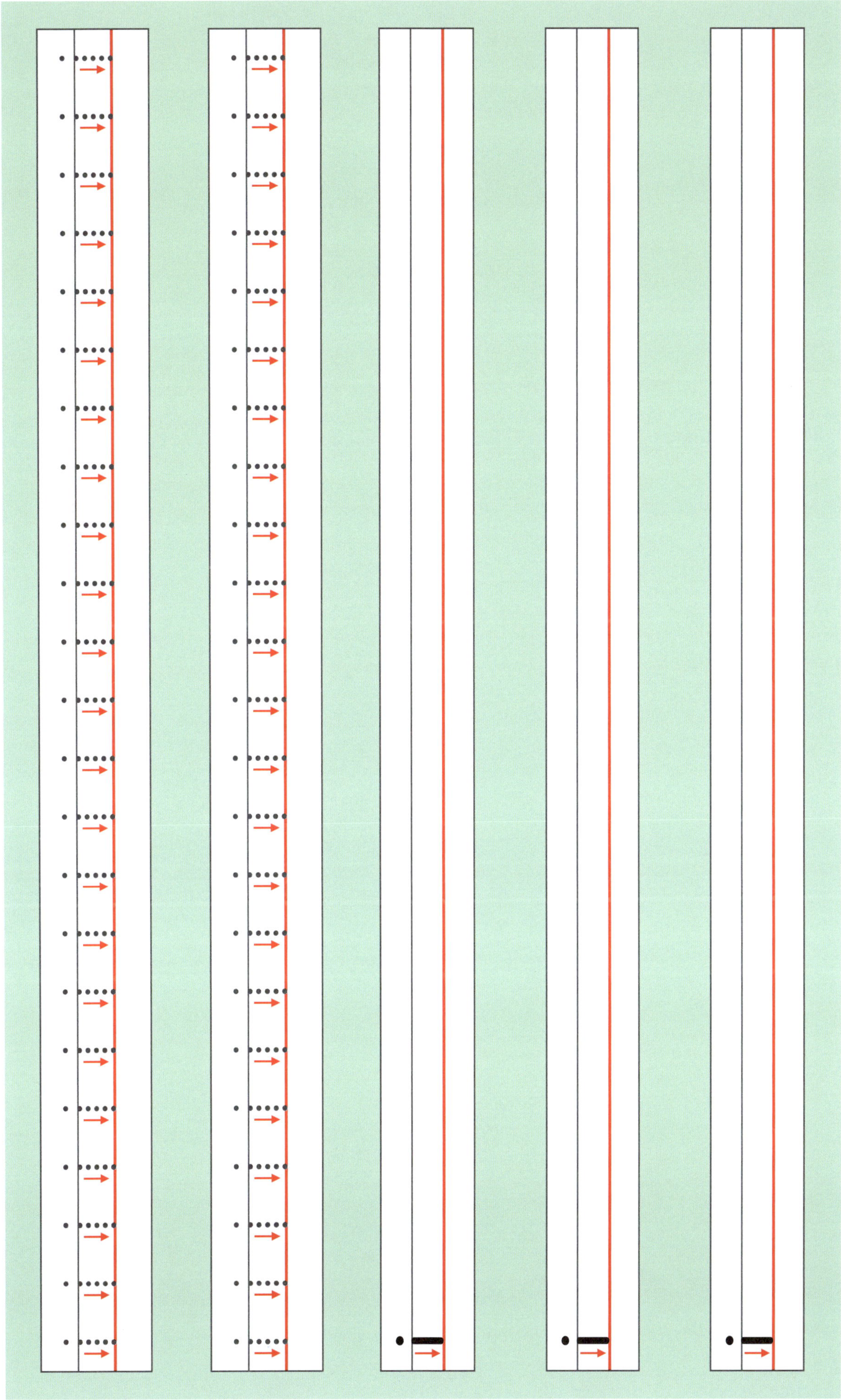

Buchstaben schreiben

Buchstaben schreiben

lesen · abdecken · schreiben

| f | s | i | n | f |

s	u	s	f	u

Diktat vorlesen · prüfen

s	s	n	i	s
f	i	i	f	f
f	s	n	n	s
s	i	i	i	n
s	s	n	n	s
f	s	i	f	n
s	i	n	i	f
s	i	i	f	s
f	s	n	n	n
f	i	n	f	s
1	2	3	4	5

Diktat schreiben

lesen · abdecken · schreiben

fi if su us as

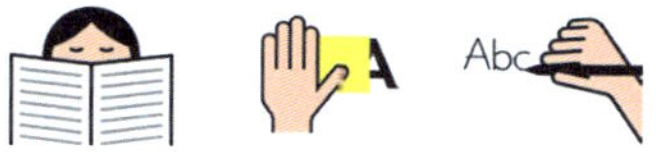

lesen · abdecken · schreiben

um

im

in

an

am

F. Jansen, U. Streit, A. Fuchs, *Schreiben lernen nach dem IntraActPlus-Konzept*

Diktat vorlesen · prüfen

1	fi	fu	fa	fi	fa	fu
2	su	us	su	us	as	is
3	an	in	in	an	in	an
4	am	am	an	an	am	an
5	im	im	in	in	im	in

Diktat schreiben

Buchstaben schreiben

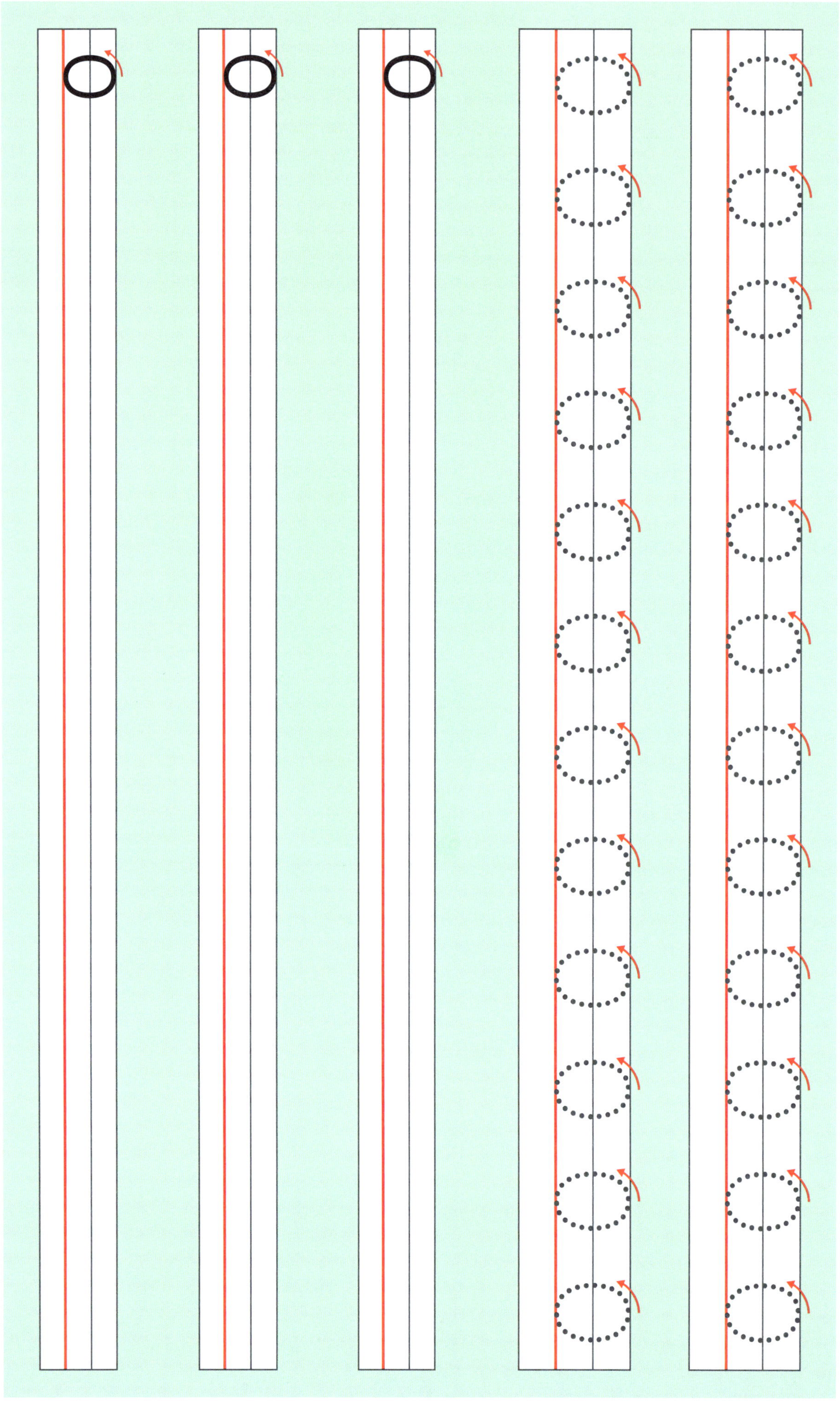

56

Buchstaben schreiben

Buchstaben schreiben

Buchstaben schreiben

lesen · abdecken · schreiben

| B | O | W | E | B |

lesen · abdecken · schreiben

W

E

B

O

W

F. Jansen, U. Streit, A. Fuchs, *Schreiben lernen nach dem IntraActPlus-Konzept*

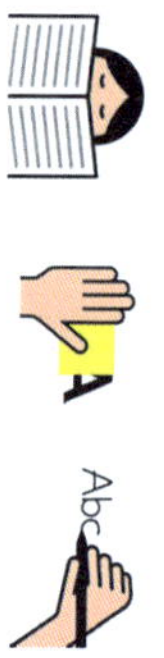

Diktat vorlesen · prüfen

1	B	B	B	B	B	B	B	B	B
2	O	O	L	O	L	O	L	O	L
3	W	W	W	W	O	W	O	W	O
4	E	E	B	B	E	B	E	B	E
5	B	O	W	E	E	W	O	B	W

lesen · abdecken · schreiben

BO BA BE BU BI

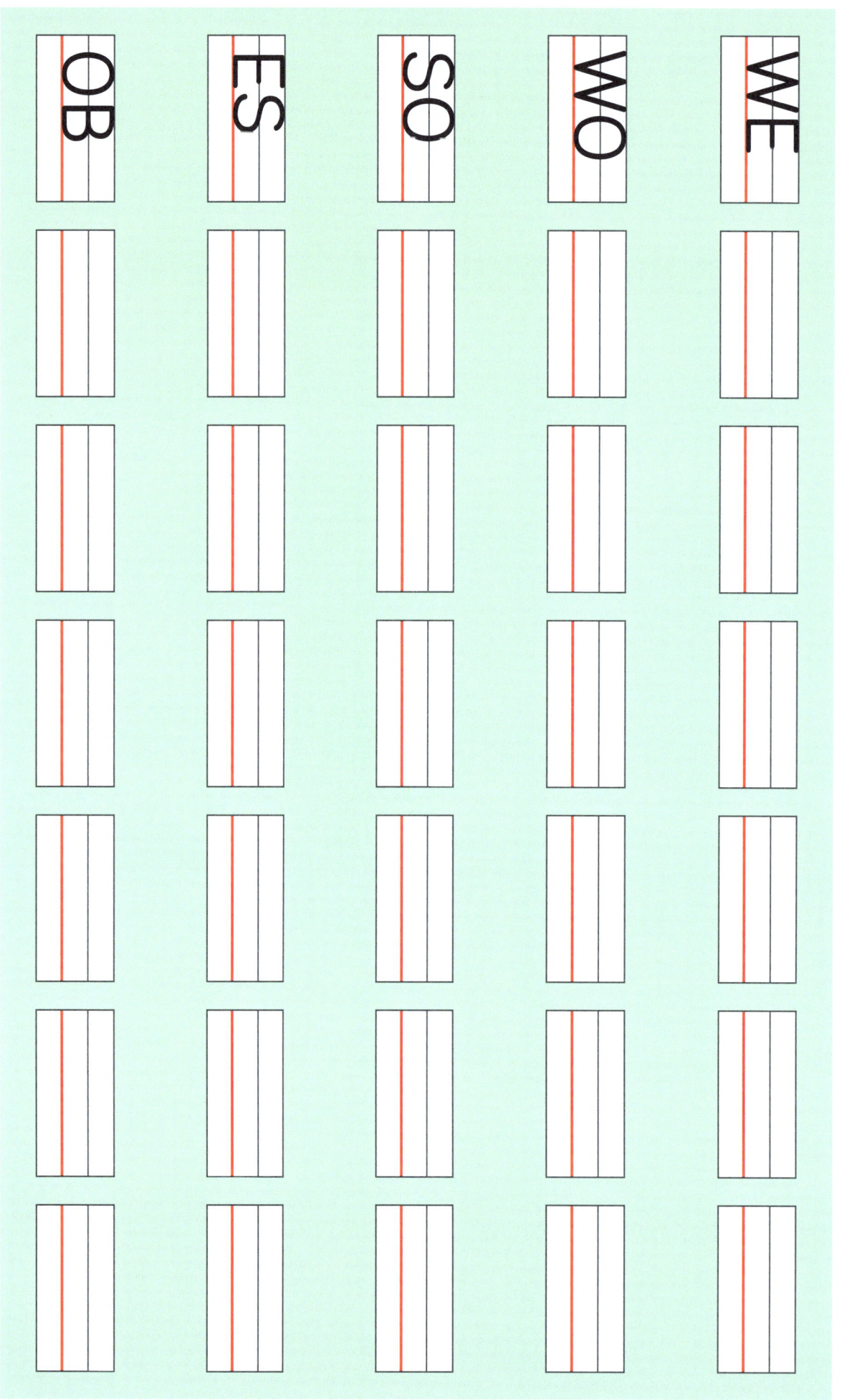

Diktat vorlesen · prüfen

1	BO	BE	BO	BO	BE
2	WE	WO	WE	WO	WE
3	BO	BE	WO	WE	BE
4	BA	BO	WO	WA	BO
5	WO	ES	OB	AB	ES	WO

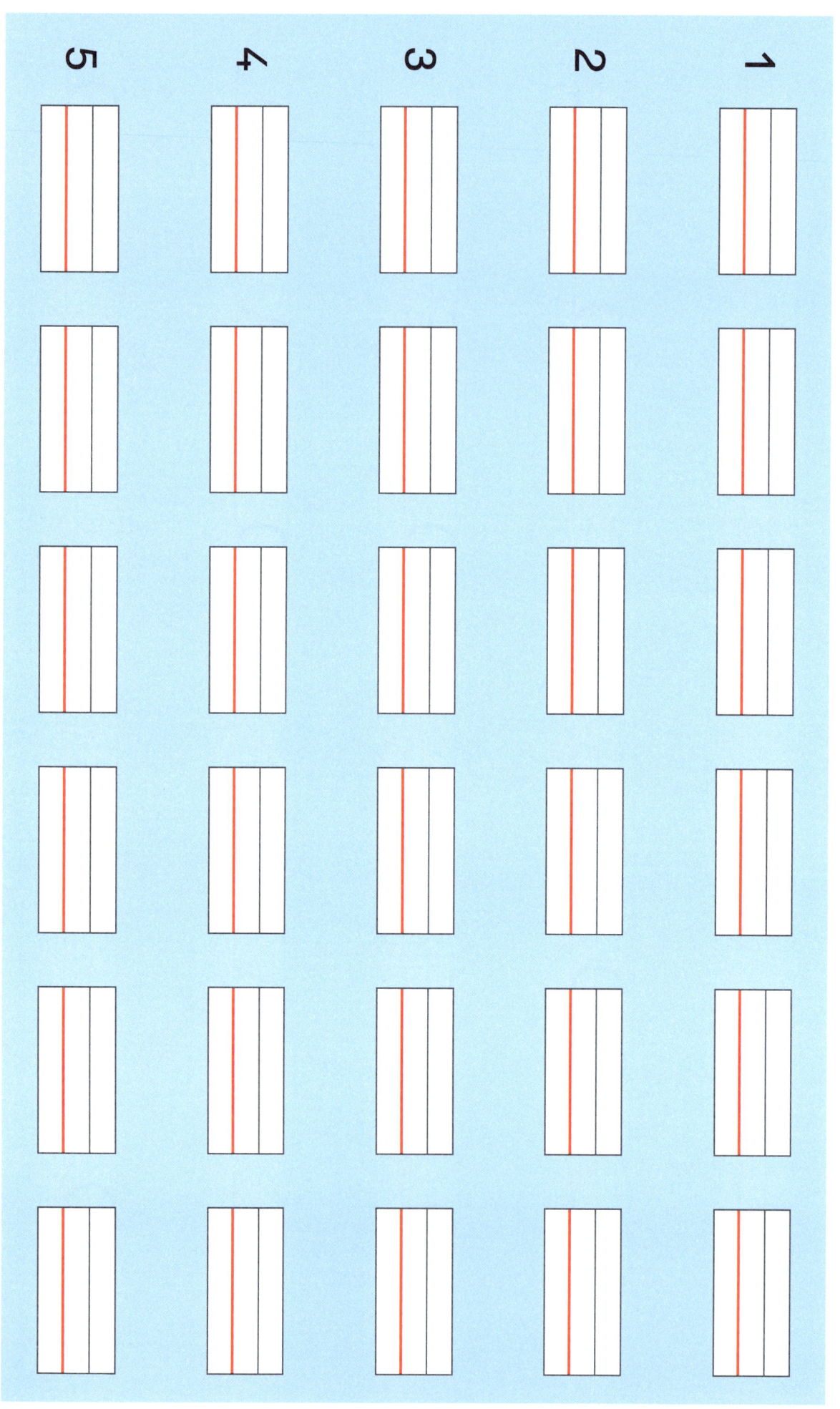

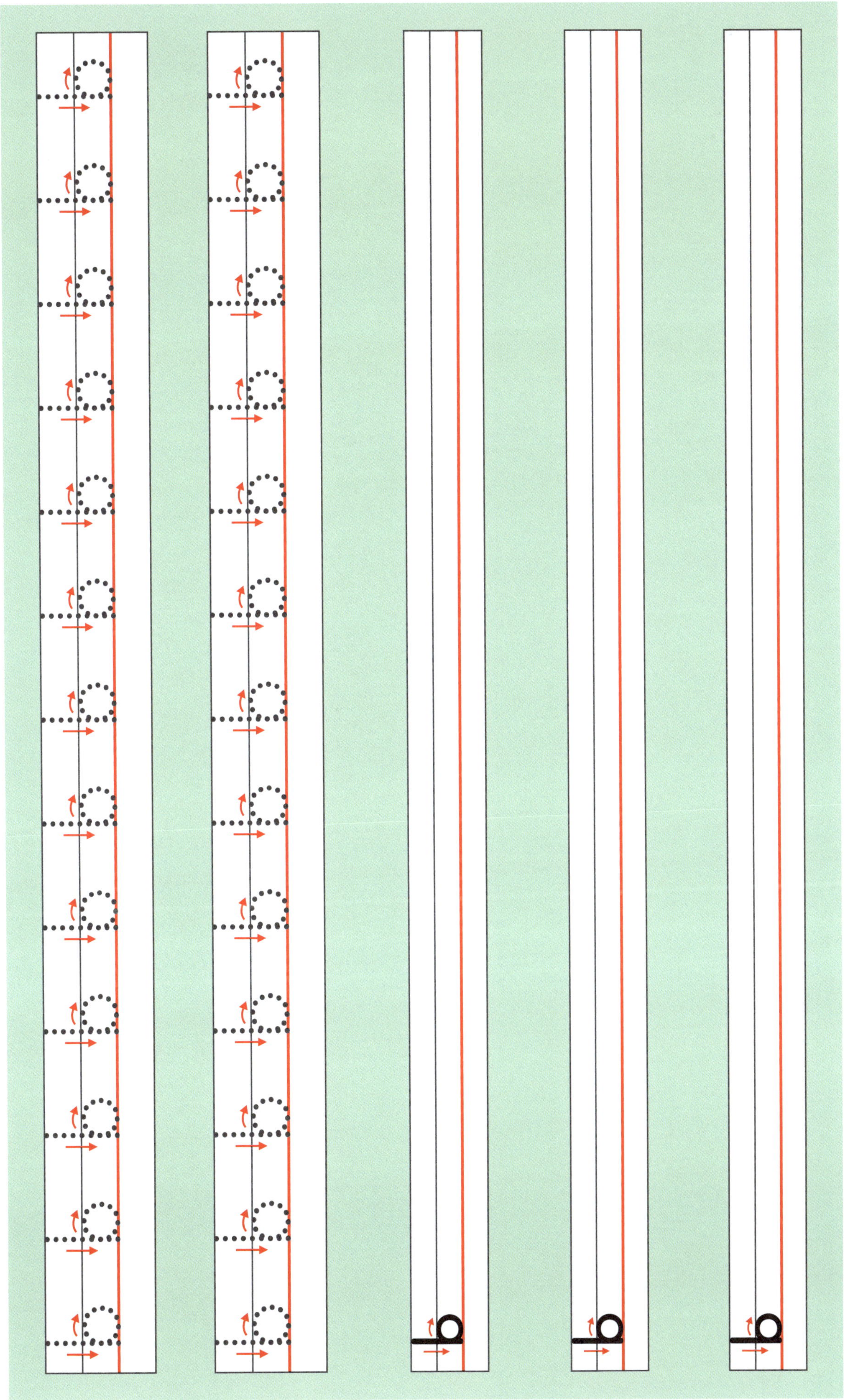

Buchstaben schreiben

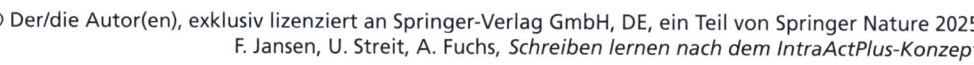

Buchstaben schreiben

69

70

Buchstaben schreiben

lesen · abdecken · schreiben

| b | o | w | e | b |

w	e	b	w	e
w	e	b	w	e

lesen · abdecken · schreiben

Diktat vorlesen · prüfen

1	b	b	i	b	i	b	b	i	b	b
2	o	o	o	o	L	o	L	L	o	o
3	w	o	w	o	w	o	w	w	o	o
4	e	e	e	e	e	b	e	b	b	e
5	b	o	w	e	w	b	e	w	b	w

lesen · abdecken · schreiben

bo ba be bu bi

ob · es · so · wo · we

lesen · abdecken · schreiben

Diktat vorlesen · prüfen

1	bo	be	bo	be	bo
2	we	wo	we	wo	we
3	bo	we	bo	we	be
4	ba	wa	bo	wo	bo
5	wo	es	ob	ab	es	wo

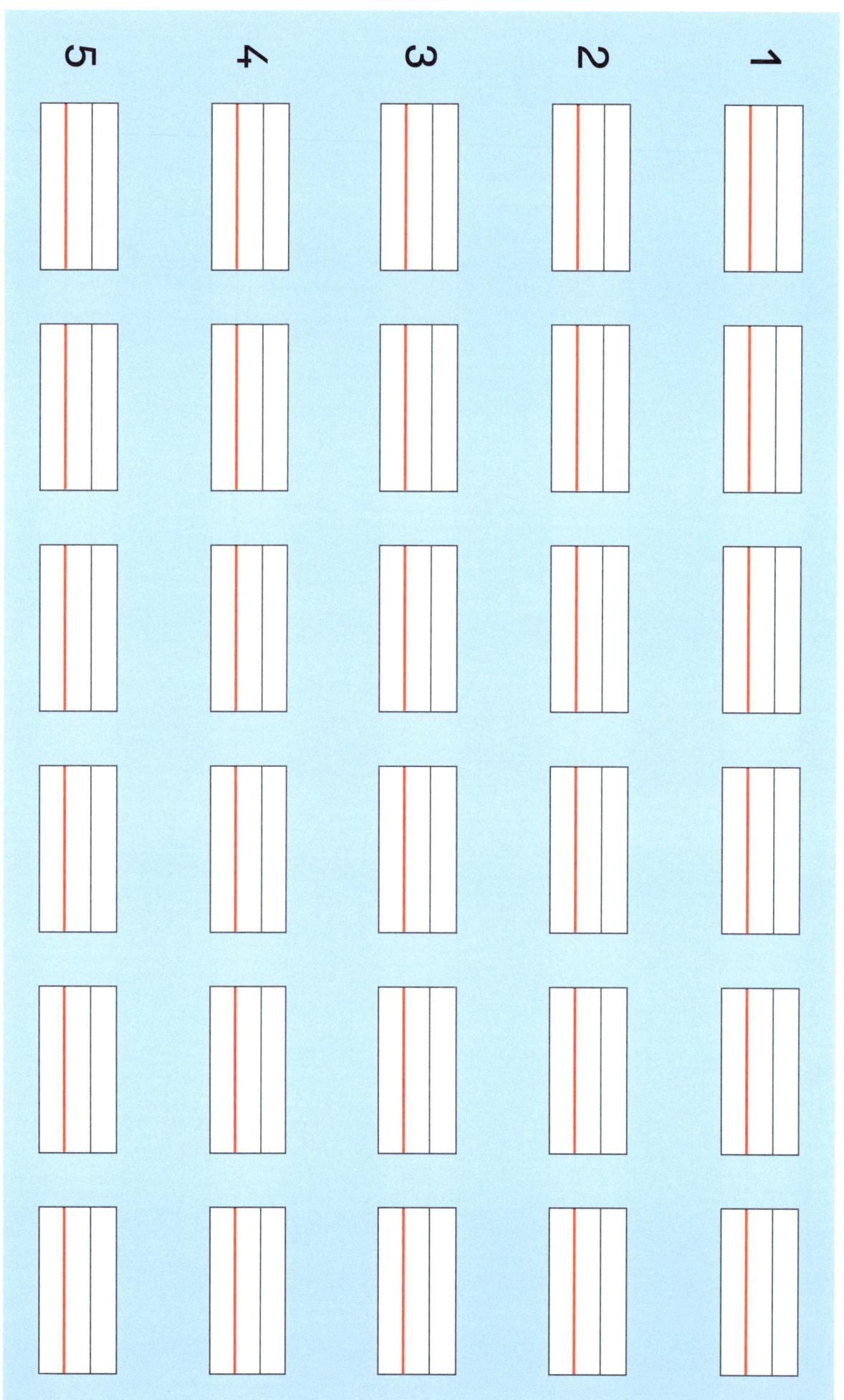

lesen • abdecken • schreiben

Mama

Oma

Omi

Lisa

Lena

Lama	Limo	Esel	Wal	Wolf

lesen · abdecken · schreiben

Diktat vorlesen • prüfen

1	Mama	Oma	Omi	Lisa	Lena
2	Lena	Lisa	Mama	Oma	Omi
3	Limo	Lama	Esel	Wal	Wolf
4	Wolf	Esel	Wal	Wolf	Wal
5	Mama	Lama	Esel	Wolf	Wal

Diktat schreiben

Name ....

Functional Skills

Maths: Number

Level 2

Course Booklet

Answers available online

CGP Books — The Choice of Champions!

He knows it.
You know it.
Everyone knows it ☺

cgpbooks.co.uk

Contents

✓ Use the tick boxes to check off the topics you've completed.

About This Booklet .... 1 ☐
Knowledge Organiser .... 2 ☐

Section One — Numbers and Calculations

Numbers over One Million .... 6 ☐
Read, write, order and compare
positive numbers of any size.

Negative Numbers .... 8 ☐
Read, write, order and compare
negative numbers of any size.

Adding and Subtracting .... 10 ☐
Carry out calculations with numbers up to one
million, including strategies to check answers.

Multiplying and Dividing .... 12 ☐
Carry out calculations with numbers up to one
million, including strategies to check answers.

Order of Operations .... 14 ☐
Follow the order of precedence of operators, including indices.

Section Two — Fractions

Fractions .... 18 ☐
Use improper fractions and mixed numbers.

Expressing a Number as a Fraction of Another .... 20 ☐
Express one number as a fraction of another.

Comparing and Ordering Fractions .... 22 ☐
Compare and order amounts or quantities using
proper and improper fractions and mixed numbers.

Adding and Subtracting Fractions .... 24 ☐
Add and subtract amounts or quantities using
proper and improper fractions and mixed numbers.

Section Three — Decimals

Comparing and Ordering Decimals .... 26 ☐
Compare and order decimals.

Rounding and Estimating Decimals .... 28 ☐
Approximate decimals.

Adding and Subtracting Decimals .... 30 ☐
Add and subtract decimals up to three decimal places.

Multiplying and Dividing Decimals .... 32 ☐
Multiply and divide decimals up to three decimal places.

Section Four — Percentages

Percentages of Amounts .... 34 ☐
Work out percentages of amounts.

Expressing Amounts as Percentages .... 36 ☐
Express one amount as a percentage of another.

Percentage Increase .... 38 ☐
Calculate percentage change (any size increase).

Percentage Decrease .... 40 ☐
Calculate percentage change (any size decrease).

Finding the Original Value .... 42 ☐
Calculate original value after percentage change.

Fractions, Decimals and Percentages .... 44 ☐
Identify and know the equivalence between
fractions, decimals and percentages.

Section Five — Ratio and Proportion

Ratios .... 48 ☐
Understand and calculate using ratios.

Direct Proportion .... 52 ☐
Understand and calculate using direct proportion.

Inverse Proportion .... 54 ☐
Understand and calculate using inverse proportion.

Section Six — Formulas

Formulas in Words...56 ☐
Evaluate expressions and make substitutions
in given formulae in words.

Formulas in Symbols..58 ☐
Evaluate expressions and make substitutions
in given formulae in symbols.

Topic-Based Questions

Numbers and Calculations..............................60 ☐
Fractions...62 ☐
Decimals...63 ☐
Percentages...64 ☐
Ratio and Proportion...65 ☐
Formulas...66 ☐

Mixed Practice

Section A..67 ☐
Section B..69 ☐

Individual Learning Plan...................................74 ☐

Unlock your Digital Extras

To get your free digital extras, go to **cgpbooks.co.uk/fs-maths** or scan the QR code below.

This will take you to:
- An answer booklet
- More Individual Learning Plan pages
- A Knowledge Retriever

Published by CGP

Written by Mike Davidson

Reviewer: Nicki Powers

Editors: Liam Dyer, Sharon Keeley-Holden and Chris Lindle.

With thanks to Glenn Rogers for the proofreading.
With thanks to Beth Linnane for the copyright research.

Specification points in Contents contain public sector information licensed under the Open Government Licence v3.0. https://www.nationalarchives.gov.uk/doc/open-government-licence/version/3/

ISBN: 978 1 83774 210 3
Printed by Elanders Ltd, Newcastle upon Tyne.
Graphics from Corel®

Text, design, layout and original illustrations © Coordination Group Publications Ltd (CGP) 2025 All rights reserved.

Photocopying this book is not permitted, even if you have a CLA licence.
Extra copies are available from CGP with next day delivery • 0800 1712 712 • www.cgpbooks.co.uk

About This Booklet

This course booklet supports your learning of the 'Using numbers and the number system' content area of the Level 2 qualification.

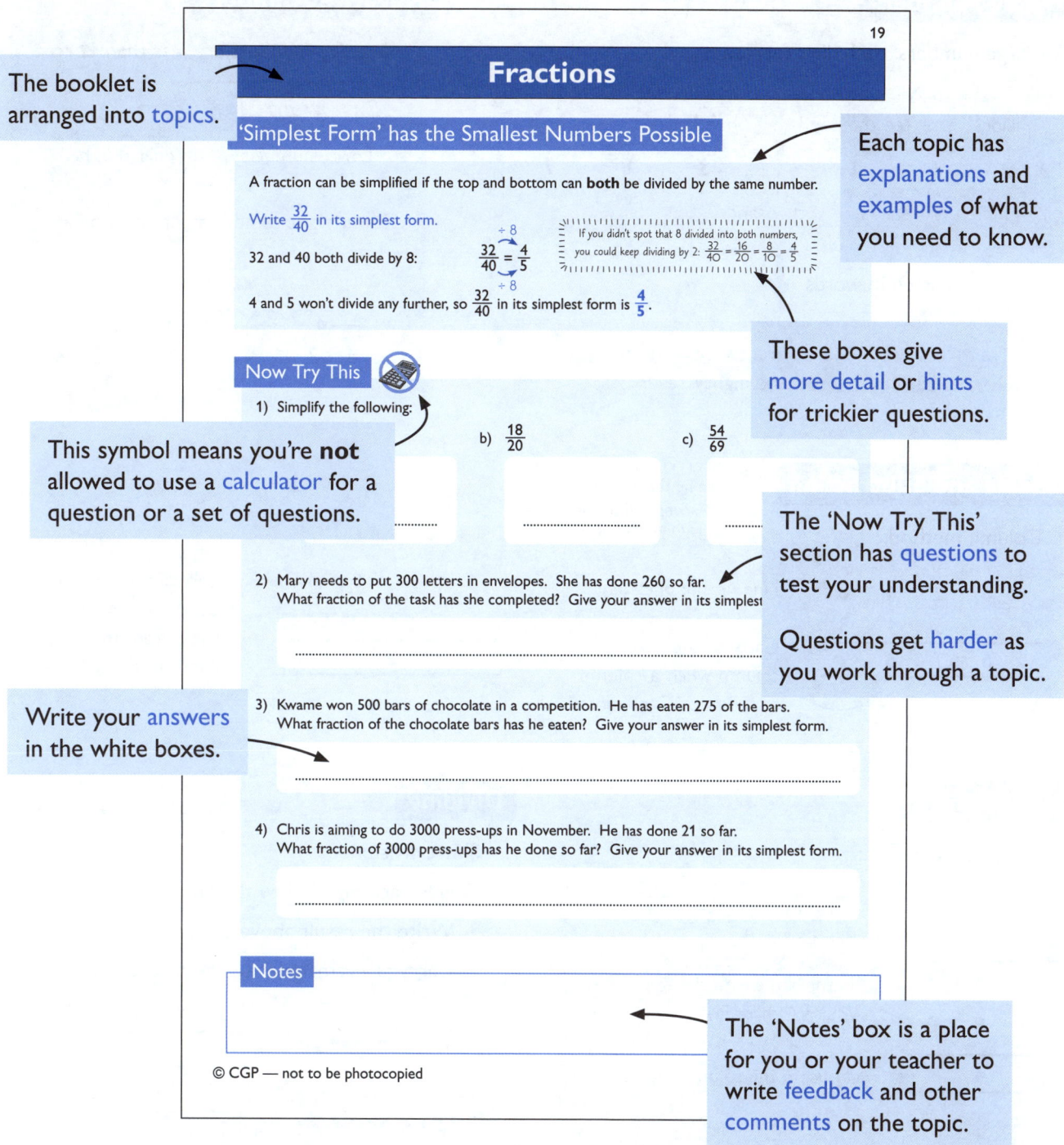

The booklet is arranged into topics.

Each topic has explanations and examples of what you need to know.

These boxes give more detail or hints for trickier questions.

This symbol means you're **not** allowed to use a calculator for a question or a set of questions.

The 'Now Try This' section has questions to test your understanding.

Questions get harder as you work through a topic.

Write your answers in the white boxes.

The 'Notes' box is a place for you or your teacher to write feedback and other comments on the topic.

At the end of the booklet, you'll find:

- **Topic-Based Questions**: more practice, split into **topics**.
- **Mixed Practice**: questions that can test you on **any** topic from the booklet — you'll need to use **more than one skill** to answer some of these.
- **Individual Learning Plan**: to track your progress towards your **learning goals**.

Knowledge Organiser

This Knowledge Organiser has everything you need to know in one place — handy!

Whole Numbers

For large numbers, each digit represents:

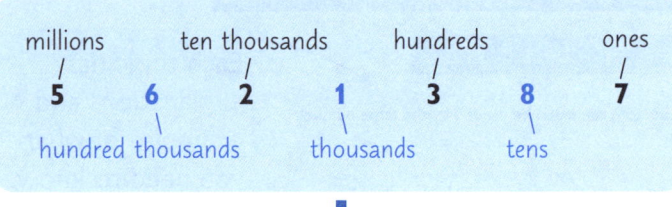

written in words

Five million, six hundred and twenty-one thousand, three hundred and eighty-seven.

Negative Numbers

Negative numbers are less than **zero**:

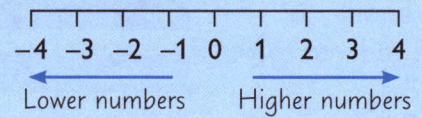

Count right to add or left to subtract:

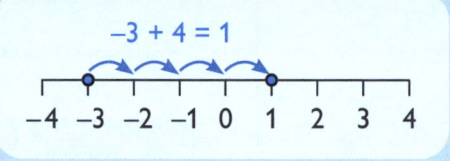

Adding and Subtracting

Line up the decimal point if working with decimals.

Column method:

```
    6  2  4  8
 +     5  1  3
 ─────────────
    6  7  6  1
          1
```

← Line up the ones digits.

← Carry to the next column when a column adds up to 10 or more.

```
    7  3  ⁸9̸  ¹2
 −        1  3  4
 ─────────────────
    7  2  5  8
```

← If top digit is smaller than bottom digit, borrow from the column to the left.

Multiplying

Long multiplication:

```
       1  6
    ×  3  4
    ───────
       6  4
       2
    4  8  0
    1
    ───────
    5  4  4
    1
```

← Multiply the ones digit by every digit in the top number...

...do the same with the tens digit. Write a 0 here first.

← Add using the column method.

To multiply a decimal...
- Do the multiplication with whole numbers, ignoring decimal points.
- Count the total number of digits after decimal points in original numbers.
- Make the answer have this number of decimal places.

Dividing

Short division:

Divide each digit below the line:
- Write the result above the line.
- Carry any remainder to the next digit.

$701 \div 6$ →
```
        1  1  6  r 5
    6 ) 7 ¹0 ⁴1
```

$2.32 \div 4$ →
```
        0 .  5  8
    4 ) 2 . ²3 ³2
```

To divide by a decimal...
- Write the division as a fraction.
- Multiply top and bottom by 10, 100, 1000 etc. to make the bottom a whole number.
- Do whole number short division.

Knowledge Organiser

BIDMAS

BIDMAS gives the order of operations:

1) **B**rackets
2) **I**ndices (e.g. squaring)
3) **D**ivision and **M**ultiplication
4) **A**ddition and **S**ubtraction

Work left to right when there's only division and multiplication OR only addition and subtraction.

Estimating and Checking

To find an **estimate**, round all the numbers in the calculation first.

You can **check** your answer by doing an opposite calculation:

addition ⟷ subtraction

multiplication ⟷ division

Fractions

To **simplify** a fraction, divide the top and bottom by the same number. Repeat until they won't divide any more.

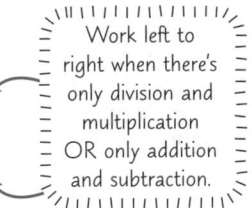

Improper fraction: top number is larger than bottom number. $\frac{7}{4}$

To change to a mixed number:
1) Divide top by bottom number.
2) Result is whole number part.
3) Remainder is top of fraction part.

$\frac{7}{4}$ ⟶ 7 ÷ 4 = 1 r 3, so $\frac{7}{4} = 1\frac{3}{4}$

Mixed number: a whole number part and a fraction part. $2\frac{1}{3}$

To change to an improper fraction:
1) Multiply whole number by bottom number.
2) Add on the top number.
3) Result is top of improper fraction.

$2\frac{1}{3}$ ⟶ 2 × 3 = 6, 6 + 1 = 7, so $2\frac{1}{3} = \frac{7}{3}$

Expressing a Number as a Fraction of Another

- Write the 1st number over the 2nd number.
- Simplify the fraction.

Write 24 as a fraction of 90:

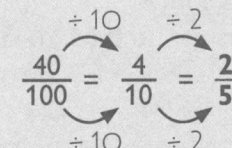

Ordering Fractions

Ascending order: small to big.
Descending order: big to small.

- Find equivalent fractions with same bottom number.
- Compare the top numbers.

E.g. Put these in ascending order: $\frac{5}{6}, \frac{7}{12}, \frac{3}{4}$

$\frac{5}{6} = \frac{10}{12}, \frac{7}{12}, \frac{3}{4} = \frac{9}{12}$, so compare 10, 7 and 9.

Order is: $\frac{7}{12}, \frac{9}{12}, \frac{10}{12} = \frac{7}{12}, \frac{3}{4}, \frac{5}{6}$

Adding and Subtracting Fractions

- Find equivalent fractions with same bottom number.
- Add (or subtract) the top numbers.

E.g. $\frac{2}{5} + \frac{1}{4} = \frac{8}{20} + \frac{5}{20} = \frac{13}{20}$

Knowledge Organiser

Decimals

E.g. a decimal with 3 decimal places (dp):

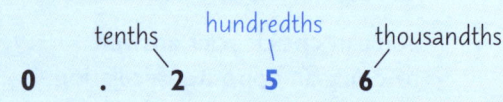

To **compare** decimals:
1) Fill in zeros so each has the same number of dp.
2) Compare the digits in each place, from left to right.

Which is larger: 0.87 or 0.892?
1) Write 0.87 as 0.87**0**.
2) Look at the tenths — they are both 8.
   Look at the hundredths. 9 is larger, so **0.892** is larger.

Rounding Decimals

1) Find the decimal place you're rounding to ('last digit').
2) Look at the digit to the right:
   - **5 or more** → round up the last digit.
   - **4 or less** → leave the last digit as it is.

E.g. Round 9.2③5 to 2 dp.
         'last digit'

The digit to the right of the last digit is 5, so round up to **9.24**

Percentages

Per cent (%) means out of 100, e.g. 30% is '30 out of 100'.

To find a percentage of an amount:
- Turn the percentage into a decimal.
- Multiply the decimal by the amount.

→ Find 60% of 900.
60% = 0.6
0.6 × 900 = **540**

To find 10%, divide by 10.
To find 1%, divide by 100.
To find 25%, divide by 4.

Percentage Change

To find a percentage **increase** or **decrease**:

1) Find the % of the original value.
2) Add this to / subtract it from original value.

OR

1) Add % to / subtract the % from 100%.
2) Convert this to a decimal.
3) Multiply by original value.

E.g. Increase £40 by 25%.

1) 25% of £40
   = £40 ÷ 4 = £10
2) £40 + £10 = **£50**

OR

1) 25% + 100% = 125%
2) 125% ÷ 100 = 1.25
3) 1.25 × £40 = **£50**

% increase: decimal is greater than 1.
% decrease: decimal is less than 1.

Finding the Original Value

1) Write the new amount as a % of original value.
2) Divide to find 1% of original value.
3) Multiply by 100 to find 100% (the original value).

A coat now costs £40 in a 20% off sale. What was the original price of the coat?
1) 80% = £40
2) 1% = £40 ÷ 80 = £0.50
3) 100% = £0.50 × 100 = **£50**

Knowledge Organiser

Common Conversions

Fraction	Decimal	Percentage
$\frac{1}{2}$	0.5	50%
$\frac{1}{4}$	0.25	25%
$\frac{3}{4}$	0.75	75%
$\frac{1}{5}$	0.2	20%
$\frac{1}{10}$	0.1	10%

How to Convert

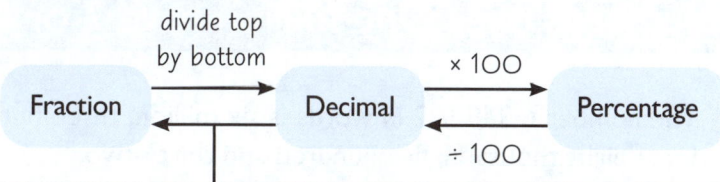

Fraction → Decimal (divide top by bottom)
Decimal → Percentage (× 100)
Percentage → Decimal (÷ 100)

- Multiply decimal by 10, 100 etc. to get a whole number.
- Write the whole number on top of the fraction.
- Write the number you multiplied by on the bottom.

Write 0.017 as a fraction. → 0.017 × 1000 = 17, so 0.017 = $\frac{17}{1000}$

Formulas

A **formula** is a rule for working out an amount. Formulas can be written in **words** or using letters.

Words: area of a circle = pi × radius²
Letters: $A = \pi r^2$

To **use** a formula, replace (substitute) letters with numbers that you're given.

Ratios

A **ratio** shows how many of one thing there is compared to another thing.

Multiply or divide all numbers in a ratio by the same number to scale up or down.

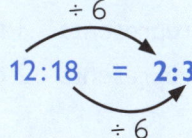

12 : 18 = 2 : 3 (÷ 6)

Ratio and Proportion

To split an amount in a certain ratio:
1) Find the total number of parts.
2) Find the value of 'one part' (total amount ÷ total number of parts)
3) Multiply each side of the ratio by the value of 'one' part.

The ratio of blue to red cars is 3 : 5. There are 32 cars. How many of each colour are there?
1) Total number of parts: 3 + 5 = 8
2) Value of 'one part':   32 ÷ 8 = 4
3) 3 × 4 = **12 blue** cars and 5 × 4 = **20 red** cars.

Direct and Inverse Proportion

Direct proportion: two amounts increase or decrease at the same rate.

1) Divide to find the amount for 'one thing'.
2) Multiply to find the amount for the number of things you want.

3 flapjacks contain 96 g of oats. How many g of oats are there in 10 flapjacks?
1) 1 flapjack has 96 g ÷ 3 = 32 g of oats
2) 10 flapjacks have 32 g × 10 = **320 g** of oats

Inverse proportion: one amount increases at the same rate as the other thing decreases.

1) Multiply to find the amount for 'one thing'.
2) Divide to find the amount for the number of things you want.

4 workers can clean a car in 15 minutes. How long would it take 5 workers?
1) 1 worker takes 4 × 15 = 60 minutes
2) 5 workers take 60 ÷ 5 = **12 minutes**

Section One — Numbers and Calculations

Numbers over One Million

It's important to know the value of each digit in big numbers — it'll help you read and order them.

Numbers over One Million have 7 or More Digits

The number 6 348 532 in words is six million, three hundred and forty-eight thousand, five hundred and thirty-two.

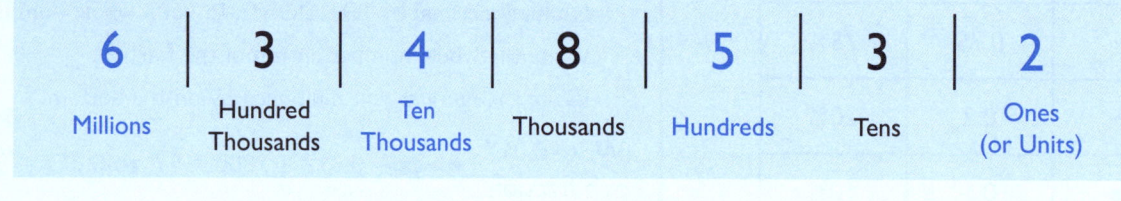

6 represents   6 millions (6 000 000)
3 represents   3 hundred thousands (or 300 000)
4 represents   4 ten thousands (or 40 000 — "forty thousand")
8 represents   8 thousands (or 8000)
5 represents   5 hundreds (or 500)
3 represents   3 tens (or 30)
2 represents   2 ones

When writing long numbers, put a comma or space between each group of 3 digits, from right to left. This makes them easier to read.

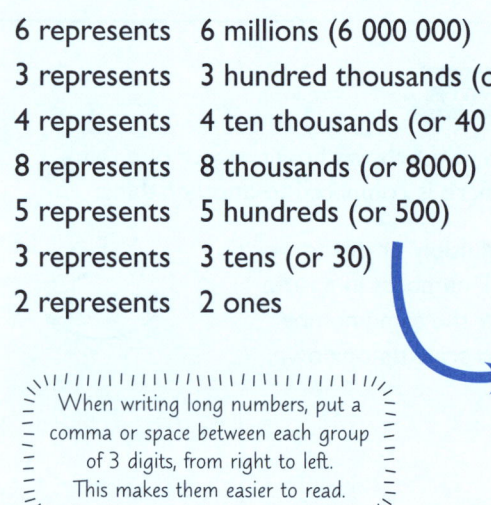

Now Try This

1) Circle the two numbers with a millions digit of 5.

   510 744   15 223 000   555 201   52 007 035   5 032 998

2) Write 7 563 297 in words.

   ....

   ....

3) Write five million, two hundred and eighty-nine thousand, one hundred and seven in digits.

   ....

Numbers over One Million

4) Write 15 870 652 in words.

   ....
   ....

5) Write twenty-one million, six thousand, two hundred and sixty-four in digits.

   ....

6) Put these numbers in order from smallest to largest.

   21 034   1204   181 006   12 901 000   100 094   67 094

   ....

7) At a bank, savings above £15 000 000 receive a higher interest rate than savings below that amount. Circle all the values below that would get the higher interest rate.

   £18 193 005   £15 421   £12 697 014   £15 901 000   £175 882

   £150 030   £16 570 049   £1 555 621   £22 001 003

8) Gita is researching the population of different countries. She finds the table below.

Country	Italy	Japan	UK	Peru	Finland
Population	58 972 000	123 930 000	67 596 300	33 725 900	5 583 400

   Put the countries in order, from smallest to largest population.

   ....

Notes

Negative Numbers

In the exciting world of negative numbers, you can count lower than zero.

Negative Numbers are Less than Zero

A **negative** number is shown with a (–) sign.
Number lines and scales are useful when working with negative numbers.

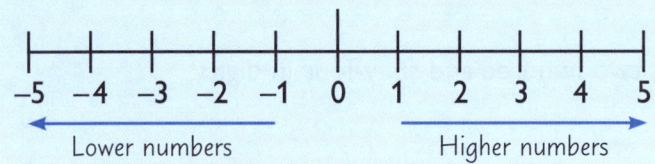

The further right you go, the higher the number,
e.g. 1 is higher than –4 and –1 is higher than –5.

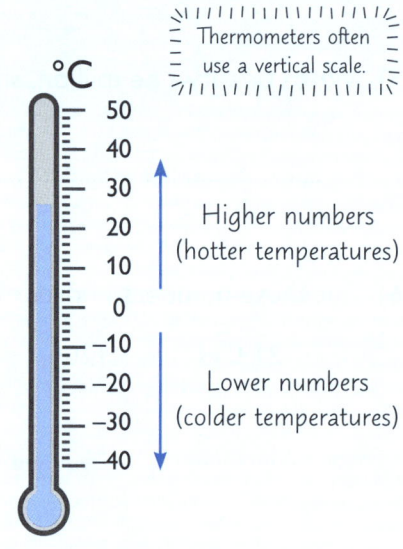

You can also work out the **difference** between
two numbers by counting the number of steps.

What is the difference between 2 and –3?

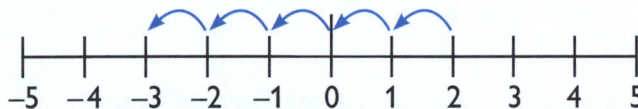

Count backwards from 2 to –3. There are 5 steps, so the difference is **5**.

Now Try This

1) Circle the higher number in each pair:

   a)   –8 or 2　　　　　b)   –17 or –13　　　　　c)   5 or –6

2) Put this list in order from lowest to highest.

   12,　–8,　11,　–4,　–12

   ....

3) In a quiz, 3 points are awarded for a correct answer and 2 points are taken away for an incorrect answer. Amir answered 4 questions correctly and 8 questions incorrectly. What was his score?

   ....

Section One — Numbers and Calculations

Negative Numbers

4) The temperature in Montreal at midnight was –12 °C. At midday, the temperature had risen by 15 °C. What was the temperature at midday?

....

5) Sean recorded the temperature at 5 different ski resorts.

Resort	Kaltenbach	Lermoos	Almenwelt	Kleine	Racines
Temperature (in °C)	–7	–10	–2	–14	1

a) Write the names of the ski resorts in order, starting with the coldest.

....

b) What is the difference in temperature between Lermoos and Almenwelt?

....

6) Myers Diving Centre has two courses: beginners and advanced.
The table below shows the depth from sea level (in feet) reached by some divers.

	Ben	Bernie	Joe	Afsha	Mikael
Beginners	–42		–12	–56	
Advanced		–108			–125

a) Who dived the furthest in the beginners course?

....

b) How much further did Bernie dive than Joe?

....

Notes

Adding and Subtracting

You need to know when to add or subtract. Examiners won't always tell you what to do in a question.

Adding and Subtracting are Opposite Calculations

Use the Column Method without a Calculator

You can work out addition and subtraction problems using the column method.
Line up the digits correctly and work from right to left.

What is 102 345 + 17 285?

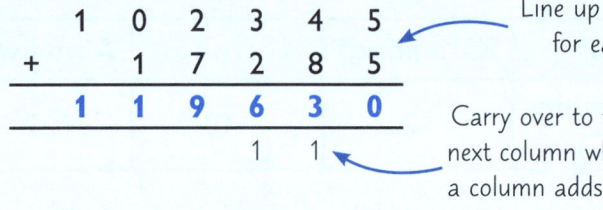

Line up the ones digits for each number.

Carry over to the next column when a column adds up to 10 or more.

Decide Whether to Add or Subtract

You'll need to work out which calculation to use in real-life context questions.

There are 12 086 home fans at a football match. There are 7069 fewer away fans. How many away fans are there?

Words like fewer and less mean you'll need to subtract. Words like more and extra mean you'll need to add.

This is a subtraction.
You need to subtract 7069 from 12 086:

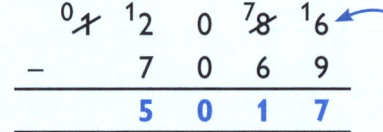

6 is smaller than 9. So borrow from the column to the left.

So there are **5017** away fans.

Do the opposite calculation (addition) to check your answer: 5017 + 7069 = 12 086 ✔

Now Try This

1) Work out each calculation. Show how you can check your answers.

   a) 58 097 + 21 068   b) 18 903 + 154   c) 1065 + 212 055

   d) 38 714 − 15 302   e) 150 667 − 43 067   f) 103 041 − 672

Adding and Subtracting

2) Polly scored 103 967 points in a video game. Parvati scored 99 005 points.

   a) Calculate the total number of points.

   b) Show a calculation to check your answer.

3) Alisha has £892. Andrew has £162 less. How much do they have in total?

   You'll need to do two calculations for question 3.

   ....

   ....

4) Look at this distance chart.

Seaport			
1789 km	Cliff Edge		
2029 km	2521 km	Box Town	
1586 km	967 km	3056 km	East City

   To find the distance between two places, go down from the first place to the row of the second place.

   a) How much further is Seaport from Box Town than it is from East City?

   ....

   ....

   b) Owen is a lorry driver. He travels from Box Town to East City, East City to Cliff Edge, then Cliff Edge back to Box Town. Calculate his total distance.

   ....

   ....

Notes

Multiplying and Dividing

You should be comfortable using written methods or a calculator to multiply and divide.

Multiplying and Dividing are Opposite Calculations

Use a Written Method without a Calculator

Long multiplication is used if both numbers have 2 digits or more.

Work out 347 × 56.

Write the larger number on top. → Multiply the **ones digit** by every digit in the top number. Start with 6 × 7 = 42.

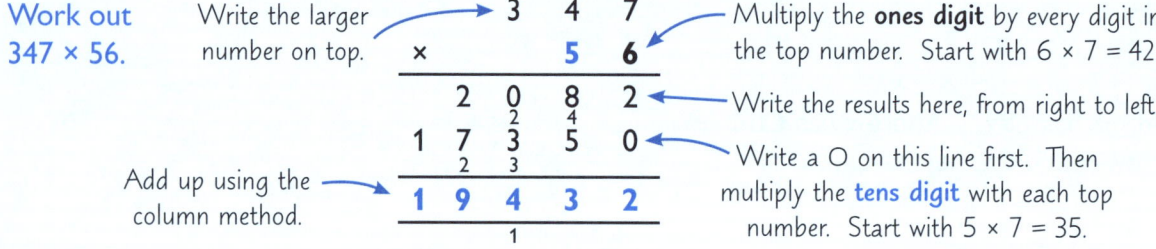

Write the results here, from right to left.

Write a 0 on this line first. Then multiply the **tens digit** with each top number. Start with 5 × 7 = 35.

Add up using the column method.

Round When it Makes Real-Life Sense

You might have to round a non-whole number up or down depending on the context.

A farm grows 7012 pumpkins. 6 pumpkins can fit in one crate. What is the smallest number of crates needed to store all the pumpkins?

This is a division. You need to divide 7012 by 6:

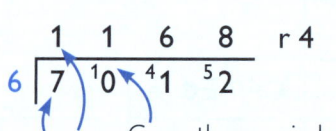

Divide the first digit by 6. Write the result on top.

Carry the remainder to the next column and repeat the process.

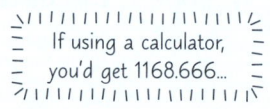

If using a calculator, you'd get 1168.666...

You must round the number of crates **up** to fit all the pumpkins in, so **1169 crates** are needed.

Now Try This

1) Work out each multiplication. Use estimation to check each of your answers.

   To estimate, round trickier numbers in the calculation to the nearest 10, 100, etc.

   a) 324 × 8   b) 32 × 68   c) 8 × 12 × 63

2) A school caretaker organises chairs for a play. He makes 18 rows, with 19 chairs in each row. How many chairs are there altogether?

....

Section One — Numbers and Calculations

Multiplying and Dividing

3) Work out: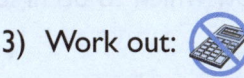

   a) 792 ÷ 9

   b) 34 512 ÷ 8

   c) 572 ÷ 11

4) Glen has £6.96 credit on his mobile phone. A message costs 12p.
   How many messages can he send?

   ....

5) A litre of paint can cover 19 m² of wall. Bob has 21 tins of paint, each holding 20 litres.
   What area can he cover with the paint? Use a reverse calculation to check your answer.

   ....

   ....

   ....

6) 892 supporters are going to watch a rugby game. Each bus can carry 38 people at most.
   Lizzie thinks 23 buses would be enough to carry all of the supporters.

   Is she correct? Explain your answer.

   ....

   ....

Notes

Order of Operations

Calculations may involve more than one operation (+ − × ÷). You need to know which to do first.

Follow BIDMAS in Calculations

BIDMAS tells you the correct order to do a calculation.

Brackets

Indices — also called powers, e.g squaring (^{2})

Division (÷)

Multiplication (×)

Addition (+)

Subtraction (−)

Work from left to right, when you are multiplying and dividing OR adding and subtracting.

What is 8 + 3 × 4?

If you do the addition first, you'd get the wrong answer of 44.

Follow BIDMAS.

Do the **M**ultiplication first: 8 + 3 × 4 = 8 + 12

Now do the **A**ddition: 8 + 12 = **20**

What is 50 − (3 × 2)^2?

Follow BIDMAS.

Do the **B**rackets first: 50 − (3 × 2)^2 = 50 − 6^2

$6^2 = 6 × 6$

Do the **I**ndices: 50 − 6^2 = 50 − 36

Now do the **S**ubtraction: 50 − 36 = **14**

Now Try This

1) Work out:

   a) 8 + 5 × 3

   b) 18 − 6 ÷ 3

   c) 22 − 6 × 2

   ....

   d) 80 + 40 ÷ 4

   e) 6 + 6 × 6

   f) 10 − 6 − 2

   ....

2) Calculate:

   a) 36 − (12 ÷ 3)

   b) (8 + 3) × 11

   c) 80 − 6 + 3 × 4

   ....

Section One — Numbers and Calculations

Order of Operations

3) Work out:

   a) $48 \div 4^2 + 7$

   b) $5^2 + 3 \times 2$

   c) $30 - 2^3 + 3 \times 4$

   d) $120 \div (6^2 + 4)$

   e) $7^2 + (2 \times 3^2)$

   f) $10^2 - (12 - 5)^2$

4) Write 'True' or 'False' for each calculation. For any that are 'False', give the correct answer.

   a) $10 \div 2 + 3 = 2$

   b) $12 + 8 \div 2 = 10$

   c) $2^3 + 12 \div 2 = 10$

   d) $6^2 - (3 + 2^3) = 5^2$

Order of Operations

There's more on BIDMAS here. You should be able to tackle calculations shown as a fraction.

Also Use BIDMAS with Fractions

Fractions are Just Like a Division

Some calculations are written as a fraction. Work out the top part and bottom part separately and then divide — you should use **BIDMAS** in each part.

What is $\dfrac{3 \times 6 + 12}{10 - 2^2}$?

Top part: $3 \times 6 + 12 = 18 + 12 = 30$
Bottom part: $10 - 2^2 = 10 - 4 = 6$

→ So the fraction is $\dfrac{30}{6} = \mathbf{5}$

Most Calculators Follow BIDMAS

If you're using a calculator, take care typing in a calculation. You'll get the wrong answer if you make a mistake.

See p.28 for more on rounding.

What is $(0.6 + 14) \div 2.7$? Give your answer to 2 d.p.

(0 · 6 + 1 4) ÷ 2 · 7 =   5.4074...

5.4074... to 2 d.p is **5.41**

*If your calculator doesn't have bracket buttons, work out the brackets **first**, then do the division.*

Now Try This

1) Work out:

a) $\dfrac{10 + 3 \times 2}{8 \div 2}$

b) $\dfrac{24 - 12 \div 2}{5 + 1^2}$

c) $15 - \left(\dfrac{4 \times 5}{2}\right)$

d) $\dfrac{18 + 12 \times 3}{81 \div 9}$

e) $\dfrac{(13 - 7) + (24 \times 3)}{18 \div 2 - 3}$

f) $\dfrac{6^2 + 4}{14 \div 7} + 5$

Order of Operations

2) Work out each calculation.
   Use a calculator to check your answers.

   a) 40 × 6 + 30 × 2

   b) 36 ÷ 3 − 2 × 4

   c) (32 − 5) + (12 ÷ 4)

3) Copy out each calculation. Draw a pair of brackets to make the calculation correct.

   a) 56 ÷ 5 + 3 = 7

   b) 18 + 12 ÷ 6 = 5

   c) 20 × 2 + 6 = 160

   d) 12 + 6 ÷ 2 + 8 = 17

   e) 2 × 6 + 1 × 3 = 42

   f) 22 ÷ 2 + 3^2 = 2

4) Use a calculator to work out each calculation. Give each answer to 2 decimal places.

   a) 12.53 + 9.6 ÷ 3.1

   b) 14.3 + 5.6 × 3.21

   c) $\dfrac{0.61 + 14.4}{2.7}$

   d) $\dfrac{9.82 \times 20}{7 + 5.5}$

If you don't have a fraction button on your calculator, do the top part and bottom part separately, then divide.

Notes

… 18

Section Two — Fractions

Fractions

Fractions show parts of something, e.g. amount of a pizza, a sum of money, or a group of people.

Improper Fractions Can Be Changed to Mixed Numbers

An **improper fraction** has a larger top number than bottom number, e.g. $\frac{19}{8}$.

A **mixed number** has a whole number part and a fraction part, e.g. $2\frac{3}{8}$.

To change an **improper fraction** into a mixed number:
- Divide the top number by the bottom number.
- The result is the whole number part. The remainder is the top number of the fraction part.
- The bottom number stays the same.

Write $\frac{13}{5}$ as a mixed number.   Top number ÷ bottom number: 13 ÷ 5 = 2 r 3

Write the mixed number: $2\frac{3}{5}$

To change a **mixed number** into an improper fraction:
- Multiply the whole number part by the bottom number of the fraction.
- Add on the top number. This is the top number of the improper fraction.
- The bottom number stays the same.

Write $5\frac{1}{4}$ as an improper fraction.   Whole number × bottom number: 5 × 4 = 20

Add on the top number: 20 + 1 = 21

Write the improper fraction: $\frac{21}{4}$

Now Try This

1) Write these improper fractions as mixed numbers:

   a) $\frac{25}{7}$ b) $\frac{15}{11}$ c) $\frac{39}{4}$

   ....

2) Write these mixed numbers as improper fractions:

   a) $6\frac{1}{3}$ b) $8\frac{3}{4}$ c) $110\frac{2}{3}$

   ....

Section Two — Fractions

Fractions

'Simplest Form' has the Smallest Numbers Possible

A fraction can be simplified if the top and bottom can **both** be divided by the same number.

Write $\frac{32}{40}$ in its simplest form.

32 and 40 both divide by 8:

$$\frac{32}{40} = \frac{4}{5}$$ (÷ 8)

If you didn't spot that 8 divided into both numbers, you could keep dividing by 2: $\frac{32}{40} = \frac{16}{20} = \frac{8}{10} = \frac{4}{5}$

4 and 5 won't divide any further, so $\frac{32}{40}$ in its simplest form is $\frac{4}{5}$.

Now Try This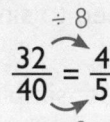

1) Simplify the following:

   a) $\frac{12}{15}$ b) $\frac{18}{20}$ c) $\frac{54}{69}$

2) Mary needs to put 300 letters in envelopes. She has done 260 so far.
   What fraction of the task has she completed? Give your answer in its simplest form.

3) Kwame won 500 bars of chocolate in a competition. He has eaten 275 of the bars.
   What fraction of the chocolate bars has he eaten? Give your answer in its simplest form.

4) Chris is aiming to do 3000 press-ups in November. He has done 21 so far.
   What fraction of 3000 press-ups has he done so far? Give your answer in its simplest form.

Notes

Expressing a Number as a Fraction of Another

When writing one number as a fraction of another, always check that it is in its simplest form.

'Express as a Fraction' Just Means 'Write as a Fraction'

To express one number as a fraction of another, put the first number on the top and the second number on the bottom. You'll usually need to simplify your answer.

Express 2 as a fraction of 20. Give your answer in its simplest form.

Write the numbers as a fraction and simplify: $\frac{2}{20} = \frac{1}{10}$ (÷ 2)

See the previous page for how to simplify a fraction.

The number on the top and the number on the bottom must be in the same unit.

Bob uses 50 g of flour out of a 1 kg bag. What fraction of the bag is used?

Convert 1 kg to 1000 g, so both numbers are in grams.

Write the numbers as a fraction and simplify: $\frac{50}{1000} = \frac{5}{100} = \frac{1}{20}$ So $\frac{1}{20}$ of the bag is used.

Now Try This

1) Express as a fraction in its simplest form:

   a) 21 out of 28   b) 20 out of 200   c) 15 out of 45

   ....

   d) 28 out of 48   e) 5.4 out of 7.2

   ....

   For e), multiply each number by 10 before simplifying.

2) What fraction of the letters in FUNCTIONAL SKILLS are:

   a) L? ....   b) N? ....

3) Ava received £90 for her birthday. She spends £48 on boots.
   What fraction of her birthday money was this? Give your answer in its simplest form.

   ....

Expressing a Number as a Fraction of Another

4) Five students take a maths test out of 60 marks. Their scores are recorded in the table below. Write each student's score as a fraction in its simplest form.

Student	Abi	Bin	Caz	Dan	Eli
Score	52	48	40	24	18
Score as a fraction	....	....	....	....	....

5) In a bag of 80 beads, 15 are yellow, 37 are red, and the rest are blue. What fraction of the beads are blue? Give your answer in its simplest form.

....

6) Pavel, Linda and Julie go to the cinema. Pavel buys popcorn for £5.40, Linda buys a hotdog for £6.60 and Julie buys nachos for £4. What fraction of the total money spent did Julie spend? Give your answer in its simplest form.

....

7) What is: *Simplify your answers where possible.*

   a) 24 minutes as a fraction of 2 hours?   b) 25 cm as a fraction of 5 m?

   ....

8) 3 litres of a drink contains 150 ml of orange juice and 200 ml of lemon juice. The rest of the drink is water. What fraction of the drink is water? Give your answer in its simplest form.

....

....

Notes

Comparing and Ordering Fractions

These pages will help you make the right decision if offered either $\frac{1}{6}$ of a cake or $\frac{1}{8}$ of a cake...

Make the Bottom Numbers the Same to Compare Fractions

If the bottom numbers are the **same**, it's easy to see which fraction is bigger.
E.g. $\frac{3}{6}$ is bigger than $\frac{1}{6}$ as 3 parts are greater than 1 part.

If the bottom numbers are **different**, make them the same using equivalent fractions.

Which fraction is bigger, $\frac{1}{2}$ or $\frac{3}{8}$?

$2 \times 4 = 8$, so multiply by 4 to get an equivalent fraction:

Now compare $\frac{4}{8}$ and $\frac{3}{8}$: $\frac{4}{8}$ is bigger, so $\frac{1}{2}$ is the bigger fraction.

$\frac{1}{2} \xrightarrow{\times 4} \frac{4}{8}$

If you have a calculator, you can change fractions to decimals then compare these — see p.26.

You'll need to change any **mixed numbers** into fractions first.

Put these values in order, starting with the smallest: $\frac{9}{4}, \frac{29}{12}$ and $2\frac{3}{8}$

Change the mixed number into a fraction: $2\frac{3}{8} = \frac{19}{8}$

4, 8 and 12 divide into 24, so make equivalent fractions: $\frac{9}{4} \xrightarrow{\times 6} \frac{54}{24}$ $\frac{29}{12} \xrightarrow{\times 2} \frac{58}{24}$ $\frac{19}{8} \xrightarrow{\times 3} \frac{57}{24}$

Compare the equivalent fractions to find the order: $\frac{9}{4}, 2\frac{3}{8}, \frac{29}{12}$

Now Try This

1) Which fraction is **larger** in each pair? Show the equivalent fractions you compare.

   a) $\frac{2}{5}$ or $\frac{3}{10}$

   b) $\frac{7}{10}$ or $\frac{8}{15}$

   ....

2) Which fraction is **smaller** in each pair? Show the equivalent fractions you compare.

   a) $\frac{3}{5}$ or $\frac{13}{20}$

   b) $\frac{15}{12}$ or $1\frac{1}{9}$

   ....

3) Adam eats $\frac{3}{4}$ of a pizza. Rebecca eats $\frac{5}{7}$ of an identical pizza. Who ate more pizza?

   ....

Section Two — Fractions

Comparing and Ordering Fractions

4) Write the following fractions in order, smallest first.

   a) $\frac{2}{3}, \frac{14}{23}, \frac{13}{20}$ ....

   b) $\frac{6}{5}, 1\frac{1}{3}, \frac{21}{15}$ ....

   c) $\frac{3}{2}, 1\frac{3}{7}, \frac{17}{14}, 2\frac{1}{4}$ ....

5) Three sports teams play the same number of games. Lindal Lions win $\frac{7}{10}$ of their games, Eskdale Egrets win $\frac{2}{3}$ of their games and Millom Manatees win $\frac{3}{5}$ of theirs. Which team won the fewest games?

   ....

6) Three jumbo bags of soil are delivered to a garden. Bag 1 contains $\frac{6}{7}$ tonnes of soil, bag 2 contains $\frac{31}{35}$ tonnes and bag 3 contains $\frac{58}{70}$ tonnes. Which bag contains the most soil?

   ....

7) Children who live more than $1\frac{3}{4}$ miles away from a school get free transport. The table below gives the distances four children live from the school. Which children will get free transport?

Child	Mohammed	Omari	Holly	Milly
Distance (km)	$\frac{19}{12}$	$\frac{16}{9}$	$\frac{17}{6}$	$\frac{5}{3}$

   ....

   ....

Notes

Adding and Subtracting Fractions

If your fractions don't have the same bottom numbers, you'll need equivalent fractions again for this lot.

Use Equivalent Fractions to Add and Subtract

To add or subtract fractions, first find equivalent fractions with the same bottom number. Then add or subtract the top numbers.

What is $\frac{2}{3} + \frac{3}{4}$?

Find equivalent fractions: $\frac{2}{3} = \frac{8}{12}$ $\frac{3}{4} = \frac{9}{12}$ ← $3 \times 4 = 12$, so multiply the top and bottom of each fraction to get 12 on the bottom.

Add the top numbers: $\frac{8}{12} + \frac{9}{12} = \frac{8+9}{12} = \frac{17}{12}$ ← Simplify your answers if possible. You may also be told to change it to a mixed number.

Now Try This

1) Work out the following. Simplify your answers where possible.

   a) $\frac{1}{5} + \frac{2}{3}$

   b) $\frac{3}{5} + \frac{4}{7}$

   ....

   ....

   c) $\frac{51}{100} - \frac{7}{20}$

   d) $\frac{3}{4} - \frac{1}{6}$

   ....

   ....

2) Amir spent $\frac{1}{2}$ of his wages on rent and $\frac{2}{7}$ on food this week. What fraction of his wages has he spent on rent and food?

   ....

3) Avril has $\frac{2}{3}$ of a litre of apple juice in a jug. She pours out $\frac{1}{4}$ of a litre into a glass. How much apple juice is left in the jug?

   ....

4) Benny says $\frac{1}{6}$ add $\frac{2}{13}$ equals $\frac{3}{19}$. Show whether Benny is right or wrong.

   ....

   ....

Section Two — Fractions

Adding and Subtracting Fractions

Split Mixed Numbers into Whole Numbers and Fractions

Deal with whole numbers and fractions **separately** when calculating with mixed numbers.

What is $3\frac{3}{4} + 4\frac{4}{5}$?

Add the whole numbers: $3 + 4 = 7$

Add the fractions: $\frac{3}{4} + \frac{4}{5} = \frac{15}{20} + \frac{16}{20} = \frac{31}{20} = 1\frac{11}{20}$ ← If you get an improper fraction, change it to a mixed number.

Put the two parts back together: $7 + 1\frac{11}{20} = 8\frac{11}{20}$

Now Try This

1) Work out the following. Simplify your answers where possible.

   a) $2\frac{8}{9} - 1\frac{1}{3}$

   b) $13\frac{1}{7} + 5\frac{5}{6}$

   c) $3\frac{5}{6} - 1\frac{4}{10}$

   d) $4\frac{2}{3} + 7\frac{4}{5}$

2) Lynne is training for a half marathon. She follows the training plan below.

Day	Monday	Tuesday	Wednesday	Thursday	Friday
Distance (miles)	$12\frac{5}{6}$	rest	$7\frac{3}{4}$	rest	$11\frac{2}{15}$

   a) What was the total distance Lynne ran on Monday and Wednesday?

   b) How much further did Lynne run on Monday than on Friday?

Notes

Section Three — Decimals

Comparing and Ordering Decimals

Decimals are numbers with a decimal point, e.g. 3.14. They show numbers between whole numbers.

Make Decimals the Same Length to Compare Them

Decimal places (dp) are the digits to the right of a decimal point.

Putting zeros at the end of a decimal doesn't change its value, e.g. 0.1 and 0.1000 are the same.

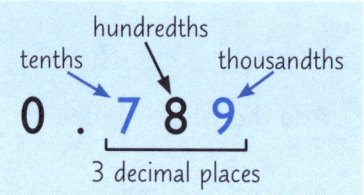

To **order** decimals:
1) Make sure all decimals have the same number of decimal places by filling in zeros.
2) Compare the digits in each position, from left to right.
   If they're different, order those decimals.
   If they're the same, move on to the next position.

Order these decimals, from smallest to largest: 3.4, 5.65, 3.34, 5.61, 2.07

1) Add a zero to the end of 3.4:   3.40   5.65   3.34   5.61   2.07

2) Compare the ones digits...   3.40   5.65   3.34   5.61   2.07

   2 is smallest, so 2.07 is the smallest number

   ...then the tenths digits...   2.07   3.40   3.34   5.65   5.61

   2.07   3.34   3.40   5.65   5.61

   3 is smaller than 4, so 3.34 is less than 3.40

   ...then the hundredths digits.   2.07   3.34   3.40   5.65   5.61

   2.07   3.34   3.4   5.61   5.65

   1 is smaller than 5, so 5.61 is less than 5.65

Now Try This

< means 'is less than'.
> means 'is greater than'.

1) Put the correct symbol (< or >) in between each pair of decimals.

   a) 3.2 .... 3.6   b) 0.9 .... 0.5   c) 4.5 .... 4.15

   d) 7.23 .... 7.8   e) 5.098 .... 5.91   f) 3.405 .... 3.43

2) Tick the two lists written in descending order (largest to smallest).

   1.9, 2.05, 2.9, 3.05 ☐   90, 89.8, 80.7, 78.6 ☐

   5.2, 5.15, 5.13, 5.11 ☐   0.09, 0.1, 0.05, 0.02 ☐

Comparing and Ordering Decimals

3) Order each list, from smallest to largest.

   a) 2.78, 2.56, 2.87, 2.03, 2.91

   ....

   b) 13.765, 13.345, 13.807, 13.008, 13.457

   ....

   c) 0.865, 0.632, 0.367, 0.329, 0.613

   ....

4) Put these volumes in order, starting with the lowest.

   48.06 litres, 54.98 litres, 46.78 litres, 54.89 litres, 48.6 litres

   ....

5) Put these weights in order, starting with the heaviest.

   4.065 kg, 4.65 kg, 3.999 kg, 4.6 kg, 3.12 kg

   ....

6) Dean and Mary are on holiday. The distances to various tourist attractions are shown in the table. Write the attractions in order, from the closest to the furthest attraction.

Attraction	Distance (miles)
Waterfall	10.23
Caves	10.03
Funfair	10.73
Market	10.5

....

....

Notes

Rounding and Estimating Decimals

Working with decimals can be awkward, but estimating can give you a rough answer quickly.

Shorten Answers by Rounding Off Decimals

You might need to **round** a decimal to a certain number of decimal places (dp):

1) Find the decimal place you're rounding to — this is the 'last digit'.
2) Look at the digit to the right of the last digit — this is the 'decider'.
3) If the decider is **5 or more**, round up the last digit by one.
   If the decider is **4 or less**, leave the last digit as it is.
4) Remove anything after the last digit.

> Round 13.309 to 1 dp.
>
> 1 3 . 3 0 9
> 'last digit'   'decider'
>
> The decider is 4 or less, so leave the last digit as it is.
>
> So the answer is **13.3**.

> Round 15.467 to 2 dp.
>
> 1 5 . 4 6 7
> 'last digit'   'decider'
>
> The decider is 5 or more, so round the last digit up.
>
> So the answer is **15.47**.

You round to a **whole number** in a similar way — the 'last digit' is the ones digit.

Now Try This

1) Round these numbers to 1 decimal place:

   a) 11.32   b) 12.864   c) 69.099   d) 1062.654

2) Round these numbers to the nearest whole number:

   a) 13.854   b) 167.3   c) 275.915   d) 98.165

3) Use a calculator to work out these calculations. Round each answer to 2 decimal places.

   a) 19 ÷ 8   b) 11.37 × 11.1   c) 1003 ÷ 16

Section Three — Decimals

Rounding and Estimating Decimals

Round Decimals to Estimate Answers

It's useful to round numbers in a calculation to work out an **approximate** answer. Then you can check if your answer makes sense.

A group of 5 friends go to a restaurant. They spend £109.89 on food and £21.09 on drinks. They decide to split the total bill equally. Estimate how much each person will pay.

You need to add the amount for food and drink together, then divide by 5.

1) Round each amount (to the nearest £10 will do) and add together: £110 + £20 = £130
2) Now do the division: £130 ÷ 5 = £26

So each person pays approximately **£26**.

Now Try This

1) George has £8.18 in two-pence pieces.
   Tick a correct estimate for the total number of coins he has.

   820 ÷ 2 ☐   820 × 2 ☐   82 ÷ 20 ☐   2 × 8180 ☐

2) Eve lays 58 planks of wood end to end. Each plank is 0.21 metres long. Use estimation to decide whether the total length of the planks is likely to be more than 10 m.

   ....

   ....

3) Thomas weighs 41.4 kg. His father is twice as heavy.
   His mother is 9.4 kg lighter than his father.
   Estimate the total weight of the three family members.

   ....

   ....

Notes

Adding and Subtracting Decimals

Luckily enough, you can add and subtract decimals using the written methods you've met before.

Line Up the Decimal Points in Written Methods

See page 10 for written methods of adding and subtracting.

To **add** or **subtract** decimals, line up the decimal points.
Then fill in zeros, so all the numbers have the same number of decimal places.

Calculate 11.53 + 4.275.

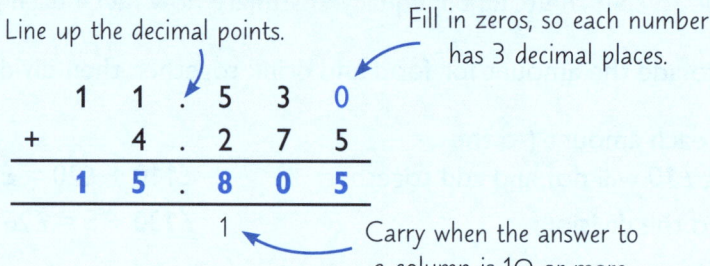

Line up the decimal points.
Fill in zeros, so each number has 3 decimal places.
Carry when the answer to a column is 10 or more.

Alan has 1.37 kg of flour. He uses 0.725 kg to bake a cake. How much flour does he have left?

This is a subtraction.
You need to subtract 0.725 from 1.37:

So he has **0.645 kg** of flour left.

0 is smaller than 5. So borrow from the column to the left.

Now Try This

1) Calculate:

   a) 15.7 + 3.8   b) 14.563 + 12.64   c) 13 + 65.829 + 17.1

   d) 54.5 − 22.3   e) 103.76 − 9.97   f) 78.84 − 23.489

2) Kai buys the items below from a corner shop.
   How much did he spend in total?

Sherbet dip	Chocolate bar	Crisps
£0.62	£1.05	£0.38

Adding and Subtracting Decimals

3) Akram pays £12.38 to have a puncture on his bike repaired. He pays with a £20 note. How much change does he get?

....

4) Roger is a 200 m sprinter. The table shows the times of his last 5 runs.

Race	1	2	3	4	5
Time (s)	20.68	20.92	24.36	22.89	20.76

a) What was the total time for the 5 races?

....

....

b) What is the difference between his fastest and slowest times?

....

5) At the supermarket checkout, Mrs Fisher's groceries come to £164.64. She uses a voucher to reduce the amount she pays to £137.89. She then goes to the petrol station and pays £48.78 for some fuel.

a) How much money did she save by using the voucher?

....

....

b) How much did she pay in total for her grocery shop and fuel?

....

....

Notes

Multiplying and Dividing Decimals

More calculating with decimals now — some of these skills are useful when splitting a bill with friends.

Ignore the Decimal Points when Multiplying

To **multiply** by a decimal, follow these steps:

1) Ignore the decimal points.
2) Do the multiplication with whole numbers.
3) Put the decimal point in the answer. Count the total number of decimal places (dp) in the original numbers. The answer has this many decimal places.

Look back at page 12 for more on multiplying.

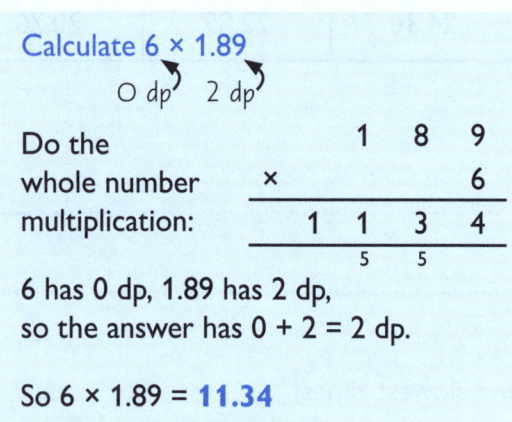

Calculate 6 × 1.89
0 dp   2 dp

Do the whole number multiplication:

```
    1 8 9
  ×     6
  1 1 3 4
    5 5
```

6 has 0 dp, 1.89 has 2 dp, so the answer has 0 + 2 = 2 dp.

So 6 × 1.89 = **11.34**

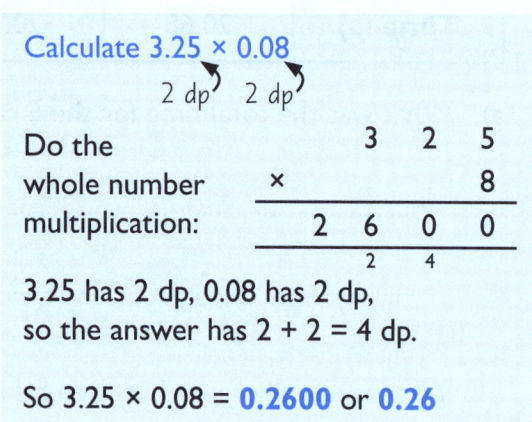

Calculate 3.25 × 0.08
2 dp   2 dp

Do the whole number multiplication:

```
    3 2 5
  ×     8
  2 6 0 0
      2 4
```

3.25 has 2 dp, 0.08 has 2 dp, so the answer has 2 + 2 = 4 dp.

So 3.25 × 0.08 = **0.2600** or **0.26**

Now Try This

1) Calculate: *Use your times tables knowledge to answer these.*

   a) 0.2 × 0.4   b) 0.07 × 0.5   c) 0.002 × 0.7   d) 0.005 × 0.012

   ....

2) Cliff is paid £12.22 per hour. He gets 1.5 times his hourly pay on a Saturday.

   a) What is his hourly pay on a Saturday?

   ....

   b) How much does he earn if he works for 8 hours on a Friday?

   ....

Section Three — Decimals

Multiplying and Dividing Decimals

Use Equivalent Fractions to Divide a Decimal

To divide a decimal by a **whole number**, e.g. 3.42 ÷ 6, use the same written method that you use for whole numbers.

$$\begin{array}{r} 0\ .\ 5\ 7 \\ 6\overline{)3\ .\ ^34\ ^42} \end{array}$$

Make sure your decimal point goes in the right place.

To divide a number by a **decimal**, write the division as a fraction. Find an equivalent fraction where the bottom number is a whole number by multiplying both the top and bottom numbers by 10, 100, etc.

What is 1.278 ÷ 0.06?

1) Write the division as a fraction:

$$\frac{1.278}{0.06} \xrightarrow{\times 100} = \frac{127.8}{6}$$

The bottom is now a whole number.

2) Use a written method to do 127.8 ÷ 6:

$$\begin{array}{r} 0\ 2\ 1\ .\ 3 \\ 6\overline{)1\ ^12\ 7\ .\ ^18} \end{array}$$

So 1.278 ÷ 0.06 = **21.3**

127.8 ÷ 6 gives the same answer as 1.278 ÷ 0.06.

Now Try This

1) Calculate:

a) 18.12 ÷ 6

b) 50.72 ÷ 8

c) 27.128 ÷ 0.4

2) Charlotte has 25.6 m of ribbon. She cuts it into 8 equal pieces. How long is each piece of ribbon?

3) It costs £0.08 to photocopy one A4 sheet. Petri paid £36.08 in total for photocopying. How many photocopies did she make?

Notes

Section Four — Percentages

Percentages of Amounts

A key thing to remember when working with percentages is that 'per cent' means 'out of 100'.

A Percentage is a Fraction of an Amount

Learn These Easy Percentages

- To find 50%, divide by 2.
- To find 25%, divide by 4.
- To find 10%, divide by 10.
- To find 1%, divide by 100.

Find 25% of 360.

360 ÷ 4 = **90**

25% is 25 out of 100, which is one quarter — that's why you divide by 4.

Find Any Percentage in Two Steps

To find a percentage of an amount:

1) Turn the percentage into a decimal by dividing by 100.
2) Multiply the decimal by the amount.

47% of 600 people responded to a survey. How many people responded?

1) 47 ÷ 100 = 0.47   2) 0.47 × 600 = **282**

Now Try This

1) Work out: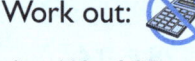

   a) 1% of 85   b) 25% of 860   c) 50% of 300

   ....

2) 10% of the 420 books in a library are fiction. How many fiction books are there?

   ....

3) Work out:

   a) 28% of 1750   b) 96% of 500   c) 52% of 575

   ....

4) A 400 g tin of soup contains 32% spinach. How many grams of spinach is in the soup?

   ....

5) Bev buys a skirt priced at £18. She has a 35% off voucher. How much will she save?

   ....

Percentages of Amounts

Break Percentages into Easy Parts

You can still work out harder percentages without a calculator. Split each percentage into easy ones, then add or subtract them.

Lynn read 49% of a 700-page book. How many pages is this?

49% = 50% − 1%
50% = 700 ÷ 2 = 350
1% = 700 ÷ 100 = 7   ⟶   49% = 350 − 7 = **343 pages**

Find 75% of 640.

75% = 50% + 25%
50% = 640 ÷ 2 = 320
25% = 640 ÷ 4 = 160

75% = 320 + 160 = **480**

Now Try This

1) Work out:

   a) 3% of 200

   b) 70% of 50

   c) 35% of 300

2) In a survey of 500 people, 76% of people said they liked bacon. How many people was this?

3) Aadan wants to buy a car for £3300. He needs a 15% deposit. How much does he need?

4) Molly and Yan took a test with 120 questions. Molly got 45% of the questions correct. Yan got 55 questions correct. Show who answered more questions correctly.

Notes

Expressing Amounts as Percentages

Percentages are one way of expressing a proportion of something. Here's how you might do it.

You Can Turn Any Fraction into a Percentage

To write one amount as a percentage of another without a calculator:

1) Write the amounts as a fraction.
2) Write an equivalent fraction over 100.
3) The top number is the percentage.

For more on converting between fractions and percentages, see p.44-47.

You may have to write an equivalent fraction in two steps.

Mike went on a 20-day holiday. It rained on 8 days. On what percentage of the days did it rain?

Write the rainy days as a fraction of the total days: $\frac{8}{20} = \frac{40}{100} \rightarrow$ **40%** (× 5)

Write 3 as a percentage of 15.

$\frac{3}{15} = \frac{1}{5} = \frac{20}{100} \rightarrow$ **20%** (÷3, ×20)

Now Try This

1) Write these proportions as percentages.

   a) 9 out of 20 ....

   b) 4 out of 25 ....

   c) 7 out of 50 ....

   d) 12 out of 40 ....

   e) 24 out of 60 ....

   f) 21 out of 75 ....

2) 450 raffle tickets are sold out of 500. What percentage of the tickets remain unsold?

   ....

3) There were 6000 spectators at a football match. 2100 of them were children. What percentage of the spectators were children?

   ....

4) There are 20 beads in a bag. Each bead is red, blue or yellow. 8 beads are red and there are an equal number of blue and yellow beads. What percentage of the beads are blue?

   ....

Section Four — Percentages

Expressing Amounts as Percentages

There's a Different Method When Using a Calculator

To write one amount as a percentage of another:

1) Divide the first number by the second to get a decimal.
2) Multiply the decimal by 100 to get a percentage.

18 out of 150 students are vegan. What is this as a percentage?

1) 18 ÷ 150 = 0.12
2) 0.12 × 100 = **12%**

Now Try This

1) Write these proportions as percentages.

   a) 644 out of 1150

   b) 13 out of 52

   c) 6.4 out of 256

   d) 2080 out of 4000

   e) 66 out of 125

   f) 825 out of 75 000

2) Rob measures an angle in a pie chart as 162°. What is this as a percentage of 360°?

3) Melissa earns a monthly wage of £540 from her part-time job. She saves £162 a month. What percentage of her monthly wage does she save?

4) Simon is fundraising for a charity. His target is £45. So far, he has raised £6.21. What percentage of his target has Simon raised so far?

Notes

Percentage Increase

If the boss gives you a 15% pay rise, you're going to want to know how much that is. Read on for how.

Add a Percentage Increase to 100%

To find the new amount after a percentage increase:
1) Work out the percentage of the original amount.
2) Add this on to the original amount.

See p.34 for how to work out a percentage of an amount.

A shop increases its prices by 25%. What is the new price of a belt that used to cost £52?
1) 25% of £52 = £52 ÷ 4 = £13
2) New cost = £52 + £13 = **£65**

If you are using a **calculator**, there is a more efficient method.
1) Add the percentage to 100%. Convert this percentage to a decimal.
2) Then multiply the original amount by the decimal.

Jo's £43 credit card bill is increased by 13%. How much does she now owe?
1) 13% + 100% = 113% → 113 ÷ 100 = 1.13
2) Amount owed = £43 × 1.13 = **£48.59**

Now Try This

1) Work out these percentage increases.

   a) Increase 60 by 50%.

   ....

   b) Increase 120 by 10%.

   ....

2) Shea paid £84 000 for a house. Its value has increased by 20%. Find its new value.

   ....

3) Work out these percentage increases.

   a) Increase 157 by 71%.

   ....

   b) Increase 115 by 18%.

   ....

4) Sue's salary is £32 428. She receives a 3% pay increase. What is her new salary?

   ....

Section Four — Percentages

Percentage Increase

Divide 'New' by 'Original' to Find the Percentage Increase

You may be given an **original amount** and the new value after a percentage increase. Follow these steps to find what the **percentage increase** was:

1) Divide the new value by the original value to get a decimal. — The decimal will be greater than 1.
2) Convert the decimal to a percentage.
3) Subtract 100% to find the percentage increase.

> The price of a toaster increased from £40 to £50. What was the percentage increase?
> 1) New value ÷ original value: 50 ÷ 40 = 1.25
> 2) Convert the decimal to a percentage: 1.25 × 100 = 125%
> 3) Subtract 100%:   125% − 100% = **25%**

Now Try This

1) A business increased its number of employees from 100 to 160. Calculate the percentage increase in the number of employees.

   ....

2) In 2020, a boxing club had 120 members. In 2024, it had 180 members. What was the percentage increase in the number of members?

   ....

3) In October 2023, a first-class stamp cost £1.25. In October 2024, it cost £1.65. Calculate the percentage increase in the price.

   ....

4) A factory increased their workforce from 4320 to 5832. Calculate the percentage increase.

   ....

Notes

Percentage Decrease

Sales are often based on a percentage decrease, e.g. 20% off. So this stuff is definitely worth learning.

Subtract a Percentage Decrease from 100%

To find the new amount after a percentage decrease:
1) Work out the percentage of the original amount.
2) Subtract this from the original amount.

These methods are similar to the ones for percentage increase on p.38.

Decrease 30 by 20%.   20% = 10% × 2
1) 20% of 30 = 30 ÷ 10 × 2 = 6   2) New amount = 30 − 6 = **24**

If you are using a **calculator**, there is a more efficient method.
1) Subtract the percentage from 100%. Convert this to a decimal.
2) Then multiply the original amount by this decimal.

A 125-mile bike ride is reduced by 28% due to bad weather. What is the new distance?
1) 100% − 28% = 72% → 72 ÷ 100 = 0.72   2) New distance = 125 × 0.72 = **90 miles**

Now Try This

1) Work out these percentage increases.

   a) Decrease 80 by 30%.

   b) Decrease 280 by 15%.

   ....

2) A new car cost £36 000. Its value has decreased by 25%. Find its new value.

   ....

3) Work out these percentage decreases.

   a) Decrease 1400 by 31%.

   b) Decrease 628 by 98%.

   ....

4) Roshin sees the offer on the right.
   How much would he pay for the tablet and pen together?

   | Pear Tablet: £109 Pen: £22 |
   | Buy both and save 15% |

   ....

   ....

Percentage Decrease

Finding a Percentage Decrease Involves a Decimal Smaller than 1

You may be given an **original amount** and the new value after a percentage decrease. Follow these steps to find what the **percentage decrease** was:

1) Divide the new value by the original value to get a decimal. ← The decimal should be smaller than 1.
2) Convert the decimal to a percentage.
3) Subtract this percentage **from** 100% to find the percentage decrease.

A jacket is reduced from £50 to £30. What was the percentage decrease?
1) New value ÷ original value: 30 ÷ 50 = 0.6
2) Convert the decimal to a percentage: 0.6 × 100 = 60%
3) Subtract from 100%:   100% − 60% = **40%**

The first two steps are the same as for finding a percentage increase on page 39.

Now Try This

1) Jon buys a suit reduced from £150 to £120. What was the percentage reduction?

   ....

2) Jan's weight decreased from 60 kg to 57 kg. Calculate her percentage decrease in weight.

   ....

3) A travel agent reduces the price of a holiday from £3240 to £2656.80. Calculate the percentage reduction.

   ....

4) Calculate the percentage the population of Tawlyn decreased by:

Year	2022	2023	2024
Population of Tawlyn	1000	750	525

   a) from 2023 to 2024.   b) from 2022 to 2024.

   ....

Notes

Finding the Original Value

You may have to work backwards to find an amount before a percentage change. Read on for how.

The Original Value is 100%

You could be given the result of a percentage change and be asked to find the **original value**. There are three steps to follow:

1) Write the amount as a percentage of the original value. ← *For a percentage increase, this will be greater than 100%. For a percentage decrease, this will be smaller than 100%.*
2) Divide to find 1%.
3) Multiply by 100 to find 100% (the original value).

> Yi Ming buys a scooter for £140 in a 20% sale. What was the original price of the scooter?
>
> 1) £140 is 100% − 20% = 80% of the original price: 80% = £140
> 2) Divide by 80 to find 1%: 1% = £1.75
> 3) Multiply to find 100%: 100% = **£175**

Now Try This

1) A lamp costs £14 in a 30% off sale. What was its original price?

   ....

   ....

2) Sharna earns £156 a week after a pay rise of 4%. How much did she earn before the pay rise?

   ....

   ....

3) The population of a village increased by 15% to 805. What was it before the increase?

   ....

   ....

4) After a haircut, a dog's weight decreased by 2% to 4.9 kg. What was its original weight?

   ....

   ....

Finding the Original Value

5) Jason removes some items from his suitcase. This decreases its weight by 10%. It now weighs 24.3 kg. How much did it weigh before he removed the items?

   ....

   ....

6) The width of a pond decreases by 8% in a drought. It now measures 248.4 m across. What was its original width?

   ....

   ....

7) Charlotte's car repair bill is £151.80. This includes VAT at 20%. How much was the bill before VAT was added?

   VAT is a tax added to most products and services sold.

   ....

   ....

8) A cleaner decides to decrease his hourly rate by 3.5%. He now charges £19.30 per hour. How much did he charge before the decrease?

   ....

   ....

9) 97% of a software update is complete. There are only 6 minutes remaining. How long will the software update take in total? Give your answer in hours and minutes.

   ....

   ....

Notes

Fractions, Decimals and Percentages

Fractions, decimals and percentages are all parts of a whole. And you can change between them.

You Need to Change Between Proportions

Learn These Equivalent Amounts

$\frac{1}{2}$	=	0.5	=	50%
$\frac{1}{4}$	=	0.25	=	25%

$\frac{3}{4}$	=	0.75	=	75%
$\frac{1}{5}$	=	0.2	=	20%

$\frac{1}{10}$	=	0.1	=	10%
$\frac{1}{1}$	=	1	=	100%

Change a Fraction into a Decimal

To change a fraction into a decimal, divide the top number by the bottom number.
Use short division if you don't have a calculator.

What is $\frac{2}{5}$ as a decimal?

$\frac{2}{5} = 2 \div 5 = $ **0.4**

What is $\frac{3}{8}$ as a decimal?

Work out $3 \div 8$:

8 won't divide into 3, so add a decimal point and zeros.

$$\begin{array}{r} 0.375 \\ 8\overline{)3.\,^30\,^60\,^40} \end{array}$$

$\frac{3}{8} = $ **0.375**

Now Try This

1) Change these into decimals:

   a) $\frac{1}{5}$ b) 75%   c) $\frac{3}{10}$

   ....

2) Use short division to write these fractions as decimals:

   a) $\frac{5}{4}$ b) $\frac{1}{8}$ c) $\frac{39}{4}$

3) 26 out of 32 of Max's ties are blue. Give the proportion of blue ties as:

   a) a fraction in its simplest form.   b) a decimal.

   ....

Fractions, Decimals and Percentages

Change a Decimal into a Fraction

There are three steps to change a decimal into a fraction:

1) Multiply the decimal by 10, 100 or 1000 etc. to make it a **whole number**.
2) Write this whole number as the **top number** of the fraction and the number you multiplied by as the **bottom number**.
3) **Simplify** using equivalent fractions.

What you multiply by depends on the number of decimal places.

What is 0.06 as a fraction?

1) Multiply by 100 to make it a whole number: 0.06 × 100 = 6

2) Write 6 as the top number of the fraction and 100 as the bottom number: $0.06 = \frac{6}{100}$

3) Divide the top and bottom by the same number to simplify: $\frac{6}{100} \underset{\div 2}{\overset{\div 2}{=}} \frac{3}{50}$

See p.19 for how to simplify fractions.

Now Try This

1) Change each decimal into a fraction in its simplest form: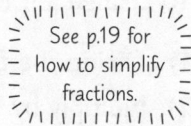

    a)   0.7   b)   0.04   c)   0.31

    ....

    d)   0.85   e)   0.125   f)   0.428

    ....

2) Order the following, from smallest to largest:

       $\frac{15}{25}$,   0.7,   0.55,   75%, $\frac{5}{10}$

Change all of these into fractions or decimals, then compare.

....

....

Notes

Fractions, Decimals and Percentages

Percentages are easier to compare than fractions or decimals, so the skills on this page are really handy.

Change a Fraction or Decimal into a Percentage

If a fraction has a bottom number of 100, the **top number** gives the percentage, e.g. $\frac{89}{100}$ = 89%.

To change a fraction into a percentage, find an equivalent fraction with 100 on the bottom.

This table shows numbers that are simple to change.

Bottom number	50	25	20	10	5	4
Multiply by	2	4	5	10	20	25

What is $\frac{3}{10}$ as a percentage?

$$\frac{3}{10} \xrightarrow{\times 10} = \frac{30}{100} = \mathbf{30\%}$$
$\times 10$

To change a fraction into a percentage with a calculator:

1) Divide the top number by the bottom.
2) Multiply by 100 and add a percentage sign.

To change a <u>decimal</u> into a percentage, just do the second step.

$\frac{18}{24}$ of learners passed their driving test. What is this as a percentage?

1) Change to a decimal: $\frac{18}{24}$ = 18 ÷ 24 = 0.75

2) Multiply by 100: 0.75 × 100 = **75%**

Now Try This

1) Change these to percentages:

    a) $\frac{3}{5}$ b) $\frac{17}{25}$ c) $\frac{9}{20}$

    ....

    d) $\frac{12}{75}$ e) $\frac{6}{15}$

Do d) and e) in two stages — first divide to get an equivalent fraction with a bottom number in the table above.

2) Vik took 3 tests. He got 28 out of 40 in English, 69% in Maths, and 50 out of 70 in Science. In which test did he get the greatest percentage?

....

....

Fractions, Decimals and Percentages

Change a Percentage into a Fraction or Decimal

To change a percentage into a **fraction**:
1) Write the percentage as the top number and 100 on the bottom.
2) Simplify using equivalent fractions.

To change a percentage into a **decimal**, divide by 100:

Write 24% as:

a) a fraction in its simplest form

$$\frac{24}{100} \overset{\div 4}{\underset{\div 4}{=}} \frac{6}{25}$$

b) a decimal

$24 \div 100 = \mathbf{0.24}$

Now Try This

1) Complete the table below by finding the equivalent fractions and decimals:

Percentage	56%	38%	3%
Fraction (simplest form)	....	....	....
Decimal	....	....	....

2) Order the following, from smallest to largest.

a) 67%, 0.61, $\frac{198}{300}$ ....

b) 82%, 0.819, $\frac{170}{200}$ ....

3) Julie, Ruth and Aanya are saving to go on holiday. Julie saves £120 out of her £500 wages, Ruth saves $\frac{1}{4}$ of her wages, and Aanya saves 22% of hers.
Show who saves the greatest proportion of their wages.

....

....

Notes

Section Five — Ratio and Proportion

Ratios

Ratios may look odd, but working through some examples will help you get your head around them.

Ratios Split Things Up into Parts

Writing a Ratio

A **ratio** shows the size of one part compared to other parts.

You write a ratio using a colon (:) to separate each part.

There were 7 dry days and 23 wet days in September. What is the ratio of dry to wet days?

dry : wet
7 : 23

Check your ratio is the correct way round. E.g. the ratio of **wet** to **dry** days would be 23 : 7.

Simplifying a Ratio

To simplify a ratio, divide all parts by the same number.

Simplify the ratio 5 : 10 : 15.

÷5 (5 : 10 : 15) ÷5
1 : 2 : 3

With tricker numbers you might need to divide both sides **more than once**. It's a lot like simplifying fractions — see p.19.

Now Try This

1) There are 14 boys and 7 girls in a class. What is the ratio of boys to girls?

For questions 1-4 make sure you simplify your ratios.

....

2) There are 20 blue cars, 30 red cars and 50 black cars in a car park. Write the ratio of blue to red to black cars.

....

3) There are 8 brown loaves and 6 white loaves. What is the ratio of white to brown loaves?

....

4) 3600 men, 900 women and 1500 children attend a football match. What is the ratio of men to women to children?

....

Ratios

Start by Finding the Value of One Part

Ratios are often used to divide a total amount into parts.

Tarsem shares £108 with his three grandchildren in the ratio of their ages.
Hari is 9 years old, Ankita is 6 and Remi is 3. How much does each child receive?

1) Find the number of parts: 9 + 6 + 3 = **18**
2) Find the value of one part: total amount ÷ number of parts
   = £108 ÷ 18 = **£6**
3) Multiply the value of one part by each age.

Hari	**Ankita**	**Remi**
£6 × 9 = **£54**	£6 × 6 = **£36**	£6 × 3 = **£18**

*You can check your answer by making sure all the parts add up to £108:
£54 + £36 + £18 = £108.*

Now Try This

1) Stephen and Laura share £50 in the ratio 3 : 2. How much money does Laura get?

   ....

2) A 60-litre bag of compost is split into small, medium and large pots in the ratio 2 : 3 : 7. How much compost is in each pot?

   ....

3) Grace adds water to concentrated screenwash to put in her car. The ratio of concentrated screenwash to water is 1 : 25. How much water is there in 1300 ml of mixed screenwash?

   ....

4) Karl has 240 tiles. There are 23 white tiles for every 25 black tiles. How many white tiles does Karl have?

   ....

Notes

Ratios

A bit more on ratios. You can also use them to work out total amounts.

Some Questions Don't Give the Total Amount

Sometimes you need to work out a value from a ratio but you aren't given a total amount. This usually involves you working out the value of one part.

Tim and Ian share money in the ratio 2 : 7. Tim gets £36.

a) How much money does Ian get?

1) Write out what you know: Tim : Ian
   2 : 7
   £36 : ?   ← ? is the value you need to work out.

2) Find the value of one part: £36 (Tim's share) ÷ 2 = £18   So one part = **£18**

3) Multiply to find the value of Ian's share: Ian has 7 parts so you can multiply to work out his share.
   Tim : Ian
   2 : 7 × 18
   £36 : ?   Ian's share = £18 × 7 = **£126**

b) What is the total amount of money they share?

1) Work out the total number of parts: 2 + 7 = **9**

2) Multiply this by the value of one part to find the total: £18 × 9 = **£162**

Check your answer: Tim and Ian's shares should add up to your total (£36 + £126 = £162).

Now Try This

1) Stephanie and Laurence share potatoes in the ratio 5 : 3. Stephanie gets 105 potatoes. How many potatoes does Laurence get?

....

....

2) Pavel and Katy are dog walkers. They split the dogs to walk between them in the ratio 3 : 13. Katy gets 26 dogs to walk. How many dogs does Pavel have to walk?

....

....

Ratios

3) A historic house is holding a behind-the-scenes open day. For safety, there must be a ratio of staff to visitors of 1 : 9. If 162 visitors are attending, how many staff members are needed?

....

....

4) A pile of sand is shovelled into a small bag, a medium bag and a large bag in the ratio 2 : 3 : 5. The medium bag contains 42 kg. Work out the weight of sand in the other two bags.

   a) small bag

   ....

   b) large bag

   ....

5) A basketball team play home and away games in a ratio of 6 home to 4 away. In a year the team play 18 home games. How many games do the team play in total?

....

6) Dan has space for one small bag and two large bags on his bike. The ratio of the volumes of the bags is 2 : 5 : 5. The small bag can hold 6 litres. What is the total volume of the bags?

....

....

7) A staff room is being redecorated. The staff have voted on the paint colour for the walls. The ratio of votes for white to yellow to blue was 4 : 2 : 8. 32 people voted for blue. How many people voted in total?

....

....

Notes

Direct Proportion

Proportion can be used to scale up or scale down. Here's how to use direct proportion.

Direct Proportion means Change by the Same Amount

Two amounts can be **directly** proportional. As one increases, the other will increase at the **same rate**. So if one amount is tripled, the other amount is tripled too.

To work out direct proportion questions:
1) Divide to find the value for 'one thing'.
2) Multiply (scale up) to find the value you need.

> 6 pencils cost £1.20. Find the cost of 5 pencils.
>
> 1) Cost of one pencil = £1.20 ÷ 6 = **£0.20**
> 2) 5 pencils = £0.20 × 5 = **£1**

If you do your working in pence, don't forget to convert back to pounds.

You may be asked to make an **assumption**.

> a) If 5 technicians can change 15 car tyres in an hour, how many tyres could 12 technicians change in an hour?
>
> 1) Find out how many tyres one technician can change per hour: 15 ÷ 5 = **3**
> 2) Multiply this by 12: 3 × 12 = **36 tyres per hour**
>
> b) What assumption are you making about the 12 technicians?
>
> All the technicians take the **same amount of time** to change a tyre.

This is the same as saying they work at the same rate.

Now Try This

1) Sharon buys 4 pouches of cat food for £1.60. Find the cost of: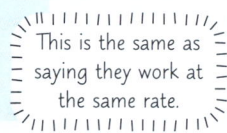

   a) 3 pouches   b) 5 pouches   c) 14 pouches

   ....

2) Five small bars of chocolate cost 80p. How much do three bars cost?

   ....

3) An electrician charges an hourly fee. They charge £140 for a 4-hour job. For a similar job that only took 3 hours, how much would the electrician charge?

   ....

Section Five — Ratio and Proportion

Direct Proportion

4) A car travels a distance of 120 miles on a motorway in 2 hours.

   a) How far does the car travel in 5 hours?

   ....

   b) How long would it take the car to travel 180 miles?

   ....

   c) What assumption did you make for parts a) and b)?

   ....

5) A recipe for 14 fairy cakes includes 112 grams of sugar. Riz wants to make 25 cakes. How much sugar does she need?

   ....

6) A team of 6 cleaners can clean 168 hotel rooms per day.

   a) How many rooms could a team of 10 cleaners clean per day?

   ....

   b) What assumption did you make?

   ....

7) The total length of eight metal poles is 288 cm. How long are 35 metal poles? Give your answer in metres.

   ....

Notes

Inverse Proportion

Inverse proportion is when one thing gets bigger as another gets smaller.

Inverse Proportion is the Opposite of Direct Proportion

If two values are **inversely** proportional, one increases at the same rate as the other decreases. E.g. speed and time are inversely proportional. If speed **halves**, the time for a journey **doubles**.

To work out inverse proportion questions:

1) Multiply to find the value for 'one thing'.
2) Divide this to find the value you need.

You often have to make assumptions, e.g. that all people work at the same rate.

> 4 workers take 6 hours to paint a fence. How long would it take 12 workers to do this?
> 1) Multiply to find how long 1 worker would take: 4 × 6 = 24 hours
> 2) Divide 24 hours between 12 workers: 24 ÷ 12 = **2 hours**

Now Try This

1) 6 tractors take 1 hour to plough a field. How long will it take 12 tractors?

   ....

2) 4 children share a box of sweets equally. They get 9 sweets each.
   How many sweets would each child get if the box was shared between 12 children?

   ....

3) 6 parents take 1 hour 30 minutes to make paper chains for a party.
   How long would it take 9 parents to make the same paper chains?

   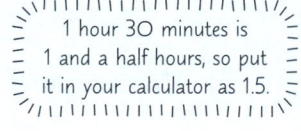

   1 hour 30 minutes is 1 and a half hours, so put it in your calculator as 1.5.

   ....

4) A box of emergency rations for 8 mountaineers will last 6 days.

   a) How long would the box last 6 mountaineers?

   ....

   b) How long would the box last 32 mountaineers?

   ....

Inverse Proportion

5) 5 teachers take 6 hours to mark a set of exam papers.
Complete the table to show how long this task would take for different numbers of teachers.

Teachers	1	6	12	15
Time	....	....	....	....

6) 11 gardeners take 15 minutes to plant some roses. How long would this take 5 gardeners?

....

7) A company is moving offices. They hire 4 delivery vans to move the office contents. Each van makes 10 trips between the offices. Each van is full on each trip.

  a) How many trips would 5 vans each have taken?

  ....

  b) State an assumption you made in part a).

  ....

8) 8 taps can fill a small pool in 45 minutes.

  a) How long would it take if 2 of the taps were turned off?

  ....

  b) State an assumption you made in part a).

  ....

Notes

Section Six — Formulas

Formulas in Words

Formulas can be written in words. But it isn't always obvious what the formula is from the question.

A Formula is a Rule for Working Out an Amount

You need to **interpret** the question and write a formula in words.

A recipe says that pork leg joints should be roasted for 40 minutes per kilogram. How long will it take to cook a 3-kilogram leg joint using this recipe?

1) Work out the formula: Cooking time = 40 × number of kilograms
2) Put the correct number in: Cooking time = 40 × **3** = **120 minutes**

Check the unit of the number you put in. It must be in kilograms.

Sometimes there are **two steps** in a formula. The order you do them in is important.

A plumber charges a call-out fee of £70, plus £50 per hour. How much will it cost for this plumber to do a job that takes 4 hours?

1) Work out the formula: Cost = 70 + (50 × number of hours)
2) Put the correct number in: Cost = 70 + (50 × **4**)
   = 70 + 200 = **£270**

The multiplication must be done first — see page 14. Putting it in brackets makes this clearer.

Now Try This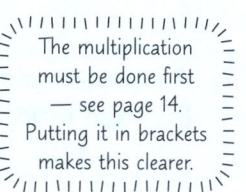

For each question, write down the formula you use.

1) 'Irene's Ironing' charges £1.20 to iron a shirt. How much will they charge for 7 shirts?

   ....

   ....

2) In a game, you score 5 points for a blue card and 10 points for a red card. Caleb has 12 blue cards and 4 red cards. What does he score?

   ....

   ....

3) A taxi has an initial fee of £5, then a cost of £2 per mile. How much will a 6-mile journey cost?

   ....

   ....

Formulas in Words

4) It takes 1 person 15 minutes to wash a car.
   How long does it take Mike and Pete to wash 13 cars if they work together?

   ....

   ....

5) Sarah's mobile phone company charges her £2 per day to use her phone abroad, plus 50p for each call made. She uses her phone abroad for 7 days and makes 20 calls in total. How much will Sarah be charged?

   You'll need to change 50p into pounds.

   ....

   ....

6) Fatima uses 10 units of electricity over 3 days.

   a) The electricity company Squid has a daily fixed charge of 61p.
      On top of this daily amount, it charges 28p per unit of electricity used.
      How much would Fatima be charged by Squid? Give your answer in pounds.

      ....

      ....

   b) The electricity company Eel also has a daily fixed charge of 61p.
      However, they charge different amounts for electricity used in the day and in the night:

      | Daytime charge per unit | 30p |
      | Night-time charge per unit | 20p |

      Fatima used 7 out of the 10 units of electricity during the day.
      How much would Fatima be charged by Eel? Give your answer in pounds.

      ....

      ....

Notes

Formulas in Symbols

Formulas often contain mysterious letters. Once you learn to decipher them, they're not so bad.

Each Letter in a Formula Represents Something

An example of a formula is $s = d \div t$ (s represents speed, d is distance and t is time). Sometimes formulas don't use '×' or '÷':

$a \times b$ can be written as ab $a \div b$ can be written as $\frac{a}{b}$ $a \times a$ can be written as a^2

You can replace the letters in a formula with numbers. This is called **substituting**. You'll often have to use BIDMAS (p.14) to decide which bit of a formula to work out first.

The cost in pounds of hiring a car, C, can be worked out using the formula below:
$C = 1.50m + 99$, where m = miles driven

Si hires a car and drives 200 miles. How much will this cost?

1) Write the formula out: Cost = $1.50m + 99$
2) Replace any letters with numbers you know.
   He drives 200 miles, so $m = 200$ Cost = $1.50 \times 200 + 99$
3) Work it out using BIDMAS.
   Do multiplication before addition.   Cost = $300 + 99 = 399$

So the cost is **£399**. ← You're told the formula gives the cost in pounds.

Now Try This

1) Find the value of:

   a) $4t + 8$, if $t = 5$ b) $5p - 2r$, if $p = 14$ and $r = 11$

2) Evaluate: *'Evaluate' means 'work out'.*

   a) abc, if $a = 5$, $b = 6$ and $c = 12$ b) $\frac{5y}{4}$ if $y = 8$

   c) $\frac{U}{V} + W$, if $U = 12$, $V = 4$ and $W = 7$ d) $st^3 - z$, if $s = 11$, $t = 2$ and $z = 21$

Formulas in Symbols

3) The cost of hiring a bike in pounds, C, is given by the formula:

   C = 35d + 20, where d = the number of days hired

   Find the cost if Uzma hires a bike for 4 days.

   ....

4) The formula used to convert between degrees Celsius (°C) and degrees Fahrenheit (°F) is:

   F = 1.8C + 32, where F is the temperature in °F and C is the temperature in °C

   Work out F if C = 30 °C.

   ....

5) A printing firm uses the formula below to calculate the cost of business cards in pence, p:

   p = N(2 + 0.11L), where N is the number of cards and L = number of letters

   Find the cost of 200 cards with 160 letters on each. Give your answer in pounds.

   ....

   ....

6) The formula for the volume of a cone, V, is:

   $V = \frac{1}{3}\pi r^2 h$,

   where r = the radius of the base and h = height

   Use the π button on your calculator. If you don't have one, use 3.14.

   Calculate the volume of a cone with a base radius of 5 cm and a height of 8 cm.

   Give your answer in cm³ to the nearest whole number.

   ....

   ....

Notes

Topic-Based Questions

These questions are all designed to give you some extra practice on the topics in this book.

Numbers and Calculations

1) Write three million, one thousand and two in digits.

   ....

2) Write 692 470 in words.

   ....

   ....

3) The average yearly temperature of 3 places is given in the table.

Place	Canada	Greenland	Sweden
Average temperature	−4 °C	−19 °C	3 °C

   a) Which of these places is the coldest on average? ....

   b) What is the difference in average temperature between Canada and Sweden?

   ....

4) The table below shows the album sales of a band.

Album name	Eat Cake	Bacon	Silence	Wild Days	Moves
Sales	185 005	3 872 052	34 386	2 754 045	34 632

   a) Put the albums in order, from smallest to largest sales.

   ....

   b) What were the total sales of 'Eat Cake' and 'Moves'?

   c) What was the difference in sales between 'Eat Cake' and 'Silence'?

Topic-Based Questions

5) Work out the following. Check your answer to each by doing the opposite calculation.

   a) 32 106 + 9478

   Check:

   b) 458 × 63

   Check:

6) A cruise ship uses 4389 dozen eggs per week. 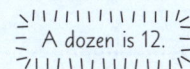 A dozen is 12.

   a) How many eggs is this in total?

   b) There are 7 kitchens on the cruise ship. Each kitchen uses the same number of eggs. How many eggs does each kitchen use?

7) Work out each calculation. Use a calculator to check your answers.

   a) $2 \times 6^2 - 20 \times 3$

   b) $10 \div (13 - 12) \times 2^2$

   c) $5 \times \left(\frac{4^2 + 5}{3} - 4 \right)$

8) Use a calculator to work out $\frac{17.6 \div 2}{7.2^2 + 0.1}$. Give your answer to 2 decimal places.

Topic-Based Questions

Fractions

1) Complete the table by finding the equivalent mixed numbers or improper fractions.

Improper fraction	$\frac{9}{7}$	....	$\frac{43}{6}$	....	$\frac{70}{9}$
Mixed number	$1\frac{2}{7}$	$3\frac{5}{6}$	....	$4\frac{2}{13}$	....

2) In a council election, the winning party won 42 out of 60 seats. What fraction of the seats is this? Give your answer in its simplest form.

....

3) Bin has £6 in his wallet. He spends 90p on a chocolate bar and £1.50 on a drink. What fraction of his money has he spent? Give your answer in its simplest form.

....

4) Four water pumps are being tested. Each pump is connected to a tank containing 2 litres of water. After the test, the amount of water in each tank is measured.
Tank 1 contains $1\frac{1}{5}$ litres, tank 2 has $\frac{7}{8}$ litres, tank 3 has $\frac{3}{4}$ litres, and tank 4 has $\frac{8}{5}$ litres.

a) Which tank contains the most water and which contains the least?

Most: .... Least: ....

b) How much more water does tank 1 contain than tank 3?

....

c) The water from tank 2 is added to tank 4. How much water is in tank 4 now? Give your answer as a mixed number.

....

5) Work out:

a) $\frac{4}{5} - \frac{3}{10} + \frac{7}{20}$

b) $5\frac{3}{8} + 2\frac{1}{4} - 4\frac{1}{3}$

Topic-Based Questions

Decimals

1) A 3 litre bottle of water costs £1.68. What is the cost per litre?

2) Rick is carpeting a 14.95 m² room. The carpet costs £11.95 per m².
   Estimate the cost of the carpet.

3) Work out:

   a) The cost of 0.8 kg of apples at £1.40 per kg.

   b) The cost of 2.6 kg of cherries at £15.65 per kg.

   c) The total cost of the apples and cherries.

4) Holly has measured the height of five trees. Her measurements are shown in the table.

Trees	1	2	3	4	5
Height (m)	7.14	7.09	8.20	8.04	7.90

   What is the difference between the largest and smallest height?

5) A 0.7 kg box of cat food costs £3.85. What is the cost of the cat food per kg?

Topic-Based Questions

Percentages

1) Bob has driven 60% of an 850 km journey. How many km has he driven?

   ....

2) The table on the right shows four employees' monthly wages and the amount they each put in a savings account.

Name	Audrey	Barbara	Colin	Debbie
Wage	£948	£756	£1034	£656
Amount saved	£56.88	£60.48	£113.74	£85.28

   Who saved the greatest percentage of their wage? Give the percentage they saved.

   ....

   ....

3) Bilal's target is to walk 9000 steps per day. By midday he has walked 2340 steps.

   a) What percentage of his daily target is this?

   ....

   b) Bilal increases his target from 9000 to 10 620 steps. What is the percentage increase?

   ....

4) A piece of rope is 39.5 m long. A second piece of rope is 14% longer. How long is the second piece of rope?

   ....

5) Gail's hens lay 560 eggs in the first year. In the second year they lay 476 eggs. What was the percentage decrease in the number of eggs laid?

   ....

6) A cricket match had 1799 supporters this week, which was 30% fewer than last week. How many supporters were there last week?

   ....

Topic-Based Questions

Ratio and Proportion

1) A cocktail has 25 ml of syrup and 200 ml of milk. What is the ratio of syrup to milk?

   ....

2) Charlotte and Sophie share £750 in the ratio 3 : 7. How much does Charlotte get?

   ....

3) A shade called 'swamp' is made by mixing green, blue and brown paint in the ratio 4 : 5 : 1. If 200 ml of green paint is used, how much 'swamp' paint will be made?

   ....

4) Every night Julia spends 1 hour reading. It takes her 2 weeks to read a book with 504 pages. How many nights will it take her to read a book with 360 pages?

   ....

5) An aircraft can travel 220 miles in 20 minutes.

   Assume the plane always travels at the same speed.

   a) How far could it travel in 36 minutes?

   ....

   b) How long would it take to travel 1089 miles? Give your answer in hours and minutes.

   ....

6) A farmer buys a bale of hay every 3 days to feed his 8 horses.

   Assume the horses always eat at the same rate.

   a) How many days would a bale of hay last if the farmer had 16 horses?

   ....

   b) How many days would the bale last if he only had 6 horses?

   ....

Topic-Based Questions

Formulas

1) Given $a = 5$, $b = 4$ and $c = 12$, find the value of:

   a) $\dfrac{2ab}{5}$

   b) $\dfrac{3c}{9} + ab$

   c) $a^2b - c$

   ....

2) The cost of hiring a kayak in pounds, C, is given by the formula:

   $$C = 15 + 3h, \text{ where } h = \text{number of hours}$$

   Find the cost of hiring a kayak for 5 hours.

   ....

3) Jo is deciding whether to buy a railcard for a country she is visiting.
   The options are shown in the table below.

Option	The Ace card	The Bee card	No railcard
Pricing	€5 + €0.15 per journey	€3 + €0.30 per journey for the first 15 journeys, then €0.20 per journey	€1.50 per journey

   She plans to make 20 journeys. Which option is cheapest and what will it cost?

   ....

   ....

4) A recipe book gives the cooking time in minutes, T, for a turkey as:

   $$T = 34w + 25, \text{ where } w = \text{weight in kg}$$

   How many minutes would it take to cook a turkey weighing 3.5 kg?

   ....

5) The grass seed needed in grams, G, for a circular lawn is given by the formula:

   $$G = 30\pi r^2, \text{ where } r = \text{radius in m}$$

   Use $\pi = 3.14$

   How much grass seed is needed for a circular lawn with a radius of 13 m?
   Give your answer to the nearest kg.

   ....

Mixed Practice

Now it's time to put your skills to the test. These questions cover everything you've seen in this book.

Section A   Don't use a calculator for Section A.

1) Write 6% as a decimal.

   ....

2) What is $\sqrt{36} \times (11 + 4)$? Tick (✓) your answer.

   70 ☐   90 ☐   400 ☐   51 ☐

3) Work out $\frac{3}{5} + \frac{2}{3}$, giving your answer as a mixed number.

   ....

4) What is 28.45 − 17.058?

   ....

5) Zoe is a vet. In one week, she weighed 14 dogs, 18 cats and 22 rabbits.

   a) What fraction of the total animals were cats? Give your answer in its simplest form.

   ....

   b) The average weight of the rabbits was 2.8936 kg.
      Write the average weight to 2 decimal places.

   ....

6) Work out:

   a) 7.3 × 8.7   b) 73.6 ÷ 0.8

Mixed Practice

7) A secretary can type 12 emails in 1 hour.
   How long would it take them, in minutes, to type 15 emails?

   ....

8) Lee drives a lorry for his work.

   a) He arrives at a junction. A signpost shows that Sea View is $5\frac{5}{8}$ miles away and Beach Head is $3\frac{3}{4}$ miles. How much further away is Sea View than Beach Head?

   ....

   ....

   b) His lorry is 415 cm tall. The maximum height allowed under a bridge is 4.2 metres. Explain whether it is safe for Lee to travel under the bridge.

   ....

9) Kai's bank account is overdrawn by £42.89.
   The next day, £320.50 of wages is paid into his account.

   'Overdrawn' means he has −£42.89 in his account.

   a) How much money is in his account now?

   ....

   b) Use estimation to check your answer to part (a).

   ....

   c) Kai withdraws £168. He shares this between Panesh and Chloe in the ratio 7 : 5. How much more money does Panesh receive than Chloe?

   ....

   ....

Mixed Practice

Section B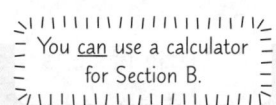

You can use a calculator for Section B.

1) Write six million, four hundred thousand and twenty-eight in digits.

   ....

2) Write the following in order. Start with the smallest value.

   $0.45 \qquad \frac{4}{10} \qquad 50\% \qquad \frac{3}{8} \qquad 46\%$

   ....

3) A teacher is buying gel pens for her students. Each gel pen costs 24p.
   There is a 20% discount off the total cost for buying more than 10 pens.
   She buys 25 pens. What change will she get if she pays with a five-pound note?

   ....

   ....

4) Erik runs 5 miles in 1 hour.

   a) How long would it take him to run 7 miles?

   ....

   b) State an assumption you have made in part (a).

   ....

5) A mobile phone company has two offers available to new customers:

   Offer A: £59.50 per month.
   Offer B: £9.89 per month, plus £499 handset cost.

   Use estimation to say which offer is better value for money on a 1-year contract.

   ....

   ....

Mixed Practice

6) Lizzie has 6 jars containing 84 sweets each. She empties them out.
She buys 2 more jars and wants to share the sweets equally between all the jars.
How many sweets would be in each jar?

....

7) A factory with 5 identical machines can produce 1200 bolts a week.
Each bolt weighs 7.1 g.

  a) What is the weight of all the bolts produced in a week? Give your answer in kg.

....

  b) If one machine broke, how many bolts could the factory produce a week?

....

....

8) Sebastien worked as both a teaching assistant and as a tutor over a year.
  • He earned £360 a week for 40 weeks as a teaching assistant.
  • He earned £300 a month for 12 months as a tutor.
What fraction of his total income was from his work as a teaching assistant?

....

....

....

9) Lisa provides food for weddings. Last year, she was booked for 64 weddings.
This year, she has been booked for 81 weddings.
She thinks her bookings increased by more than a quarter. Is she correct?

....

....

....

Mixed Practice

10) Last year, Liam bought 16 trophies for a dog show. Each trophy cost £28.50.
This year, Liam bought 19 trophies. He spent the same amount in total as last year.
What is the price of a trophy this year?

....

....

11) Ian and his two brothers are bricklayers. They take 4 hours to lay a total of 450 bricks.
If Ian is ill, how long would it take the two brothers to lay the same number of bricks?

....

....

Assume the brothers lay bricks at the same rate as Ian.

12) Geoff owns a sports shop.

a) He orders basketballs, footballs and netballs in the ratio 3:2:4.
If he orders 117 balls in total, how many of each type does he order?

....

....

b) Geoff advertises that all trainers are at least 40% off.
One pair shows a new price of £111, reduced from £180.
Has he correctly advertised the percentage off? Show how you know.

....

....

....

13) Look at the formula on the right.
Find the value of t when $b = 8.6$ and $y = 7.12$.
Give your answer to 3 decimal places.

$$t = \frac{3.4b}{3y}$$

....

Mixed Practice

14) Habib and Hannah are part of a sailing club.
They record the distance they sail each day.

Show that Habib did **not** sail more than 70% further than Hannah this weekend.

	Saturday	Sunday
Habib	12.5 km	18.4 km
Hannah	15.3 km	8.7 km

....

....

....

15) Cas owns a bakery. Last month, she ordered 480 kg of flour.

   a) This month she increased her order by 12%. How much flour did she order?

   ....

   b) Cas bakes bread in an oven at 450 °F.
   Use the formula below to convert this temperature to °C and give it to 2 decimal places.
   $C = (F - 32) \div 1.8$, where C is temperature in °C and F is temperature in °F.

   ....

   ....

16) Aisha buys a used motorbike for £5600, which is 30% less than it costs new.

   a) Work out what the motorbike would cost new. Show your working.

   ....

   ....

   b) Aisha adds some petrol to her motorbike's fuel tank. The amount in the tank increased by 60% to 4.2 gallons. How many gallons of petrol were in the tank originally?

   ....

   ....

Mixed Practice

17) Katy and Josef are looking to share a flat. They will pay the rent in the ratio of how much they earn. Katy earns £25 000 and Josef earns £30 000.

They find a flat to rent that costs £1100 per month.
Show that Katy's share of the rent would be less than £600.

....
....
....

18) Ekun uses the information below to calculate his energy bill.

Electricity: 59.2 pence per day, plus 27.4 pence per unit used.

Gas: 28.1 pence per day, plus 6.9 pence per unit used.

Calculate the amount he would pay over 30 days, if he used 290 units of electricity and 550 units of gas. Show your working.

....
....
....

19) Sienna mixes red, blue and white paint in the ratio 5:3:2 to make a certain shade of purple. She has 800 ml of red paint, 420 ml of blue paint and 250 ml of white paint. How much of this shade of paint can she make?

....
....
....

Notes

Individual Learning Plan

After each lesson or topic, use the table below to record your progress. Then you and your teacher can identify what you still don't feel confident with, why you found it difficult and what you can do to improve.

1. What I Can Do Now	2. What I Found Hard
Example: Use written methods for calculations	Using BIDMAS correctly

Individual Learning Plan © CGP — not to be photocopied

Individual Learning Plan

If you want more space to write your plan, go to: cgpbooks.co.uk/fs-maths
or scan the QR code in the header to find a printable PDF of this table.

3. What I Need To Improve On	4. What I Will Do To Improve
Remembering to deal with brackets first	Make a checklist for BIDMAS questions

CGP

www.cgpbooks.co.uk

Name ....

Functional Skills

Maths: Measures, Shape and Space

Level 2

Course Booklet

Answers available online

CGP Books — The Choice of Champions!

He knows it.
You know it.
Everyone knows it ☺

cgpbooks.co.uk

Contents

✓ Use the tick boxes to check off the topics you've completed.

About This Booklet...1 ☐
Knowledge Organiser..2 ☐

Section One — Money

Money and Rates of Pay..6 ☐
Calculate amounts of money and calculate rates of pay.

Using Percentages with Money...............................8 ☐
Calculate compound interest,
percentage increases and decreases.

Tax and Budgeting..10 ☐
Calculate tax, simple budgeting.

Section Two — Units and Measures

Converting Units...12 ☐
Convert between metric and imperial units of length,
weight and capacity using a conversion factor.

Conversion Graphs..14 ☐
Convert between metric and imperial units of length,
weight and capacity using a conversion graph.

Speed, Distance and Time....................................16 ☐
Calculate using compound measures including speed.

Density, Mass and Volume...................................18 ☐
Calculate using compound measures including density.

Section Three — Angles, Coordinates and Scale Drawings

Angles in Triangles...20 ☐
Calculate values of angles with 2D shapes.

Angles in Quadrilaterals.......................................22 ☐
Calculate values of angles with 2D shapes.

Coordinates..24 ☐
Use coordinates in 2D, positive and negative,
to specify the position of points.

Scale Drawings...28 ☐
Calculate actual dimensions from scale drawings and
create a scale diagram given actual measurements.

Section Four — Perimeter and Area

Perimeter..32 ☐
Calculate perimeters of 2D shapes including triangles and
circles and composite shapes including non-rectangular shapes.

Area..36 ☐
Calculate areas of 2D shapes including triangles and circles
and composite shapes including non-rectangular shapes.

Section Five — 3D Shapes

Nets..40 ☐
Understand and use common
2D representations of 3D objects.

Plans and Elevations..44 ☐
Draw 3D shapes to include plans and elevations.

Surface Area..48 ☐
Use formulae to find surface areas
of 3D shapes including cylinders.

Volume...50 ☐
Use formulae to find volumes of
3D shapes including cylinders.

Topic-Based Questions

Money 52
Units and Measures 53
Angles and Coordinates 54
Scale Drawings 55
Perimeter and Area 56
Nets, Plans and Elevations 57
Surface Area and Volume 58

Mixed Practice

Section A 59
Section B 61

Individual Learning Plan 66

Unlock your Digital Extras

To get your free digital extras, go to **cgpbooks.co.uk/fs-maths** or scan the QR code below.

This will take you to:
- An answer booklet
- More Individual Learning Plan pages
- A Knowledge Retriever

Published by CGP

Written by Eva Cowlishaw

Reviewer: Linda Walker

Editors: Liam Dyer, Sharon Keeley-Holden, Chris Lindle and Claire Plowman.

With thanks to Glenn Rogers for the proofreading.
With thanks to Beth Linnane for the copyright research.

Specification points in Contents contain public sector information licensed under the Open Government Licence v3.0. https://www.nationalarchives.gov.uk/doc/open-government-licence/version/3/

ISBN: 978 1 83774 210 3
Printed by Elanders Ltd, Newcastle upon Tyne.
Graphics from Corel®

Text, design, layout and original illustrations © Coordination Group Publications Ltd (CGP) 2025 All rights reserved.

Photocopying this book is not permitted, even if you have a CLA licence.
Extra copies are available from CGP with next day delivery • 0800 1712 712 • www.cgpbooks.co.uk

About This Booklet

This course booklet supports your learning of the 'Using measures, shape and space' content area of the Level 2 qualification.

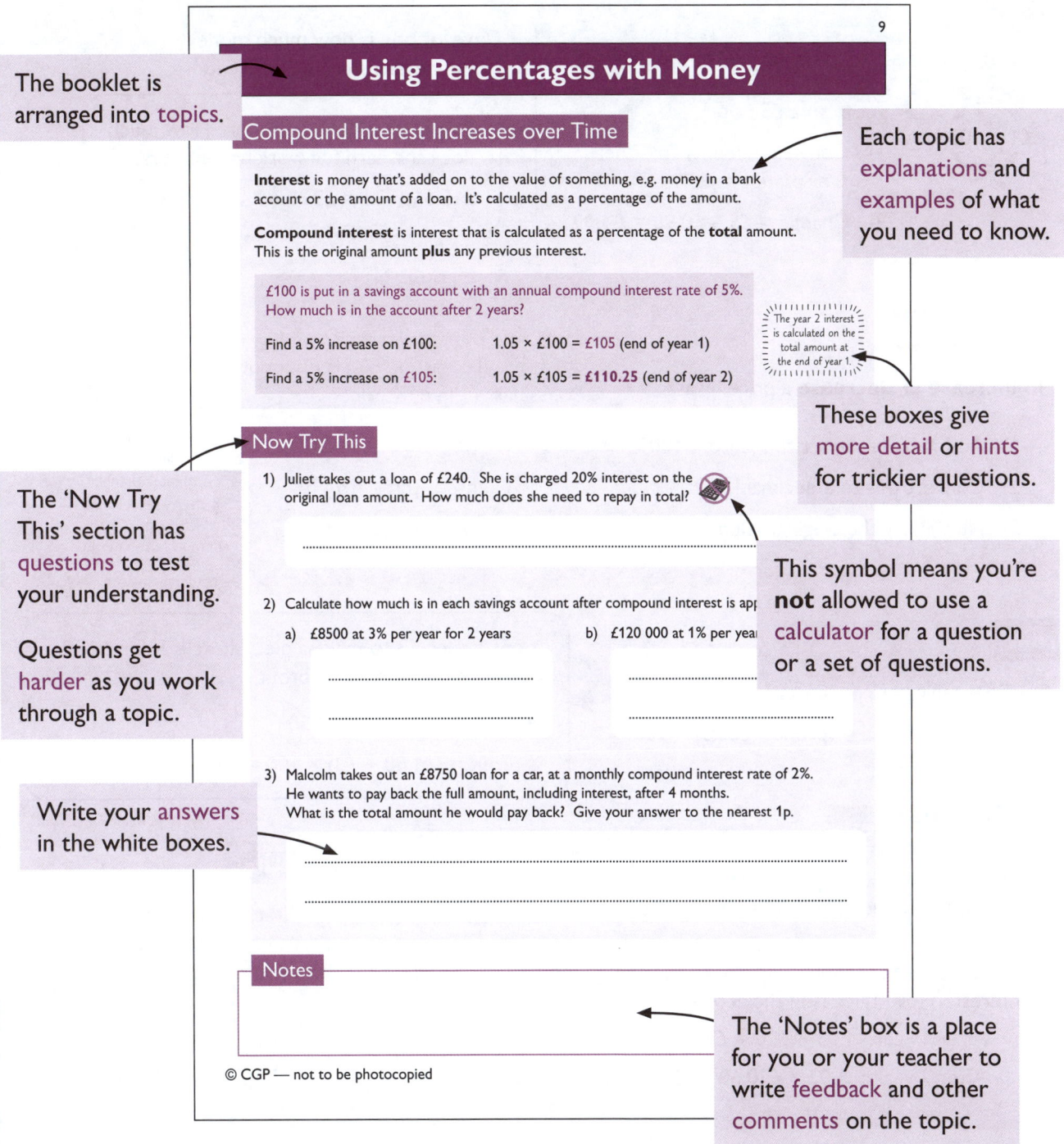

- The booklet is arranged into topics.
- Each topic has explanations and examples of what you need to know.
- These boxes give more detail or hints for trickier questions.
- The 'Now Try This' section has questions to test your understanding.
- Questions get harder as you work through a topic.
- This symbol means you're **not** allowed to use a calculator for a question or a set of questions.
- Write your answers in the white boxes.
- The 'Notes' box is a place for you or your teacher to write feedback and other comments on the topic.

At the end of the booklet, you'll find:

- **Topic-Based Questions**: more practice, split into **topics**.
- **Mixed Practice**: questions that can test you on **any** topic from the booklet — you'll need to use **more than one skill** to answer some of these.
- **Individual Learning Plan**: to track your progress towards your **learning goals**.

Knowledge Organiser

These pages contain the key info you need. They're great to refer to if you need to know what's what.

Money

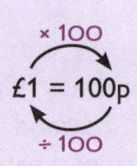

Jez buys a cucumber for 98p. How much change does he get from a £5 note?

1) Convert amounts to either £ or p: 98p = £0.98
2) Change = £5 − £0.98 = **£4.02**

Rate of pay is how much money someone earns per unit of time.

Bev earns £15.65 per hour. How much does she earn for working 24 hours?

£15.65 × 24 = **£375.60**

Money is always given to 2 dp.

Price Changes

To **increase** or **decrease** a price by a %:

1) Add % to / subtract the % from 100%.
2) Convert this to a decimal.
3) Multiply by the original value.

A hoodie costing £60 is discounted by 25%. What is the new price?

1) 100% − 25% = 75%
2) 75% ÷ 100 = 0.75
3) 0.75 × £60 = **£45**

% increase: decimal is greater than 1. % decrease: decimal is less than 1.

Profit

Profit = selling price − costs

Percentage profit = (profit ÷ costs) × 100

It costs Alec £3 to make a pie. He sells it for £4.50. Calculate his percentage profit.

Profit = £4.50 − £3 = £1.50

% profit = (£1.50 ÷ £3) × 100 = **50%**

Compound Interest

Compound interest is a percentage of the total amount, including previous interest earned.

£20 is put in an account with 3% annual compound interest. How much is in the account after 2 years?
- After 1 year: 1.03 × £20 = £20.60
- After 2 years: 1.03 × £20.60 = **£21.22** (to nearest 1p)

Budgeting

Budgeting for essential costs, e.g. rent or food, can help you manage your money.

Disposable income = income − essential costs

Tax

Tax is an amount paid to the Government. E.g. income tax, VAT, council tax.

A garage bill is £376, plus VAT at 20%. Calculate the total bill.

Total = 1.2 × £376 = **£451.20**

Sienna pays 20% tax on earnings above £12 570. She earns £15 000. How much tax does she pay?

1) Subtract £12 570 from earnings: £15 000 − £12 570 = £2430
2) Find 20% of £2430: 0.2 × £2430 = **£486**

Knowledge Organiser

Metric to Metric Conversions

Length

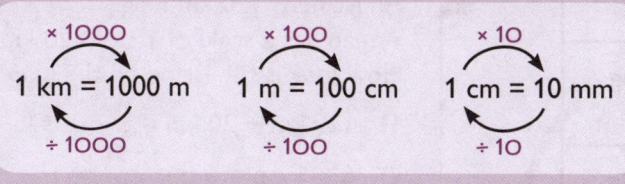

Weight (mass)

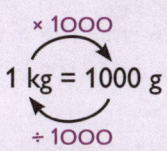

Capacity

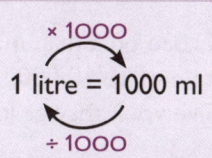

Metric to Imperial Conversions

Use the conversion factor or graph:

E.g. Convert 2 inches to cm.

1 inch ≈ 2.5 cm.

2 inches ≈ 2 × 2.5 = **5 cm**

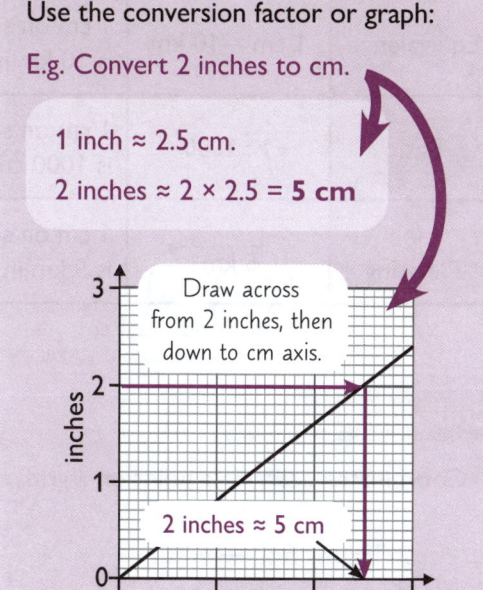

Compound Measures

Cover the letter you want to find to get the formula.

Speed = distance ÷ time

Boris walks 12 km in 4 hours. Find his speed.

Speed = distance ÷ time
= 12 ÷ 4 = **3 km/h**

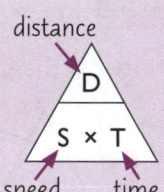

Density = mass ÷ volume

A metal has a density of 5 g/cm^3. Find the volume of a sample with a mass of 15 g.

Volume = mass ÷ density
= 15 ÷ 5 = **3 cm^3**

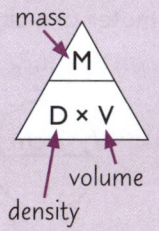

Angles in Triangles

Angles in a triangle add up to **180°**.

Calculate the size of angles A and B.

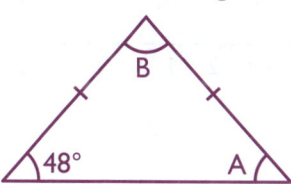

1) An isosceles triangle has two equal angles, so A = **48°**

2) Find B by subtracting the two other angles from 180°.
B = 180° − 48° − 48° = **84°**

Angles in Quadrilaterals

Angles in a quadrilateral add up to **360°**.
Use other properties of quadrilaterals too:

E.g. parallelograms have two pairs of equal angles, so E = 113°, F = G.

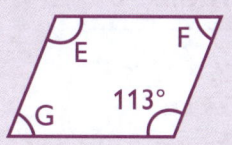

Calculate the size of angle D.

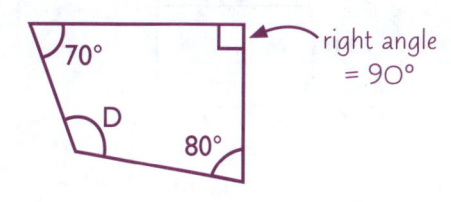

right angle = 90°

D = 360° − 70° − 80° − 90° = **120°**

Knowledge Organiser

Scale Drawings

Equivalence	1 cm = 10 km	1 cm on scale drawing is 10 km in real life.
Ratio	1 : 1000	1 cm on scale drawing is 1000 cm in real life.
Line Drawing	⊢—⊣ 5 km (Line measures 1 cm.)	1 cm on scale drawing is 5 km in real life.

An island is 120 km long.
A map has a scale of 1 cm = 20 km.
How long is the island on the map?

1) 120 km ÷ 20 km = 6
2) 6 × 1 cm = **6 cm**

A road on a map measures 3.6 cm. The map uses a scale of 1 : 10 000. How long is the road in real life? Give your answer in km.

1) 1 cm on map = 10 000 cm in real life, so 3.6 cm = 36 000 cm
2) 36 000 cm = 360 m = **0.36 km**
   ÷ 100   ÷ 1000

Coordinates

Coordinates describe a point on a grid.

x-coordinate is first ⟶ (x, y)

Points can be joined to make shapes.

(−3, 1) means −3 units along x-axis and 1 unit along the y-axis.

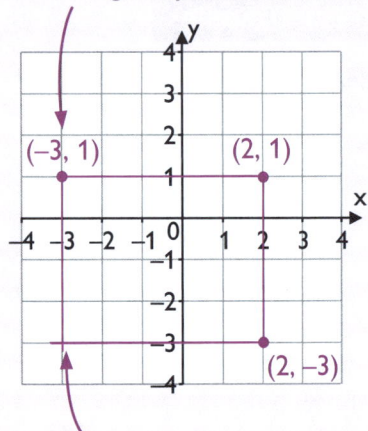

Missing corner of rectangle is (−3, −3).

Perimeter

Perimeter is the distance around the outside of a shape.

An isosceles triangle has two sides the same length.

5 cm, 6 cm

Perimeter = 5 + 5 + 6 = **16 cm**

Perimeter of a circle is the circumference.
Circumference = π × diameter

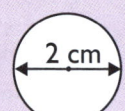

Circumference = π × diameter
= 3.14 × 2
= **6.28 cm**

Area

Area is the space inside a shape.

π = 3.14 has been used here.

Area of rectangle = length × width

8 m, 4 m

Area = 8 × 4 = **32 m²**

Area of triangle = ½ × base × height

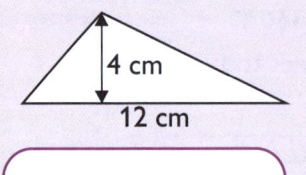

4 cm, 12 cm

Area = ½ × 12 × 4 = **24 cm²**

Area of circle = π × radius²

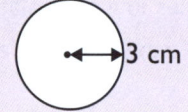

3 cm

Area = 3.14 × 3²
= **28.26 cm²**

Knowledge Organiser

Nets

A **net** shows a 3D shape unfolded into a 2D shape.

cube	cuboid	triangular prism	cylinder	square-based pyramid

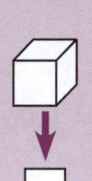
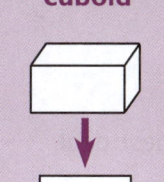

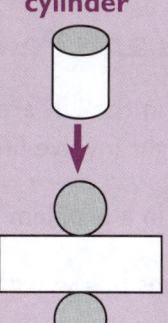
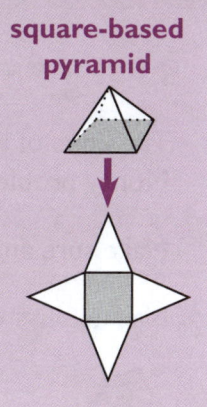

Surface Area

Surface area of a 3D shape is the area of each face added together.

Surface area of cube
= area of square face × 6
= length² × 6

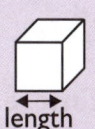

Surface area of cylinder
= (circle area × 2) + rectangle area
        ↑
       π × r²

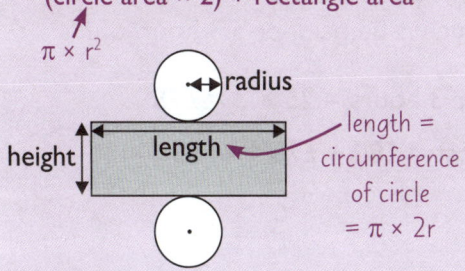

length = circumference of circle = π × 2r

Plans and Elevations

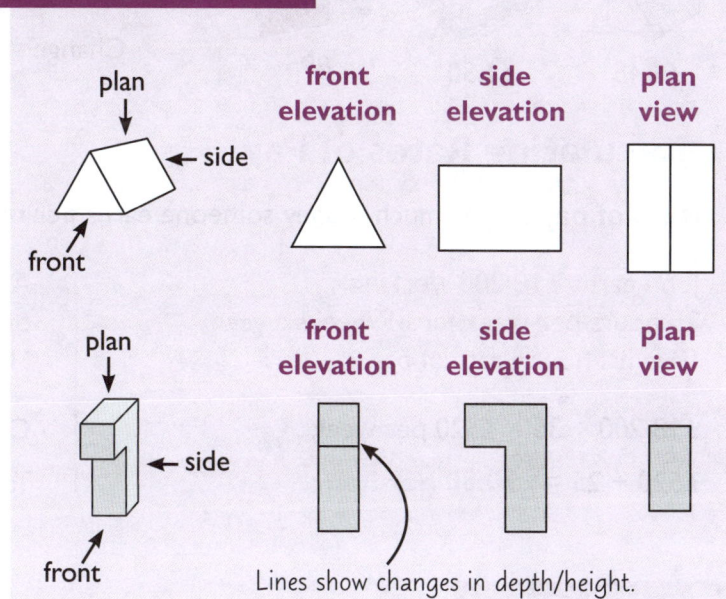

Lines show changes in depth/height.

Volume

volume of cuboid = length × width × height

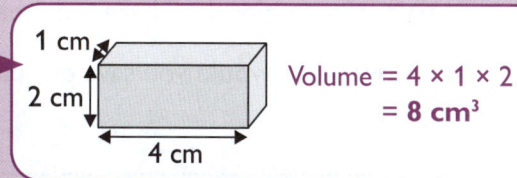

Volume = 4 × 1 × 2 = **8 cm³**

volume of prism = cross-sectional area × length

volume of triangular prism = ½ × base × height × length

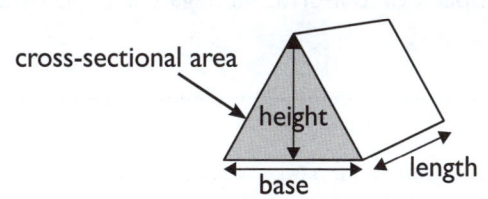

volume of cylinder = π × radius² × length

Section One — Money

Money and Rates of Pay

Here comes a very useful set of pages. Time to learn all about spending and earning money.

Rate of Pay is Usually in Pounds per Hour

Using Pounds and Pence

The units of money in the UK are pounds (£) and pence (p).
Money problems might involve finding change, a total amount or a best deal.

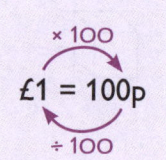

Make sure amounts in a problem are either all in pounds or all in pence.

Nadine buys the items below with a £5 note. How much change will she get?

£1.45   £1.50   89p

Cost of chocolate bar (in £) = 89p ÷ 100 = £0.89

Total cost = £1.45 + £1.50 + £0.89 = £3.84

Change = £5 − £3.84 = **£1.16**

Calculating Rates of Pay

Rate of pay is how much money someone earns per **unit of time**, e.g. £20 per hour.

John earns £18 200 working
25 hours per week for 35 weeks a year.
Give his hourly rate of pay.

£18 200 ÷ 35 = £520 per week

£520 ÷ 25 = **£20.80 per hour**

A tiler charges a fixed fee
of £80, plus £25 per hour.
How much is he paid for a 3 hour job?

Cost for 3 hours = 25 × 3 = £75

Total cost = £80 + £75 = **£155**

Now Try This

1) A supermarket sells individual bags of crisps for 65p. The same crisps are also sold as part of a multipack. There are 6 bags of crisps in the multipack, which costs £3.

   a) How much would you save per bag by buying a multipack instead of 6 individual bags?

   ....

   b) The supermarket starts a 'buy 2, get 1 free' offer on the individual bags of crisps. Explain whether it is cheaper to buy a multipack or 6 individual bags with this offer.

   ....

   ....

Money and Rates of Pay

2) Tony earns £14.55 per hour. How much does he earn if he works:

   a) 30 hours?

   ....

   b) 12 hours?

   ....

3) Molly buys a car for £12 500. Each year, breakdown cover costs her £52 and all other running costs come to £430. How much has she spent on the car in total after 2 years?

   ....

   ....

4) Harry has a pay-as-you-go SIM card. He pays 3p per minute for calls and 2p per text.

   a) Harry talks on the phone for half an hour. How much does this cost him?

   ....

   b) Each month, Harry spends an average of 550 minutes on calls and sends 300 texts. Would it be cheaper for Harry to get a £20 monthly contract with unlimited calls and texts instead of his pay-as-you-go SIM? Explain your answer.

   ....

   ....

5) Jacob makes T-shirts. He makes 22 shirts per hour. He is paid 65p for each T-shirt he makes. Martha works at a supermarket. She works 32 hours per week for £416. Show that Jacob's hourly rate of pay is more than Martha's hourly rate of pay.

   ....

   ....

Notes

Using Percentages with Money

You'll see percentages in everyday life — shops often reduce prices by a percentage in a sale.

Price Changes and Profits may be Given as Percentages

Percentage Increases and Decreases

You may have to find the new price after a **percentage** increase or decrease (discount).

A skirt priced at £45 is reduced by 17% in a sale. What is its sale price?

1) Find the new percentage.   100% – 17% = 83%
   Change this to a decimal.   83 ÷ 100 = 0.83
2) Multiply by the original amount: 0.83 × £45 = **£37.35**

The decimal is always smaller than 1 for a decrease and greater than 1 for an increase.

If you don't have a calculator, work out the percentage of the original amount and add it to or subtract it from the original amount.

Calculating Profit

Profit is the price you sell something for, minus costs. You can also find the **percentage profit**.

profit = selling price – costs
% profit = (profit ÷ costs) × 100

Omar spends £15 on a bracelet. He sells it for £18. Calculate his percentage profit.

He makes £18 – £15 = £3 profit, so his % profit = (£3 ÷ £15) × 100 = **20%**

Now Try This

1) Calculate the new cost of these items after they are discounted by 8%.

   a) a T-shirt priced at £12.

   b) a pair of jeans priced at £72.

   ....

2) Aashvi rents her shop for £895 per month. Her landlord increases the rent by 22%. What is her new rent?

   ....

3) Bob buys a broken PC for £20 and spends £12 to repair it. He sells the fixed PC for £52.

   a) What was his profit?

   b) What was his percentage profit?

   ....

Using Percentages with Money

Compound Interest Increases over Time

Interest is money that's added on to the value of something, e.g. money in a bank account or the amount of a loan. It's calculated as a percentage of the amount.

Compound interest is interest that is calculated as a percentage of the **total** amount. This is the original amount **plus** any previous interest.

£100 is put in a savings account with an annual compound interest rate of 5%. How much is in the account after 2 years?

Find a 5% increase on £100:   1.05 × £100 = £105 (end of year 1)

Find a 5% increase on £105:   1.05 × £105 = **£110.25** (end of year 2)

The year 2 interest is calculated on the total amount at the end of year 1.

Now Try This

1) Juliet takes out a loan of £240. She is charged 20% interest on the original loan amount. How much does she need to repay in total?

   ....

2) Calculate how much is in each savings account after compound interest is applied:

   a) £8500 at 3% per year for 2 years

   b) £120 000 at 1% per year for 3 years

3) Malcolm takes out an £8750 loan for a car, at a monthly compound interest rate of 2%. He wants to pay back the full amount, including interest, after 4 months. What is the total amount he would pay back? Give your answer to the nearest 1p.

Notes

Tax and Budgeting

You'll more than likely have to pay tax at some point. It's dull and complicated, but it is important.

Tax is an Amount Paid to the Government

Income tax is a tax paid on your income.
The amount paid depends on how much you earn.

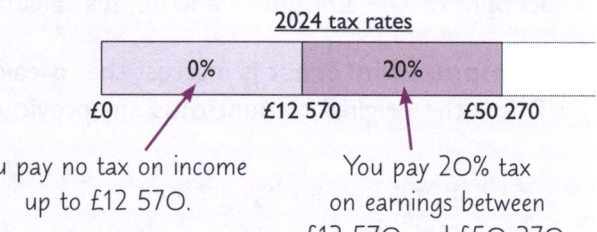

There are higher rates of 40% and 45% too.

2024 tax rates

You pay no tax on income up to £12 570.

You pay 20% tax on earnings between £12 570 and £50 270.

Katie earned £19 500 in 2024.
How much income tax did she pay?

1) Subtract £12 570 from her income: £19 500 − £12 570 = £6930
2) Find 20% of £6930: 0.2 × £6930 = £1386, so she paid **£1386** income tax.

Other examples of tax include:
- **VAT (value-added tax)** — a charge added to the cost of some items or services.
- **council tax** — a charge based on the value of your home.

Now Try This

1) The standard rate of VAT is 20%. A plumber charges £125 without VAT. Work out what they would charge including VAT.

    ....

2) The table on the right shows some council tax charges.
   Jiya's house is in Band B. As she lives alone, she gets a 25% discount.
   Calculate the council tax she pays.

Band A	£1369
Band B	£1545
Band C	£1862

    ....

3) How much income tax would be paid on a salary of £28 750 in 2024?

   Use the information at the top of the page for Q3 and Q4.

    ....

4) Matt earned £24 500 in 2024. Delia earned £29 720 in the same year.
   How much more income tax did Delia pay than Matt?

    ....

    ....

Tax and Budgeting

A Budget Helps You Manage Your Money

A **budget** helps you to plan how you spend your money.
Disposable income is the money you have left over after paying for essentials, e.g. bills.

Noah earns £1950 each month after tax. He budgets for his essential costs this month.

Item	Rent	Bills	Shopping	Transport
Cost	£830	£270	£260	£340

a) What percentage of his costs are on transport?

Total = 830 + 270 + 260 + 340 = **£1700**

(340 ÷ 1700) × 100 = **20%**

b) How much disposable income does he have?

Income − essential costs
= £1950 − £1700 = **£250**

Now Try This

1) Mei is organising a bowling party.
She wants to spend less than £320 in total.
Use the table on the right to find the maximum number of guests she could invite.

Item	Cost (per guest)
Lane hire	£7.50
Food and drink	£10

....

2) Shane earns £2700 a month after tax.
If he sticks to his budget shown on the right, he has £1298 left at the end of the month.

Expense	Amount (per month)
Rent	£920
Bills	£125
Groceries	

a) Fill in the amount he spends on groceries each month in the table.

b) How much disposable income would Shane have if his rent increased by 10%?

....

....

Notes

Section Two — Units and Measures

Converting Units

The UK uses old imperial units for some measures, such as pints of milk and beer, and road distances.

Use a Conversion Factor to Change the Units

Metric to Metric Conversions

Multiply or divide by the **conversion factor** to convert between different metric units.

What is 3500 m in km?   3500 ÷ 1000 = **3.5 km**

How many grams are in 4 kg?   4 × 1000 = **4000 g**

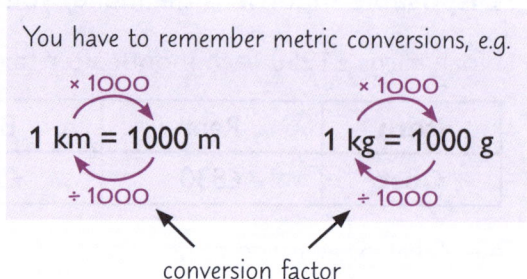

You have to remember metric conversions, e.g.

× 1000
1 km = 1000 m
÷ 1000

× 1000
1 kg = 1000 g
÷ 1000

conversion factor

Metric to Imperial Conversions

You'll be told the conversion factor to use between metric and imperial units.

A marathon is 26 miles. How far is this in kilometres?
1 mile ≈ 1.6 km.

≈ means approximately equal to.

26 × 1.6 = **41.6 km** ← 1 km is smaller than 1 mile, so the same distance is more in kilometres than in miles.

Fred is going on a flight. He can take a carry-on bag that weighs no more than 15 kg. His bag weighs 35 lb (pounds). Is his bag within the limits? Use 1 kg ≈ 2.2 lb.

35 lb ÷ 2.2 = 15.909... kg, so **no**, Fred's bag is too heavy. ← The weight is in pounds, so you need to divide to work backwards to kilograms.

Now Try This

1) Convert the following metric units.

   a) 5 m in cm
   b) 3400 cm in m
   c) 2.4 km in m

   ....
   ....
   ....

   d) 350 g in kg
   e) 26 400 ml in litres
   f) 2.08 litres in ml

   ....
   ....
   ....

2) Use the conversion 1 mile ≈ 1.6 km to convert these distances.

   a) 5 miles in km
   b) 12 miles in km
   c) 18 km in miles

   ....
   ....
   ....

Converting Units

3) Use the conversion 1 kg ≈ 2.2 lb to convert these weights.

   a) 5 kg in lb

   b) 35 kg in lb

   c) 66 lb in kg

4) Use the following conversions to answer the questions below.
   1 gallon ≈ 4.5 litres, 1 pint ≈ 0.568 litres.

   a) A fuel tank in a small car holds 12 gallons of petrol.
      How many litres of petrol would be needed to fill it from empty?

   b) Jay buys 4 pints of milk. How many litres is this?

   c) A pub has a 50 litre barrel of beer. How many full pint glasses of beer can they pour?

5) 1 mile is roughly equal to 1.6 km.

   a) The speed limit on some motorways in Europe is 130 km per hour.
      Is this faster than the 70 miles per hour speed limit on UK motorways?

   b) Ash is driving at 45 km per hour. Roughly how fast is she going in miles per hour?

Notes

Conversion Graphs

Calculators away and rulers out — it's time to do some conversions using lovely graphs instead.

Convert Between Units Using Conversion Graphs

Conversion graphs are **straight-line graphs** that can be used to convert one unit to another.

Here is a graph to convert kilometres to miles. Use the graph to convert 4 km to miles.

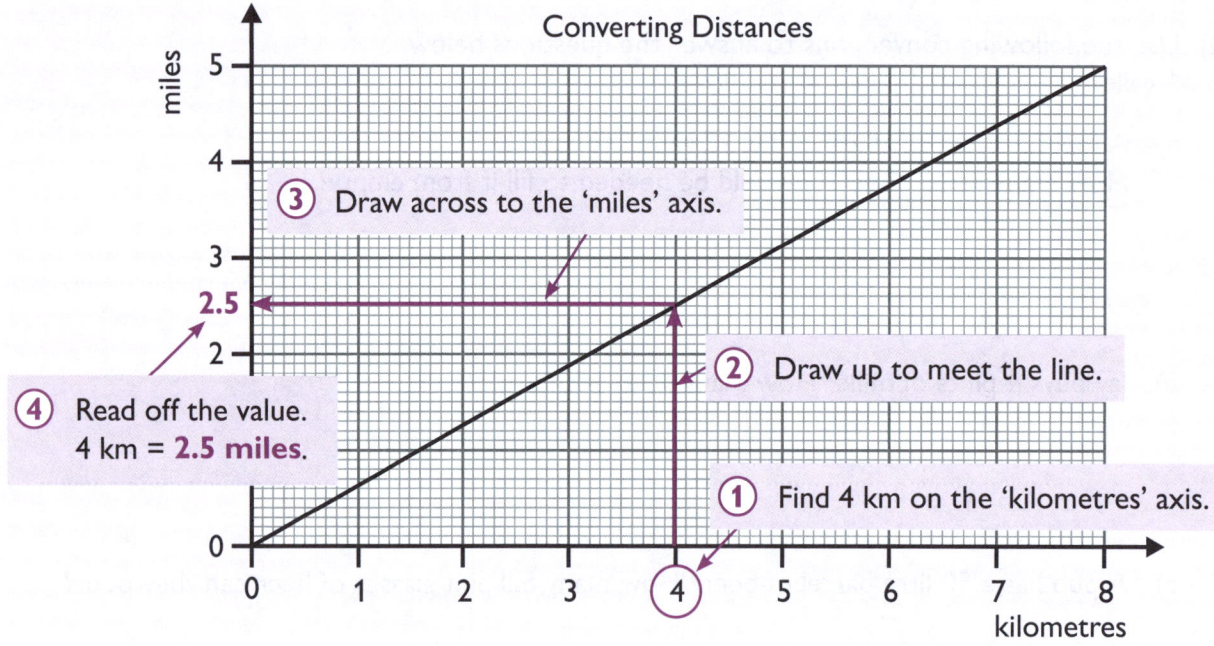

To convert from miles to kilometres, do the opposite. Start from the miles axis (vertical), draw across to the line, then draw down to the kilometres axis.

Conversion graphs can be used to convert between currencies in the same way.

Now Try This

1) This graph shows the conversion between gallons and litres. Use the graph to convert:

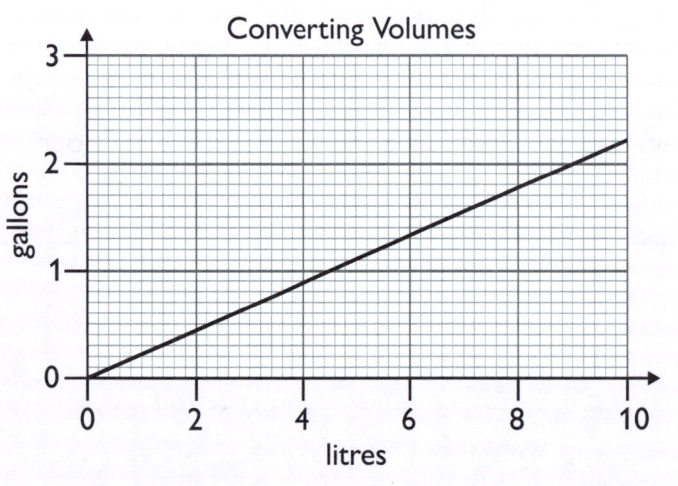

a) 5 litres to gallons.

....

b) 2 gallons to litres.

....

c) 0.8 gallons to litres.

....

Section Two — Units and Measures

Conversion Graphs

2) Here is a conversion graph between kilograms (kg) and pounds (lb). Convert:

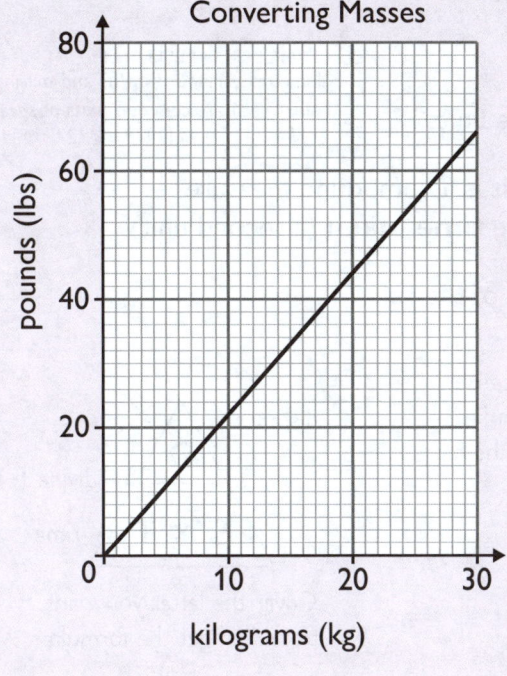

a) 25 kg to pounds.

b) 22 lb to kilograms.

c) 100 kg to pounds.

d) 88 lb to kilograms.

Hint: to find 100 kg, first find 10 kg then scale up (× 10).

3) The graph below shows the conversion between centimetres and inches.

a) Mya is 88 cm tall. Hari is 31 inches. Who is taller?

b) Mo is 150 cm tall. Jin is 56 inches. Who is taller?

c) Max is 60 cm tall. Tili is 27 inches. How much taller is Tili than Max in cm?

Speed, Distance and Time

Speed, distance and time are all connected. If you know two of them, you can work out the third.

Compound Measures Include Two Different Units

Calculating Speed

Compound measures are made up of two or more units.

Kilometres per hour (km/h) and miles per hour (mph) are common units of speed.

Speed is a measure of how fast something is going. It is a compound measure — the **distance** travelled (the first unit) is divided by the **time taken** (a second unit).

A car travels 100 km in 2 hours. Calculate the speed of the car.

speed = distance ÷ time
= 100 ÷ 2 = **50 km/h**

This is km/h because the distance is in km and the time is in hours.

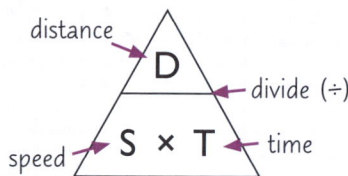

Cover the letter you want to find to get the formula.

Calculating Distance and Time

You can also calculate the distance or the time taken. Use the formula triangle to find the formulas:

distance = speed × time   **time = distance ÷ speed**

A train travelled at 125 km/h for 48 minutes. How far did it travel?

The speed is given in km/h. So change 48 minutes into hours so the units match:

$\frac{48 \text{ minutes}}{60 \text{ minutes}} = \frac{4}{5}$ hours

Use the formula triangle and cover distance (D).

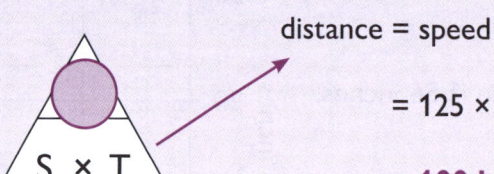

distance = speed × time

$= 125 \times \frac{4}{5}$

= **100 km**

Now Try This

1) Calculate the speed in km/h of a lorry that travels **180 kilometres** in **3 hours**.

....

2) Andrew drives 40 km at a speed of 80 km/h. How long does his journey take?

....

Speed, Distance and Time

3) A car travels **180 km** in **2½ hours**.
   Calculate the speed of the car in km/h.

   Remember that half an hour is the same as 0.5 hours.

   ....

4) A bus travels at **35 km/h** for **75 minutes**. Calculate the distance travelled in kilometres.

   ....

   ....

5) Melanie jogs each morning for **20 minutes** at **12 km/h**. How far does Melanie jog each day?
   How far does she jog in a week?

   ....

   ....

6) Jafar drives **38 miles** in **45 minutes**. Calculate his speed in miles per hour.
   Give your answer to 2 decimal places.

   ....

   ....

7) The extreme cycling challenge from Land's End to John O'Groats covers around **839 miles**.
   Mary can cycle at **9 mph** for **11 hours** per day.
   How many days will Mary need to complete the challenge?

   ....

   ....

Notes

Density, Mass and Volume

Density is how much 'stuff' is in a given volume — a box of feathers is less dense than a box of bricks.

Density is Mass Divided by Volume

Calculating Density

Density is a compound measure found by dividing the **mass** (weight) of an object by its **volume**.

Grams per centimetre cubed (g/cm³) and kilograms per metre cubed (kg/m³) are common units of density.

What is the density of a 2.5 m³ tub of mud weighing 4000 kg?

density = mass ÷ volume
= 4000 ÷ 2.5
= **1600 kg/m³**

Don't forget, the units for mass and volume should be the same as those for the density (the compound measure).

Calculating Mass and Volume

To find mass or volume, use the formula triangle or remember the formulas:

mass = density × volume   **volume = mass ÷ density**

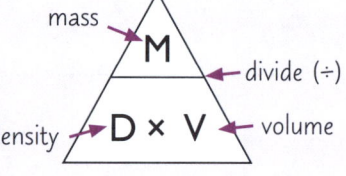

Find the mass of a concrete tile with a density of 2 g/cm³ and a volume of 75 cm³.

Cover the measure you want to find.

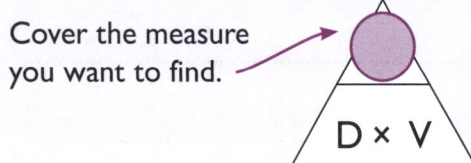

mass = density × volume
= 2 × 75
= **150 g**

Now Try This

1) Find the density of a block of wood with a mass of 50 g and volume of 100 cm³.

....

2) A sheet of foam has a mass of 4.0 kg and a volume of 0.2 m³. Calculate the density of the foam.

....

Density, Mass and Volume

3) Work out the mass of a rock that has a density of 6 g/cm³ and volume of 55 cm³.

....

4) The table below shows the density, mass and volume of different objects.
Complete the table.

Object	Mass	Volume	Density
Feathers	15 kg	5 m³	
Metal		100 cm³	4 g/cm³
Salt	81 g		2.7 g/cm³

5) The density of water is 1 g/cm³. Anything less dense than water will float. Calculate the density of each object. Which of the objects will float?

Convert the units of mass to grams first.

Object	Mass (kg)	Volume (cm³)	Density (g/cm³)	Does it float?
Ice	0.0046	5		
Sand	0.0384	24		
Gold	0.00965	0.5		
Milk	0.412	400		
Olive oil	1.08	1200		

6) A full jar of syrup weighs 0.45 kg and has a density of 1.2 g/cm³.
What is the volume of the jar in litres? 1 litre = 1000 cm³.

....

....

Notes

Angles in Triangles

There's an angle at each corner of a triangle and these pages will show you how to work them out.

Use Properties of Triangles to Work Out Missing Angles

All triangles follow this rule: All the angles in a triangle add up to **180°**.

Use this rule and the properties of isosceles, right-angled and equilateral triangles to find missing angles.

Find the values of angle A and B.

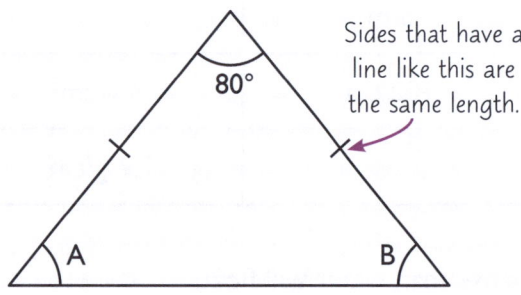

Sides that have a line like this are the same length.

1) A + B + 80° = 180°,
   so A + B = 180° − 80° = 100°

2) It's an isosceles triangle, so A = B.
   So A and B are 100 ÷ 2 = **50°**

Find the size of angle C.

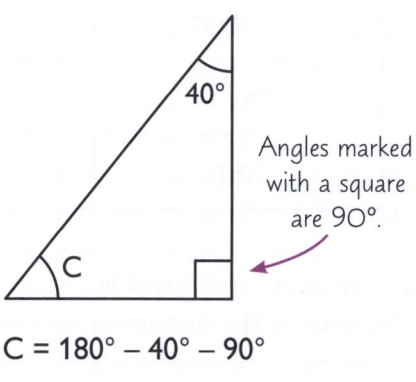

Angles marked with a square are 90°.

C = 180° − 40° − 90°
  = **50°**

Now Try This

1) What is the size of each angle in an equilateral triangle?

....

2) Calculate the size of angle A in this triangle.

....

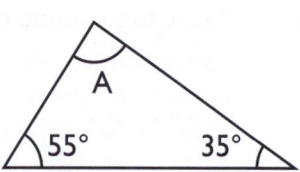

3) Calculate the size of angle B in this isosceles triangle.

....

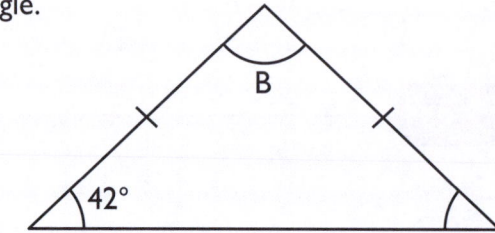

....

Angles in Triangles

4) Calculate the size of angle C in each of these triangles.

a)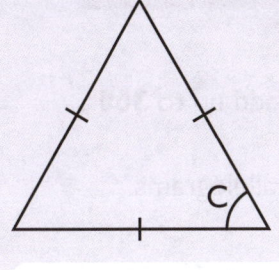

b)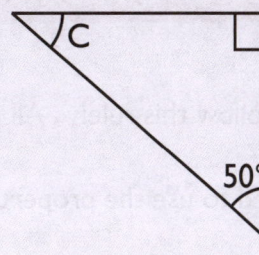

....

....

5) Calculate the size of angle D in this triangle.

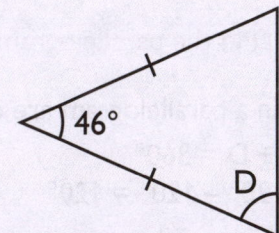

....

....

6) A ladder leans against a wall, as shown in the diagram.
Calculate the size of the angle that the top of the ladder makes with the wall.

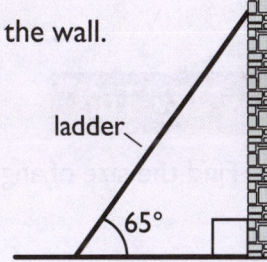

....

....

7) In the kite shown, EF = EH and FG = GH.
Show how you can use triangle properties to calculate the size of angle H.

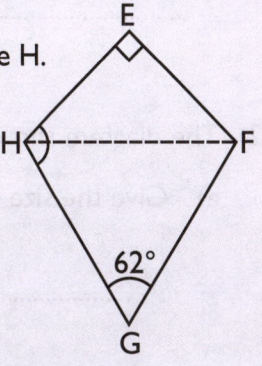

....

....

....

Notes

Angles in Quadrilaterals

Quadrilaterals have one more angle for you to deal with than triangles do.

Use Properties of Quadrilaterals to Find Missing Angles

All quadrilaterals follow this rule: All the angles in a quadrilateral add up to **360°**.

You might also need to use the properties of quadrilaterals, e.g. parallelograms.

Find the value of angle A in this quadrilateral.

A + 80° + 115° + 90° = 360°
So A = 360° − 80° − 115° − 90° = **75°**

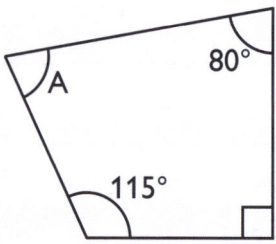

Find angles B, C and D in the parallelogram below.

1) Opposite angles in a parallelogram are equal, so C = **120°**
2) 120° + 120° + B + D = 360°
   B + D = 360° − 120° − 120° = 120°
3) Angles B and D are opposite,
   so B = D = 120° ÷ 2 = **60°**

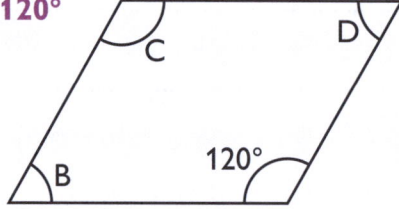

Now Try This

1) Find the size of angle A in the quadrilateral.

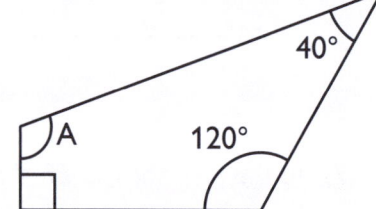

....

....

2) The diagram shows a parallelogram.

   a) Give the size of angle B.

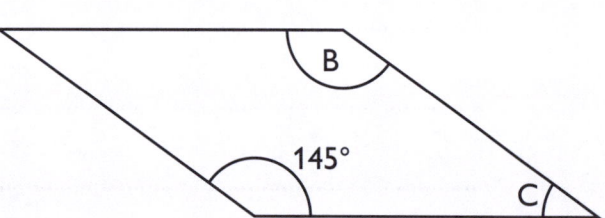

   ....

   b) Calculate the size of angle C.

....

Section Three — Angles, Coordinates and Scale Drawings

Angles in Quadrilaterals

3) Two angles of a quadrilateral add up to 170°.
   Which of the following could be the sizes of the other angles? Tick the correct box.

   100° and 100° ☐   80° and 90° ☐   50° and 60° ☐   100° and 90° ☐

4) Calculate the size of angle D in this parallelogram.

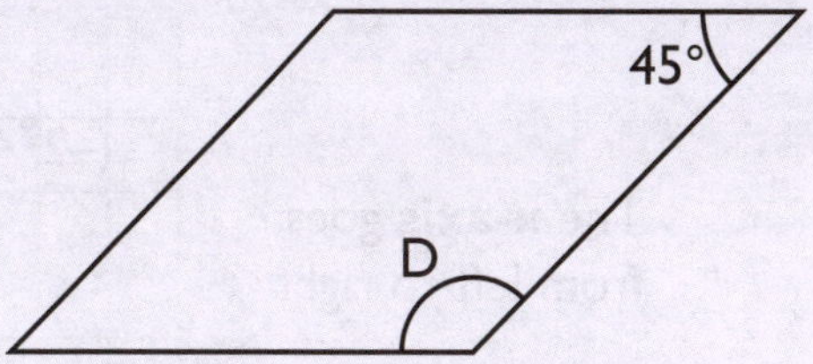

   ....

   ....

5) Calculate the size of angle E in this quadrilateral.

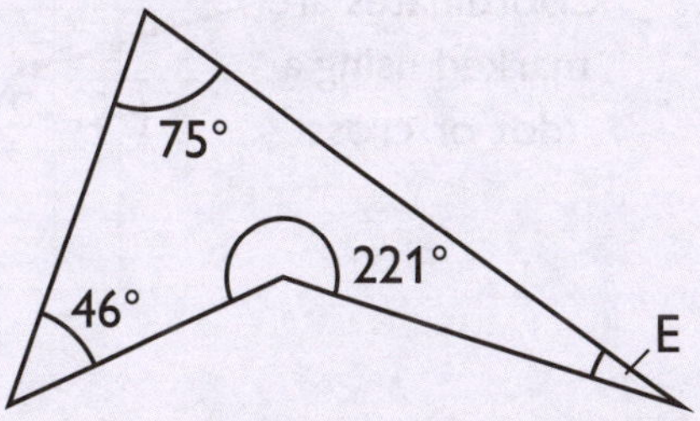

   ....

   ....

6) The diagram shows a kite with one line of symmetry.
   Calculate the size of angles F and G.

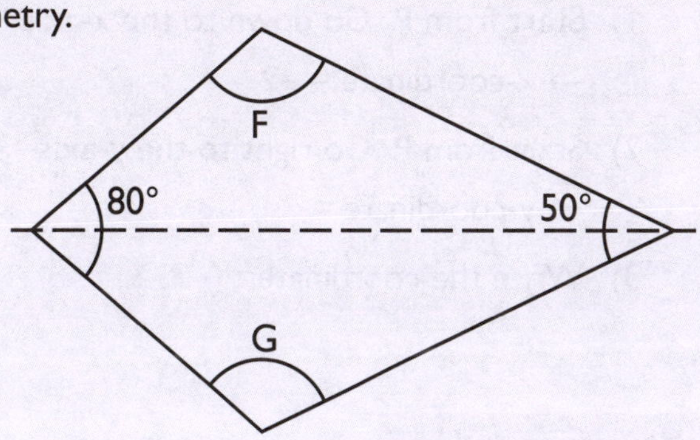

   ....

   ....

   ....

7) Calculate the size of angle H in this pentagon.

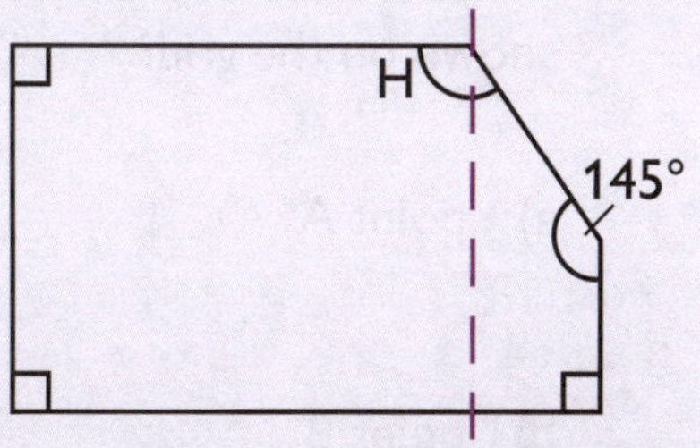

   ....

   ....

   ....

   The dashed line shows where you can split the shape into two quadrilaterals.

Notes

Coordinates

Coordinates have lots of real-life uses, e.g. in navigation and computer graphics. They're really handy.

Coordinates Describe Points on a Grid

Coordinates describe the position of a point on a coordinate grid.
Coordinates are given as a pair of numbers (x, y) — the x-coordinate always comes first.

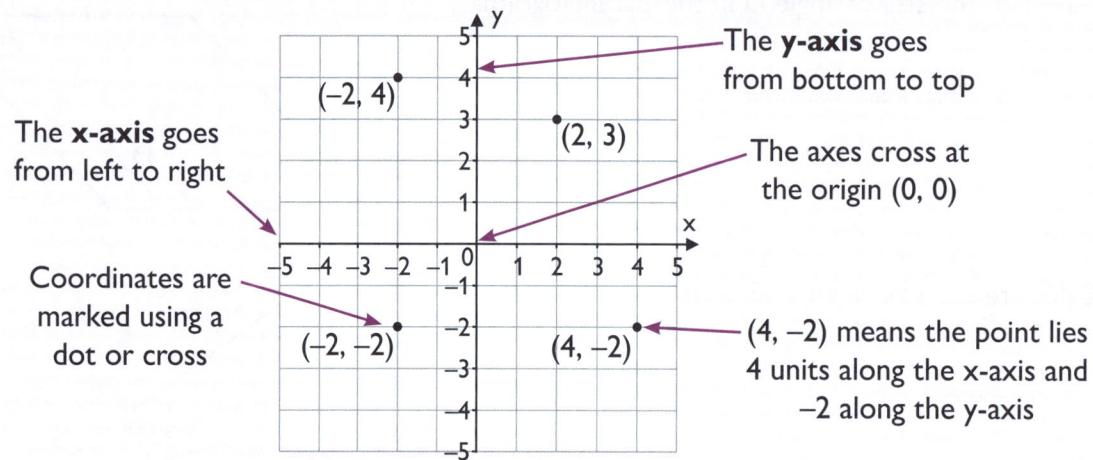

What are the coordinates of point P shown on the grid?

1) Start from P. Go down to the x-axis
 → x-coordinate = −2

2) Start from P. Go right to the y-axis
 → y-coordinate = 3

3) Write the coordinates: **(−2, 3)**

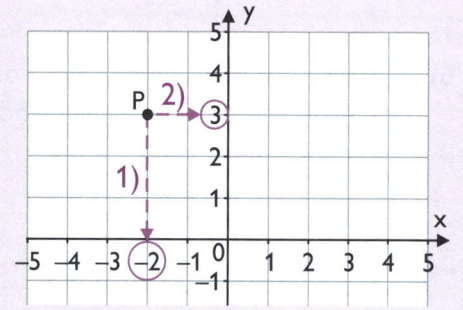

Now Try This

1) What are the coordinates of the points shown on the grid?

a) point A ....

b) point B ....

c) point C ....

d) point D ....

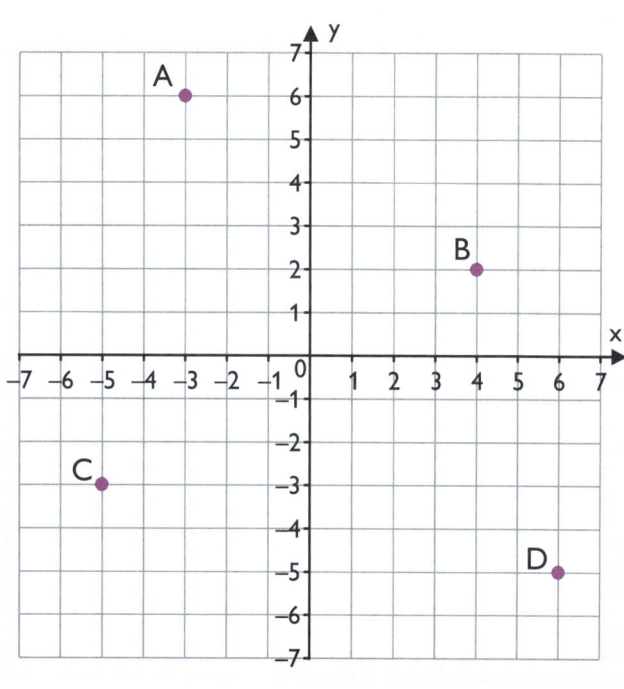

Section Three — Angles, Coordinates and Scale Drawings

Coordinates

Move Across Then Up (or Down) to Plot Coordinates

Here's how to plot coordinates:

1) Start at the origin. Move left or right to find the x-coordinate.
2) Move up or down until you're in line with the y-coordinate.
3) Put a dot or cross at this position.

Saying 'along the hall and up the stairs' can remind you that the x-coordinate comes before the y-coordinate.

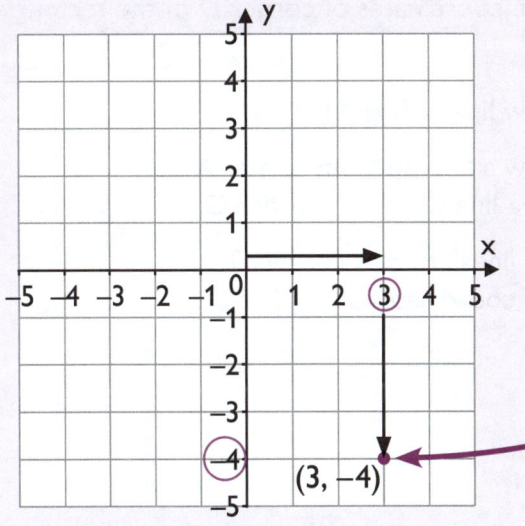

Plot the coordinates (3, −4) on the grid.

1) Move right from the origin to find 3 on the x-axis.
2) Move your finger down until you're in line with −4 on the y-axis.
3) Mark this point.

Now Try This

1) Plot the following coordinates on the grid.

   a) (3, 2)
   b) (−3, −3)
   c) (1, 0)
   d) (−4, 3)
   e) (1, −4)
   f) (4, −3)

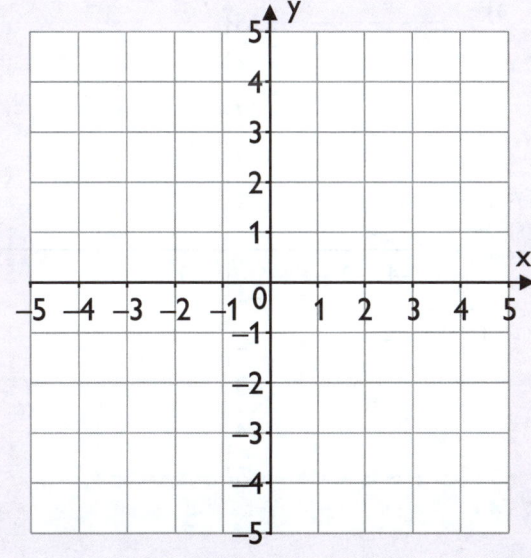

Notes

Coordinates

Coordinates aren't only used for plotting single points. You can join up the points using lines.

Plot Points to Make 2D Shapes

Coordinates can be joined together using straight lines to make 2D shapes.

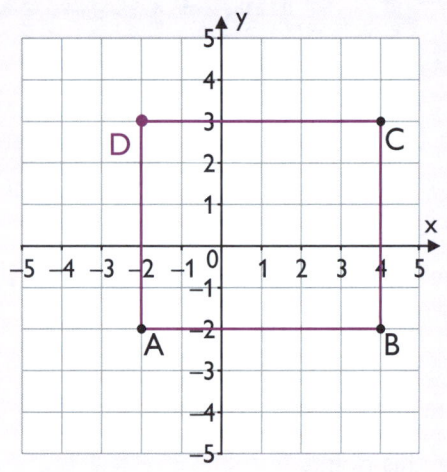

The points A, B and C are three corners of a rectangle. Draw lines to complete the shape.

Give the coordinates of corner D of the rectangle.

- Draw lines AB and BC.
- Draw a line **up** from corner A and a line **left** from corner C.
- The lines cross at corner D. The coordinates are **(–2, 3)**.

Now Try This

1) Corners A and B of a square ABCD have been plotted on each grid below. Plot and label the remaining two corners (C and D) and give their coordinates.

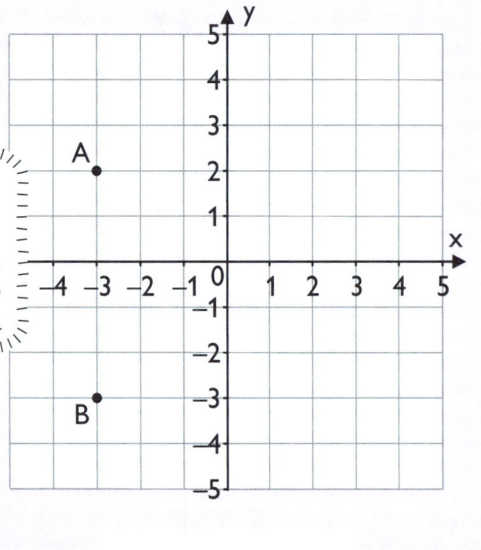

Label C and D so that you get a square if you join the points in the order ABCD (then back to A).

a)

C = ...

D = ...

b)

C = ...

D = ...

Section Three — Angles, Coordinates and Scale Drawings

Coordinates

2) Two corners (A and B) of an isosceles triangle have been plotted on each grid below. For each triangle, side AB = side AC. Give the coordinates for corner C of each triangle.

a)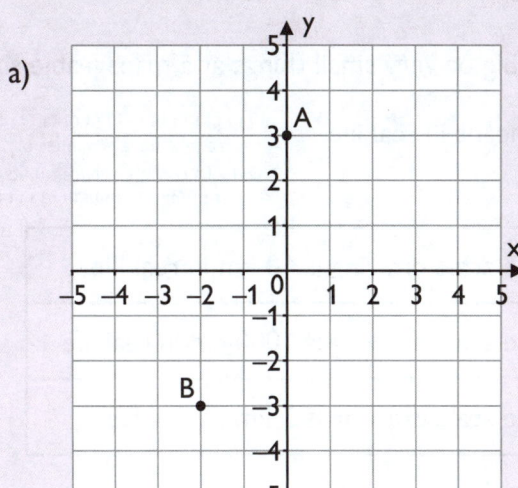

C = ...

b)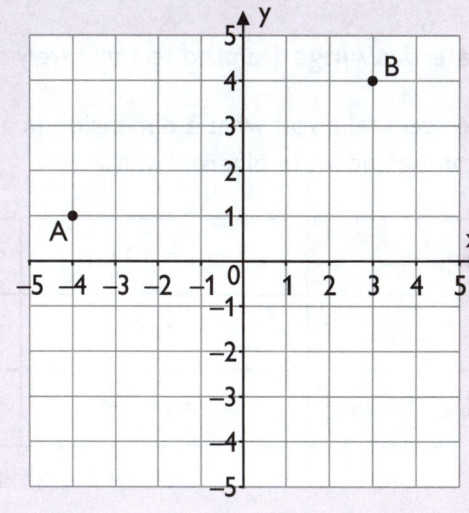

C = ...

3) The points A and B on the grid below are two corners of a right-angled triangle, ABC. The right angle of the triangle is at B. The triangle has an area of 9 cm².

See p.36 for how to work out the area of a triangle.

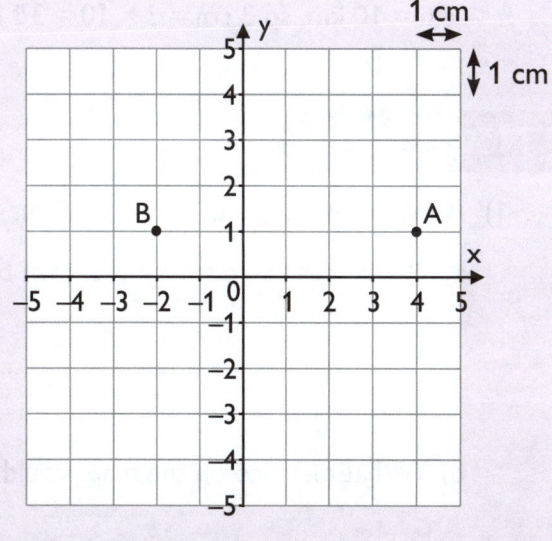

a) What is the length of side BC?

....

....

b) Give two possible pairs of coordinates for point C.

C = ...

C = ...

Notes

Section Three — Angles, Coordinates and Scale Drawings

Scale Drawings

Scale drawings are used in floor plans and maps. You'll need a ruler for this topic.

A Scale Drawing is an Accurate Diagram of Something

Scale drawings are used to accurately show very big or very small things at a manageable size.

The scale tells you what a dimension in a drawing means in real life. It can be shown in different ways:

See p.12 for a reminder of how to convert between units.

Equivalence	1 cm = 10 km	1 cm on the scale drawing is 10 km in real life
Ratio	1 : 1000	1 cm on the scale drawing is 1000 cm in real life
Line Drawing	⊢—⊣ 5 km	1 cm on the scale drawing is 5 km in real life

This line measures exactly 1 cm.

Look at the map on the right.
Find the real-life distance between Asforth and Baldon.
The scale is 1 cm = 10 km.

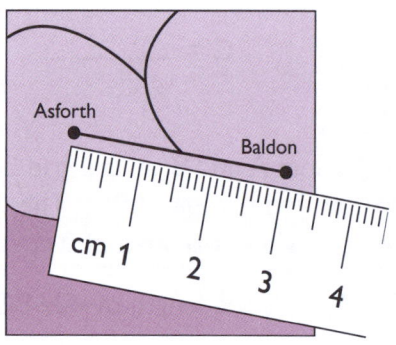

1) Use a ruler to measure the distance on the map.
   The scale drawing shows
   that the towns are 3 cm apart.

2) Use the scale to convert to the real-life distance:
   1 cm = 10 km, so 3 cm = 3 × 10 = **30 km**

Now Try This

1) A map uses a scale of 1 cm = 200 m.

   a) What real-life distance is shown by 4 cm on the map?

   ....

   b) What distance on the map would represent a real distance of 2 km?   *Convert 2 km to m.*

   ....

2) A scale drawing of an insect uses a scale of 1 cm = 2 mm.
   The insect's real length is 12 mm. What is its length on the scale drawing?

   ....

Section Three — Angles, Coordinates and Scale Drawings

Scale Drawings

3) A post office is 1.25 km from a school. A map is drawn using the scale 1 cm = 250 m.
Work out the distance between the post office and school on the map, in cm.

....

....

4) The map on the right shows a scale drawing of a village.
Estimate the real-life distance (in a straight line) between the
two buildings labelled A and B. Give your answer in m.

....

....

....

5) A map uses a scale of 1 : 200 000.
What is the real distance shown by 4.5 cm on the map?
Give your answer in km.

You'll need to convert to m, then to km, for this question.

....

....

6) The real distance between Ealon and Cradon is 80 km.
What is the scale for the map shown, written as a ratio?

....

....

....

Notes

Scale Drawings

Right, now to put pencil to paper and make some scale drawings of your own.

Use the Scale to Work Out the Dimensions

To make a scale drawing, use the scale and real-life dimensions to work out the lengths to draw.

Draw a scale drawing of a rectangular parking space with length 5 m and width 3 m. Use a scale of 1 : 100. Each grid square is 1 cm².

1 : 100 means 1 cm on the scale drawing represents 100 cm in real life.

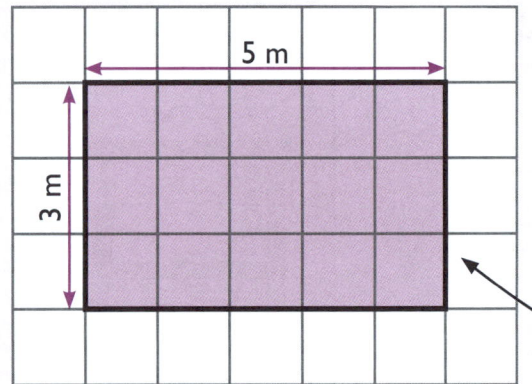

1) Convert the real-life measurements into cm.
   real length: 5 × 100 = 500 cm
   real width: 3 × 100 = 300 cm

2) Use the scale factor (divide by 100).
   drawing length: 500 ÷ 100 = **5 cm**
   drawing width: 300 ÷ 100 = **3 cm**

3) Draw the rectangle, labelling the dimensions with the real-life measurements.

Now Try This

1) Isla is building a rectangular wall. The wall is 18 m long and 4 m tall.
   Use the scale 1 cm = 2 m to draw a scale drawing of the wall below.

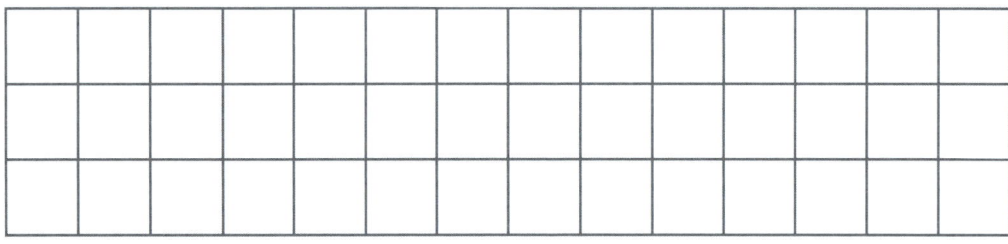

Each grid square is 1 cm².

2) A swimming pool has dimensions of 12 m by 8 m.

   Use a scale of 1 : 200 to make a scale drawing of the pool on the right.

   Each grid square is 1 cm².

Scale Drawings

3) The scale drawing on the right shows the plan view of a room. The scale used is 1 : 100.

   a) Give the real-life dimensions (in m) of the:

   bed ....

   drawers ....

   b) Draw a 2 m by 1 m wardrobe on the plan.

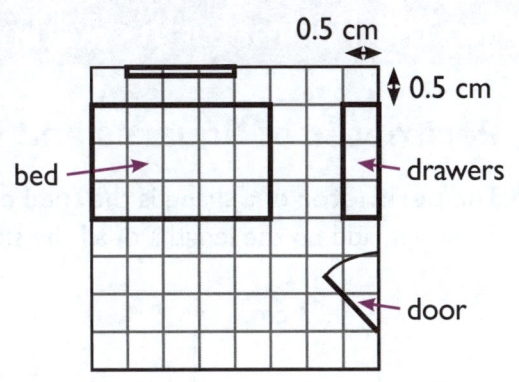

4) A rectangular flower bed has an area of 16 000 cm². Use a scale of 1 : 40 to draw a possible scale drawing for the flower bed.

See p.36 for area of a rectangle.

Each grid square is 1 cm².

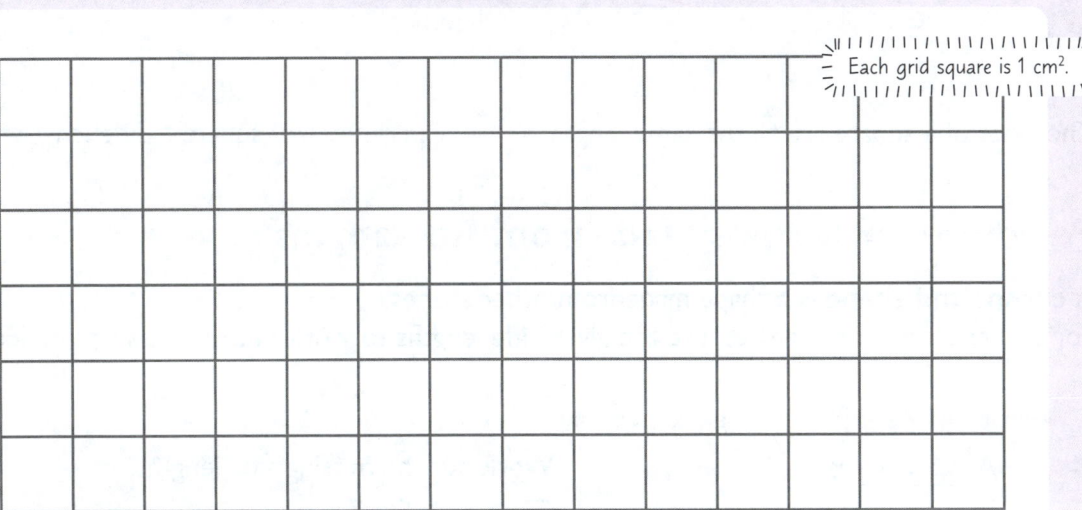

5) Harley sketched the flag below.

   Draw an accurate scale drawing of his flag, using the scale 20 mm = 1 m.

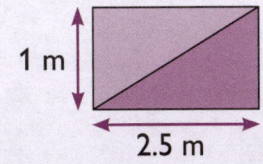

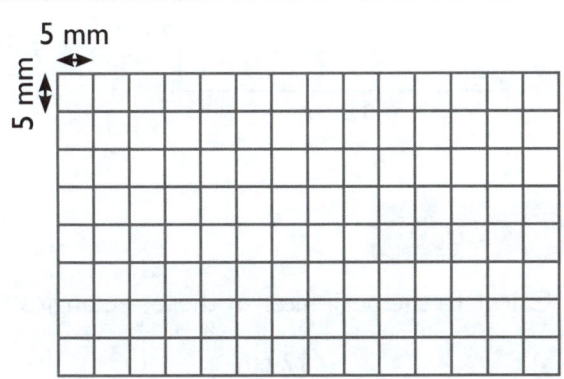

Section Four — Perimeter and Area

Perimeter

If you need to put up a fence, or like running in straight lines, this is the topic for you.

Find the Perimeter by Adding Up the Side Lengths

Perimeter of Squares and Rectangles

The **perimeter** of a shape is the total distance around the outside. To find it, add up the lengths of all the sides.

Make sure all the lengths are in the same units.

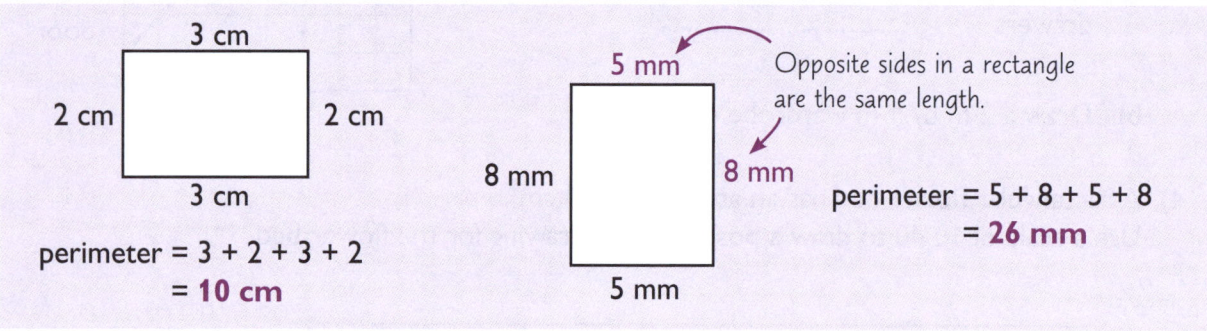

The sides of a square are all the same length. → perimeter of square = side length × 4

Perimeter of Shapes Made from Rectangles

A **compound shape** is a shape made from other shapes.
For shapes made of rectangles, use the given side lengths to work out the missing side lengths.

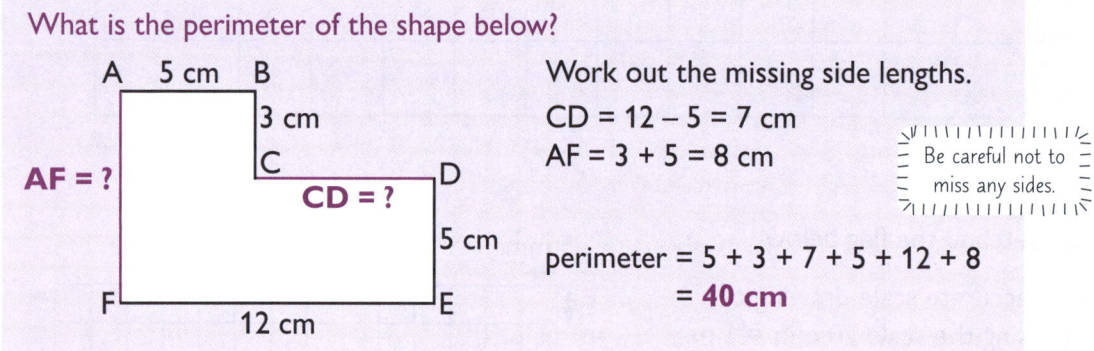

Now Try This

1) Calculate the perimeter of these rectangles.

   a) 12 cm, 7 cm

   b) 8 cm, 6 cm

   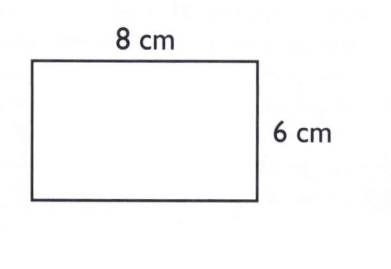

   ....

Perimeter

2) Find the missing side lengths for these shapes. Then calculate the perimeter of each shape.

a)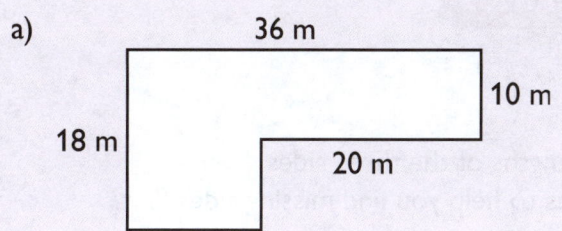

b)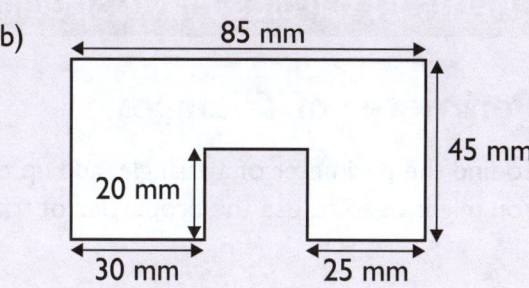

....
....
....

....
....
....

3) The diagram shows the route of a delivery driver. How far did they drive?

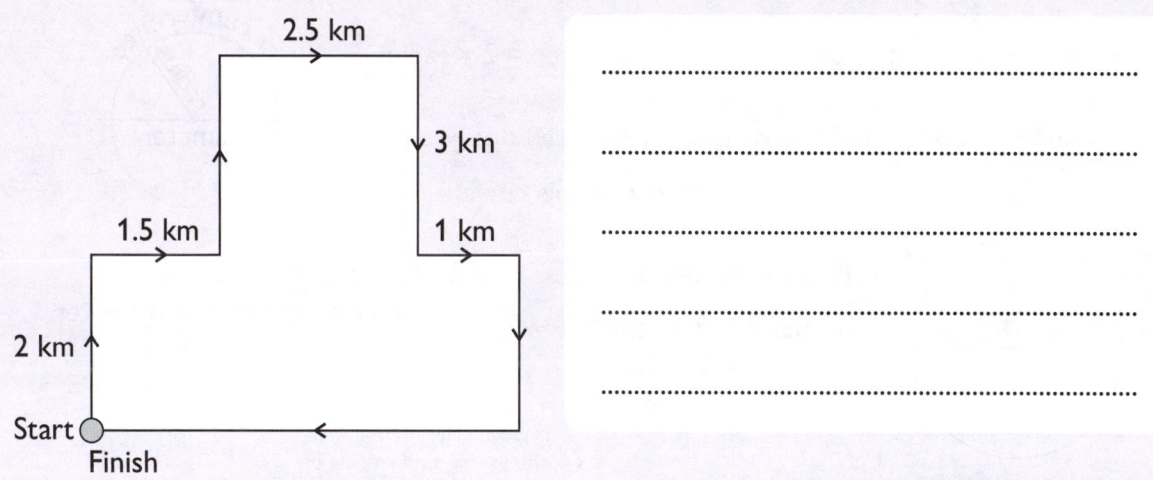

....
....
....
....
....

4) The outside edges of a square frame are 250 mm long. The perimeter of the inside of the frame is 200 mm shorter than the perimeter of the outside. How long are the inside edges?

....
....

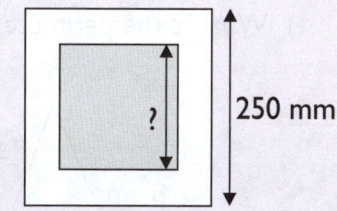

Notes

Perimeter

Circles and triangles pop up everywhere — here's how to find the distance round the edge of them.

Lengths in Circles Have Special Names

Perimeter of Triangles

To find the perimeter of a triangle, add up the lengths of the three sides.
You might need to use the properties of triangles to help you find missing sides first.

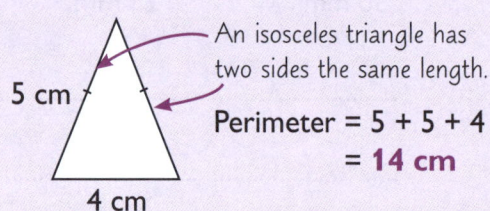

An isosceles triangle has two sides the same length.

Perimeter = 5 + 5 + 4
= **14 cm**

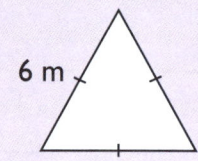

An equilateral triangle has three sides the same length.

Perimeter = 6 + 6 + 6
= **18 m**

Circumference of Circles

The perimeter of a circle is called the **circumference**.

circumference = π × diameter   diameter = 2 × radius

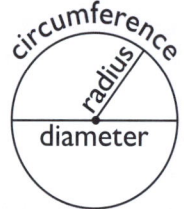

This symbol is called pi. It's a special number (about 3.14) that goes on forever.

Using π = 3.14, calculate the circumference of this circle.

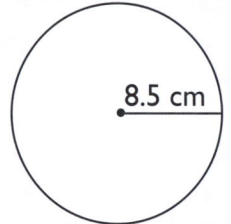

1) Find the diameter.
   diameter = 2 × radius
   = 2 × 8.5
   = 17 cm

2) Find the circumference.
   circumference = π × diameter
   = 3.14 × 17
   = **53.38 cm**

A question might tell you what value to use for π. If not, use the π button on your calculator.

Now Try This

1) What is the perimeter of these triangles?

a)

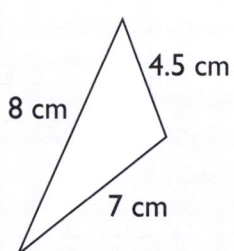

8 cm, 4.5 cm, 7 cm

b)

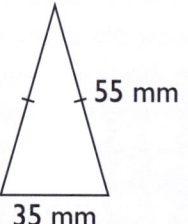

55 mm, 35 mm

....

Section Four — Perimeter and Area

Perimeter

2) A triangle has a perimeter of 20 cm. One side is 7 cm and one side is 4 cm. Find the length of the third side.

....

3) Calculate the circumference of each circle to 1 decimal place. Use π = 3.142.

a) 5 cm

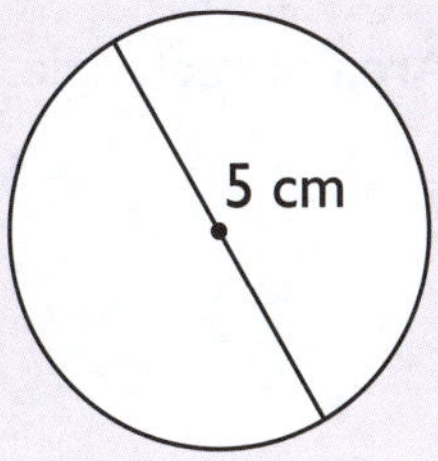

b) 12 mm

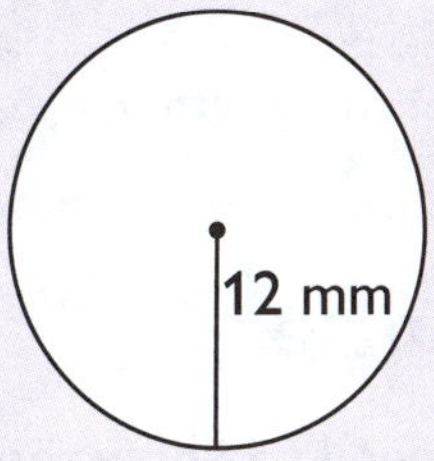

Hint: you're shown the radius here.

4) Part of Jade's roof is shown in the diagram. The perimeter of this part of the roof is 40 m. The two sloped sides are of equal length. What is the length of each sloped side?

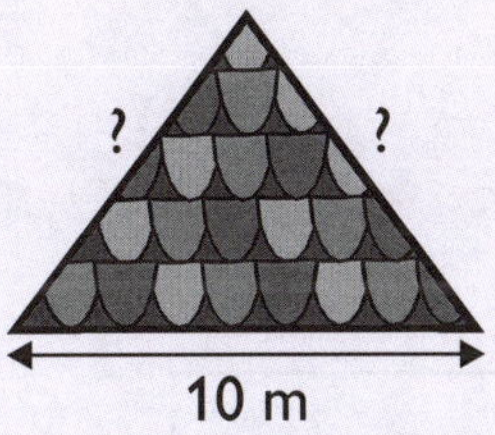

10 m

5) The wheels on Kamal's bike have a diameter of 26 inches. How far does his bike travel each time the wheels make a full turn? Use π = 3.14.

Notes

Area

Time to look at the inside of shapes. Knowing how much space something covers can be super useful.

Area is the Space Inside a Shape

Area of Rectangles

The area of a shape is the space within the shape. It is found by multiplying lengths together.

Area of rectangle = length × width

Find the area of this rectangle.

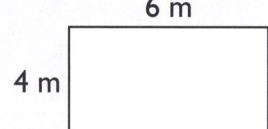

Area of rectangle = 6 × 4
= **24 m²**

Area of Triangles

For triangles, you need to know the base and height.

Area of triangle = ½ × base × height

Find the area of this triangle.

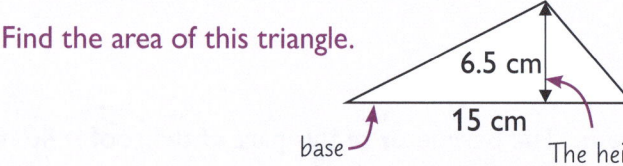

Area of triangle = ½ × base × height
= ½ × 15 × 6.5
= **48.75 cm²**

The height is the vertical height, not the length of the slope.

Now Try This

1) Find the area of these rectangles.

   a)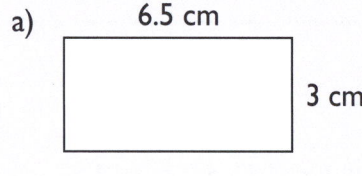

   ....

   b)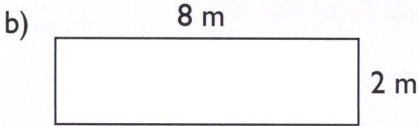

   ....

2) Find the area of these triangles.

   a)

   7 cm

   8 cm

   ....

   b)

   5 cm

   10 cm

   Don't forget to include the units. If the measurements are in cm, the area will be in cm².

   ....

Area

3) The area of this rectangle is 320 cm². Calculate the width of the rectangle.

Area = 320 cm², 40 cm, ? cm

....

4) Sharon is tiling the floor of her rectangular kitchen. She measures the length of her kitchen as 3.5 m and the width as 2.8 m. What is the area of her kitchen?

....

5) The area of a triangle is 54 cm².
If the base length of the triangle is 12 cm, what is the height of the triangle?

....

6) Cheryl is designing a new business card for her company, shown in the diagram below. Calculate how much of the total area is purple and how much is white.

....

....

....

7) The stained glass window shown below is made of 5 identical triangles. What is the total area of the window?

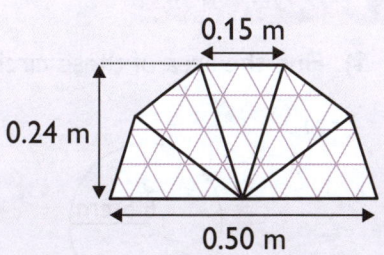

....

....

....

Notes

Area

If you can find the area of basic shapes, you can use that to find the area of much trickier ones.

Area of a Circle is π × Radius Squared

Area of Circles

Area of circle = π × radius²

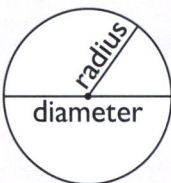

To square a number, multiply it by itself. Or use the 'squared' button on your calculator.

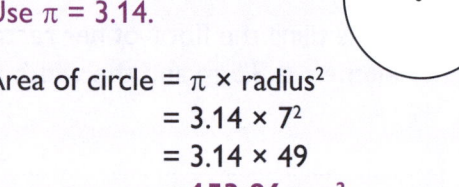

Find the area of this circle. Use π = 3.14.

Area of circle = π × radius²
= 3.14 × 7²
= 3.14 × 49
= **153.86 cm²**

Area of Compound Shapes

To find the area of a compound shape:
1) Split into rectangles, triangles and circles.
2) Find the area of each shape.
3) Add the areas together.

Claire has made the logo below. What is the total area of her logo?

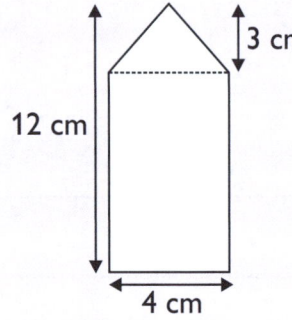

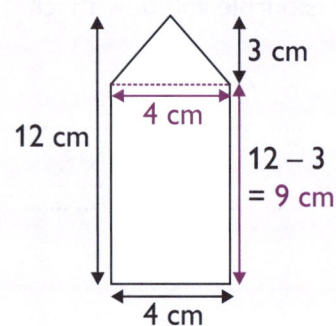

Area of triangle = ½ × 4 × 3
= 6 cm²

Area of rectangle = 9 × 4
= 36 cm²

Total area = 6 + 36
= **42 cm²**

Now Try This

1) Find the area of these circles. Use π = 3.14.

a)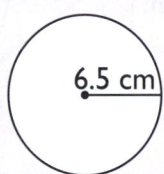

b)

c)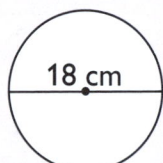

....

....

Area

2) Find the area of the compound shape below.

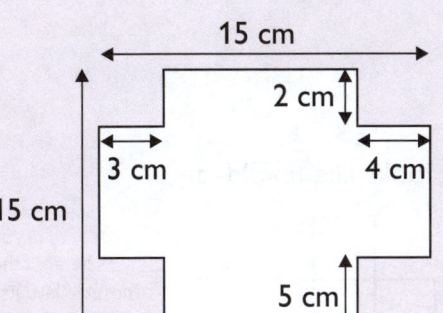

....
....
....
....

3) The diagram below shows Neil's door. A 200 ml tin of paint will cover 1.2 m². If Neil has one tin, does he have enough paint to cover the side of the door shown? Use π = 3.

To find the area of a semicircle, find the area of the circle then divide by 2.

....
....
....
....
....

4) Harri is making cards for a new game. The card with the smallest area will be the cheapest to print. Which shape card will be cheapest to print? Use π = 3.14.

A 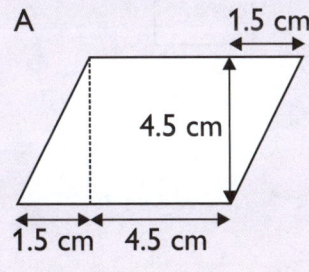 B 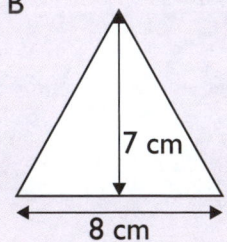 C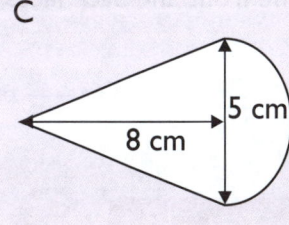

....
....

Notes

Nets

Next time you finish a box of cereal or get a parcel, unfold the box and take a look at its net.

Nets Show 3D Shapes Unfolded

Nets of Cubes

A **net** is a 2D drawing of a 3D shape — it shows what it looks like unfolded.

A cube has **6 faces**. All edges are the same length.
So the net of a cube has 6 squares like this.

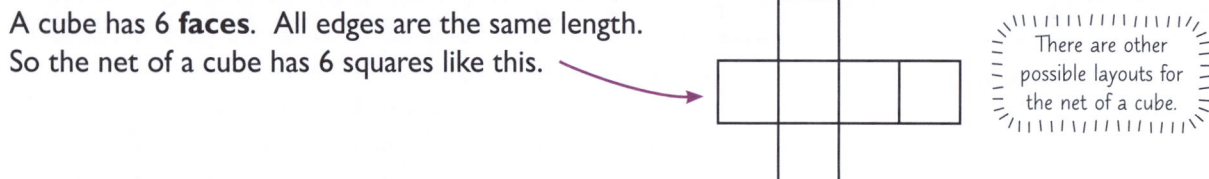

There are other possible layouts for the net of a cube.

Nets of Cuboids

Nets of cuboids have the same basic layout as cubes.
A cuboid has **6 faces**, so the net of the cuboid is made up of 6 rectangles.

Draw a net of this cuboid.

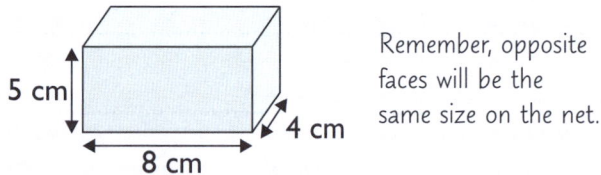

Remember, opposite faces will be the same size on the net.

Draw each face, labelling the dimension of each side:

- The top and bottom faces are 8 cm by 4 cm.
- The side faces are 5 cm by 4 cm.
- The front and back faces are 8 cm by 5 cm.

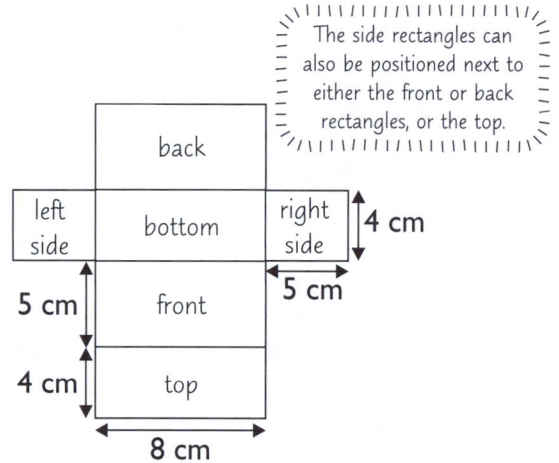

The side rectangles can also be positioned next to either the front or back rectangles, or the top.

Now Try This

1) Each side of a cube is 2 cm. Draw two different possible nets. Each grid square = 1 cm².

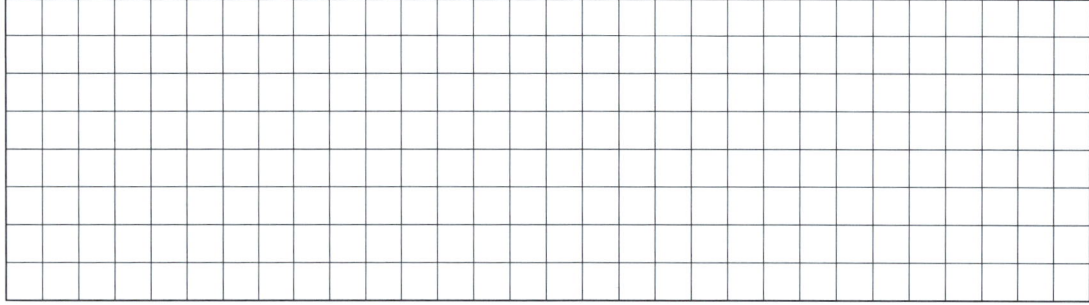

Nets

2) Draw a net of the cuboid on the right. Each grid square = 1 cm².

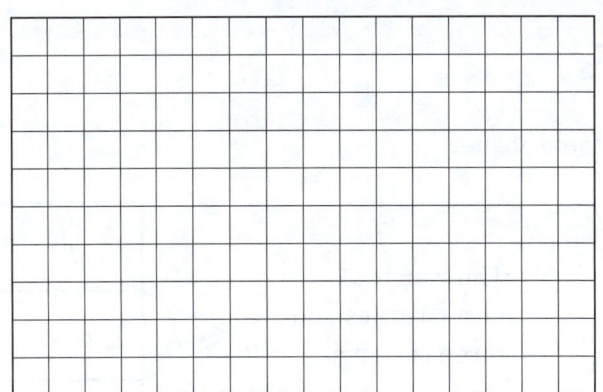
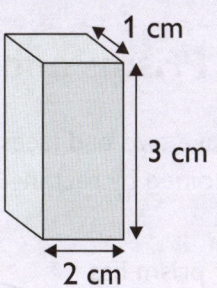

3) Tick all of the nets which would fold up into this cuboid.

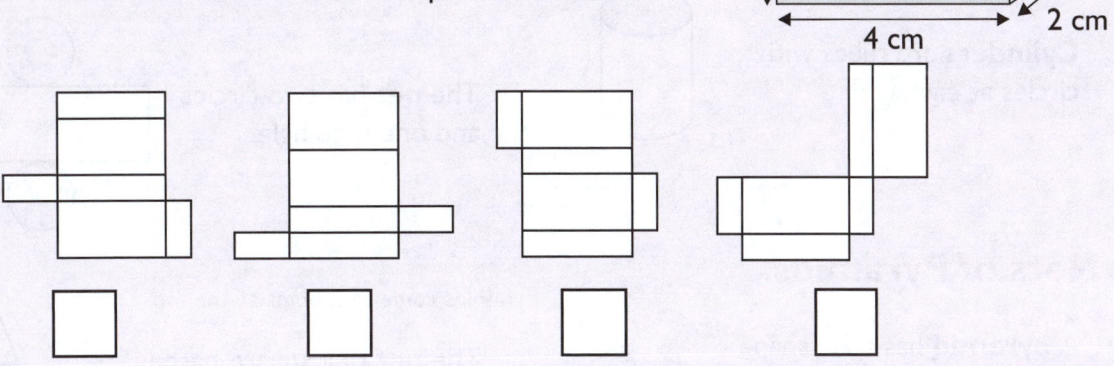

4) TJ wants to make the box below. Draw a net of the box and the lid.
Label the dimensions and mark the approximate position of the slit in the lid.

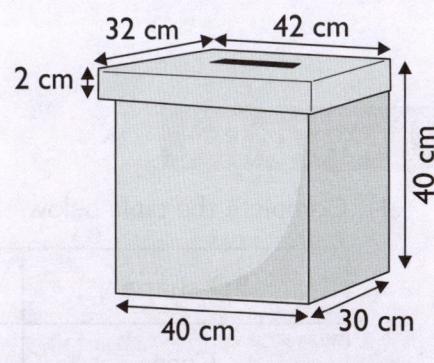

Section Five — 3D Shapes

Nets

Other 3D shapes are a bit trickier. But with a bit of brain gymnastics and this handy page, you'll be fine.

Nets of Prisms and Pyramids Have Different Shapes

Nets of Prisms and Cylinders

Prisms have two end faces that are the same shape. They are joined by rectangular faces.

A triangular prism has triangles at each end.

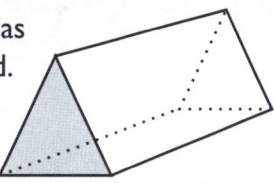

The **net** has two triangles and three rectangles.

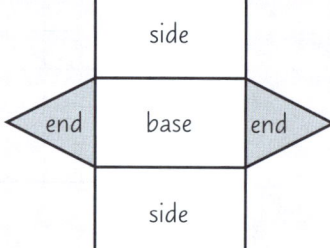

Cylinders are tubes with circles at each end.

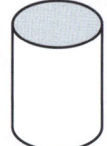

The **net** has two circles and one rectangle.

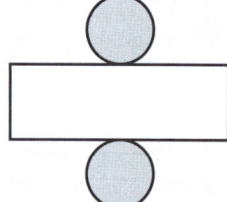

Nets of Pyramids

A **pyramid** has a 2D shape as its base. Each edge is joined to a triangular face.

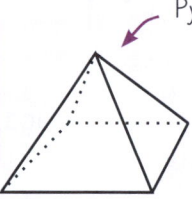

Pyramids come to a point at the top.

The **net** of a square-based pyramid will have one square surrounded by four triangles.

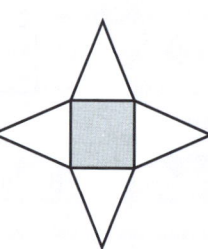

Now Try This

1) Complete the table below.

3D shape	Shapes of faces and number of each shape
Cube	
Triangular prism	
Cylinder	
Square-based pyramid	

Nets

2) Draw lines to match each 3D shape to its net.

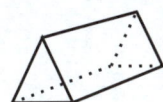   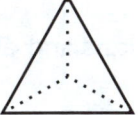

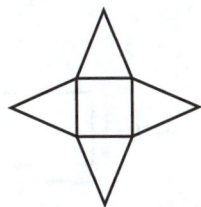 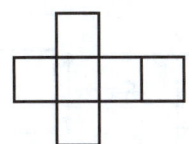 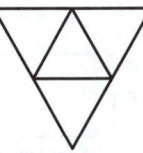 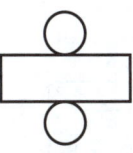 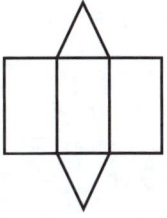

3) Which net would have more rectangles: a hexagonal prism or an octagonal prism?

....

4) A triangular prism is shown below. Draw a net for this prism on the grid. Each grid square = 1 cm².

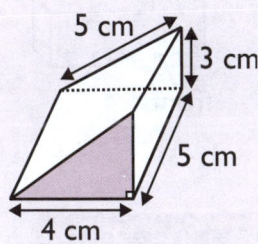

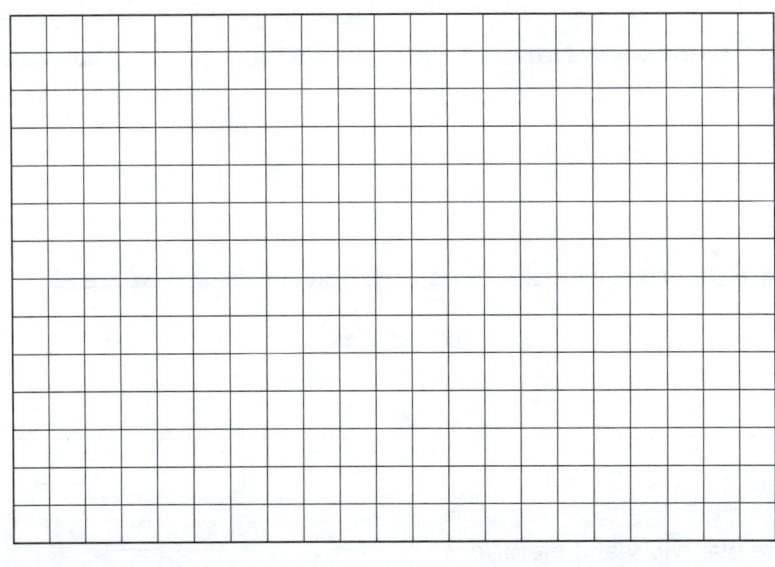

Notes

Plans and Elevations

These pages are perfect for wannabe architects or designers. Or if you like tying your brain in knots.

Plans and Elevations Show 3D Shapes in 2D

Plans and **elevations** are ways of representing 3D shapes in 2D.

- The view from the front is called the **front elevation**.
- The view from the side is called the **side elevation**.
- The view from above is called the **plan** or **plan view**.

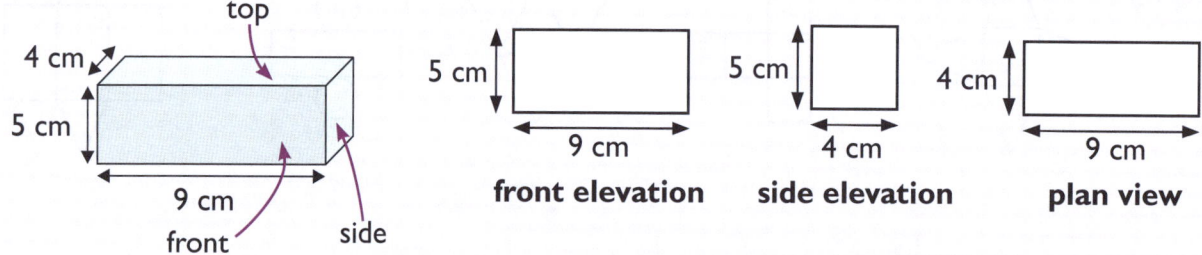

You can also draw plans and elevations for trickier shapes.

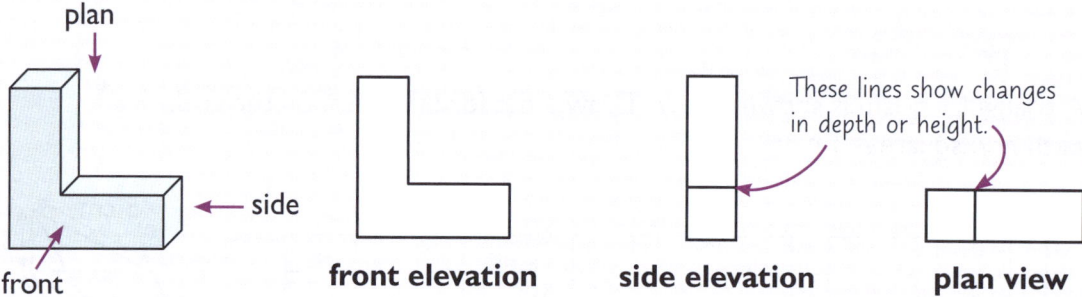

Now Try This

1) Name the 3D shape where the front elevation, side elevation and plan view are all:

   a) squares.

   b) circles.

   ....

2) Name the shape from the plan view and elevations.

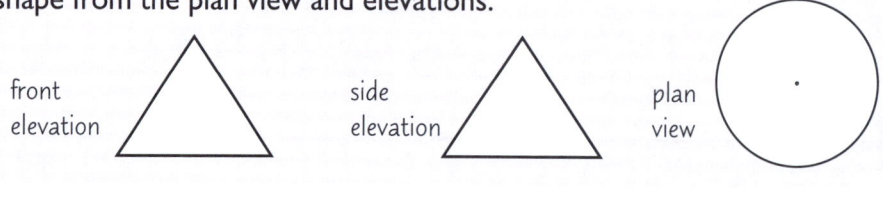

....

Section Five — 3D Shapes

Plans and Elevations

3) Draw lines to match each 3D shape with its plan view and front elevation.

plan view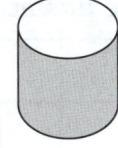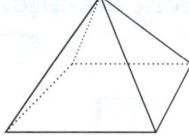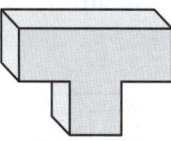

3D shape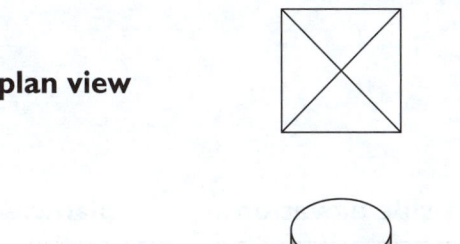

front elevation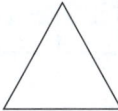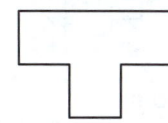

4) Label the plans and elevations for each shape below.
Choose 'front elevation', 'side elevation' or 'plan view'.

a)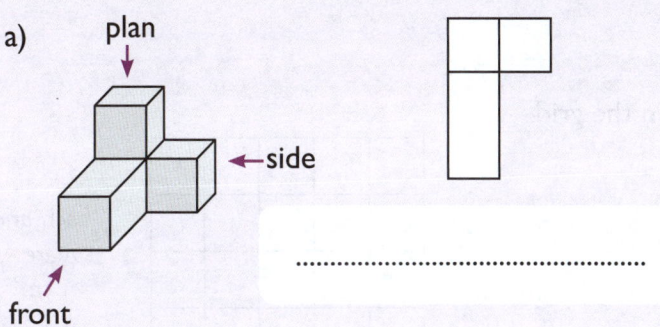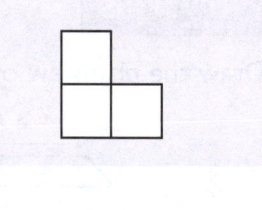

....

b)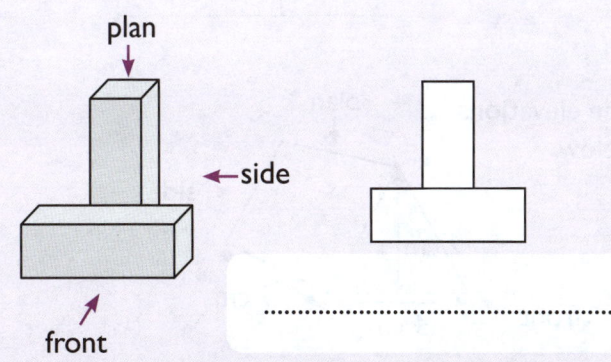

....

Notes

Plans and Elevations

It's one thing to interpret plans and elevations and quite another to draw them yourself. Here goes.

Draw Lines to Show Changes in Height or Depth

You might need to draw **plans** and **elevations** on a grid.

Here is a shape made from identical 1 cm cubes.

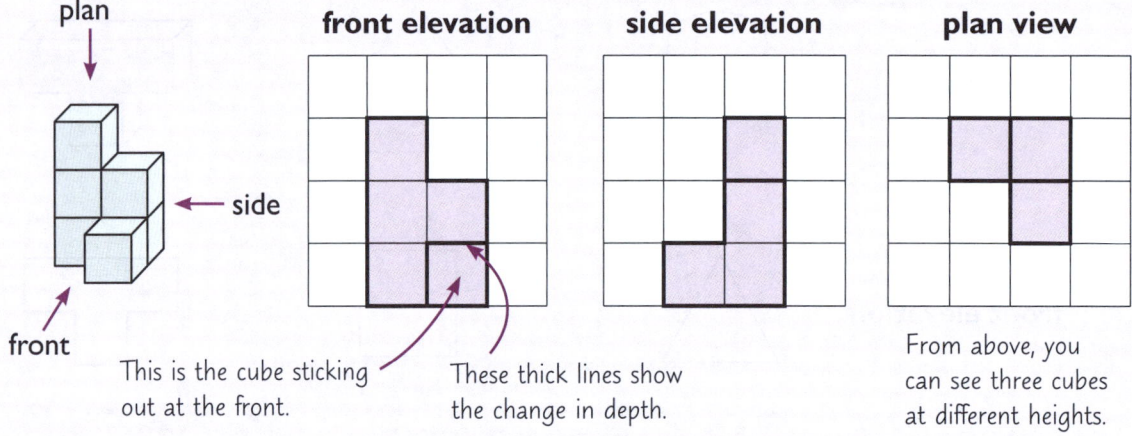

This is the cube sticking out at the front.

These thick lines show the change in depth.

From above, you can see three cubes at different heights.

Now Try This

1) Draw the plan view of this cuboid on the grid.

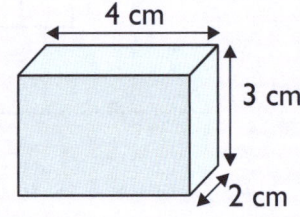

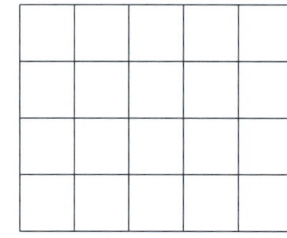

Each grid square = 1 cm².

2) Draw the plan view, and front and side elevations of this triangular prism on the grid below.

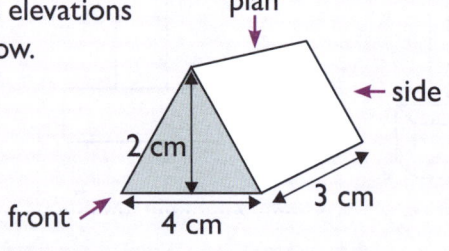

plan view

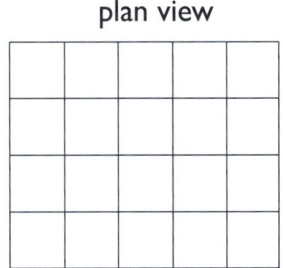

front elevation

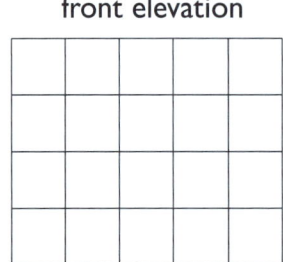

side elevation

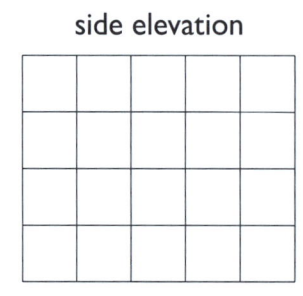

Each grid square = 1 cm².

Plans and Elevations

3) Draw the plan view, front elevation and side elevation of each shape. Each shape is made from identical cubes with side lengths of 1 cm.

a) Each grid square = 1 cm².

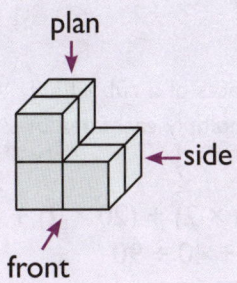 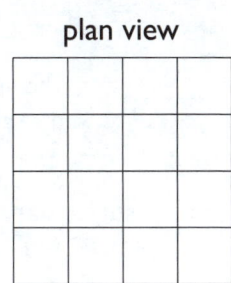 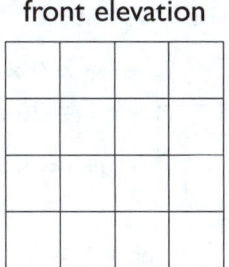 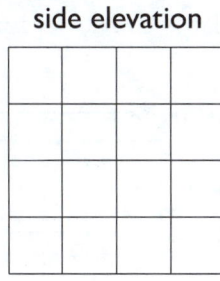

b) Each grid square = 1 cm².

 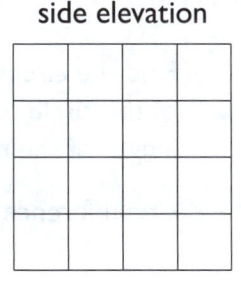 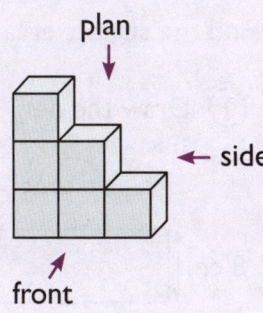 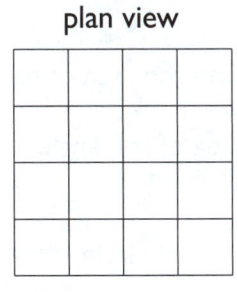

c) Each grid square = 1 cm².

Surface Area

If you've forgotten how to find areas, look back at p.36-39. Area and nets will see you through this lot.

Surface Area is the Total Area of All the Faces

The **surface area** of a 3D shape is the area of all the faces added together.

What is the surface area of this cuboid?

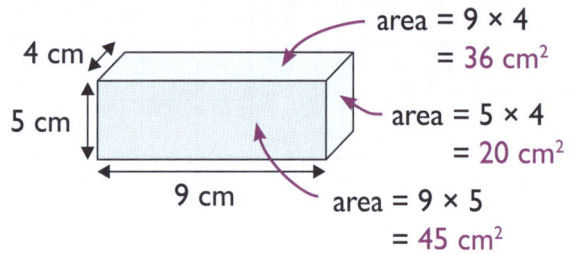

area = 9 × 4 = 36 cm²

area = 5 × 4 = 20 cm²

area = 9 × 5 = 45 cm²

The opposite faces of a cuboid are the same, so multiply each area by 2.

surface area = (36 × 2) + (20 × 2) + (45 × 2)
= 72 + 40 + 90
= **202 cm²**

Draw a net to find the surface area of more complicated shapes.

Find the surface area of the cylinder on the right. Use π = 3.14.

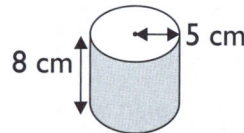

① Draw the net.

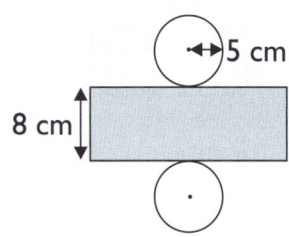

② Find the circumference of the circle to give the length of the rectangle.

circumference = π × diameter
= π × 2 × radius
= 31.4 cm

③ Find the area of each shape.

area of rectangle = 8 × 31.4
= 251.2 cm²

area of circle = π × radius²
= π × 5²
= 3.14 × 25
= 78.5 cm²

1 circle at each end.

See p.34 and p.38 for these circle formulas.

surface area = (78.5 × 2) + 251.2
= **408.2 cm²**

Now Try This

1) A cube has a side length of 5 cm. Work out the surface area of the cube.

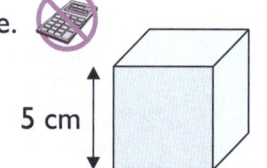

....

2) Find the total surface area of the cuboid below.

Surface Area

3) Calculate the surface area of this triangular prism.

   ....

   ....

   ....

4) Find the surface area of this cylinder to the nearest square centimetre. Use $\pi = 3.14$.

   ....

   ....

5) Naomi needs to paint the four outside walls of this storage unit (not the top or bottom). Each tin of paint will cover 15 m² and costs £34. Work out the total cost of the paint Naomi needs to buy to cover the storage unit walls.

   ....

   ....

   ....

   ....

6) The formula for the total surface area of a sphere is $4\pi r^2$ (r = radius of sphere). A ball has a diameter of 7 cm. Work out the surface area of the ball to 1 decimal place, using $\pi = 3.14$.

   ....

   ....

Notes

Volume

How big a box do I need? Will all the ingredients fit in my pan? Time for some volume calculations...

Volume is the Space Inside a Shape

Volume of Cuboids

The **volume** is the amount of space a 3D shape takes up:

volume of cuboid
= length × width × height

What is the volume of this tissue box?

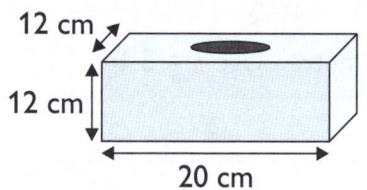

volume = length × width × height
= 20 × 12 × 12
= **2880 cm³**

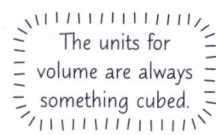
The units for volume are always something cubed.

Volume of Prisms and Cylinders

Use these formulas for prisms and cylinders:

volume of prism = cross-sectional area × length

volume of cylinder = πr² × length

πr² gives the area of a circle (the cross-section).

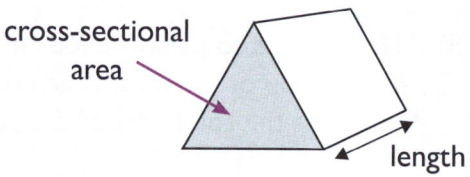
cross-sectional area, length

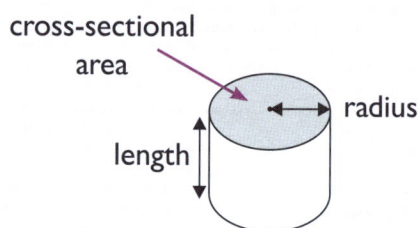
cross-sectional area, radius, length

What is the volume of this drinks can? Use π = 3.14.

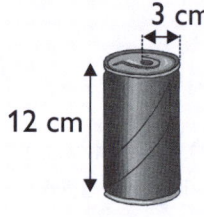

volume of cylinder = πr² × length
= 3.14 × 3² × 12
= 3.14 × 9 × 12
= **339.12 cm³**

Now Try This

1) The sides of a cube are each 6 cm. What is its volume?

....

2) Calculate the volume of this pizza box.

....

Section Five — 3D Shapes

Volume

3) Find the volume of a cylinder with a radius of 7 m and length of 12 m. Use π = 3.14.

....

....

4) The box for a chocolate bar is a triangular prism with a length of 30 cm. The triangular faces each have a 5 cm base and a 6 cm vertical height. What is the volume of the box?

....

....

5) Kyla posts a tube of sweets and a book separately. Use the table to work out the total cost of postage. Show your working.

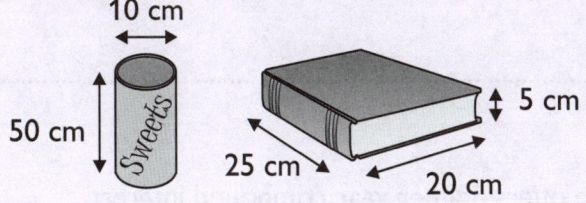

Volume of object	Postage cost
up to 3000 cm³	£3.25
3000 to 3500 cm³	£3.50
3500 to 4000 cm³	£3.75

....

....

....

6) How many cube-shaped boxes with side length 50 cm fit in a cube-shaped container with side length 2 m?

....

....

Notes

Topic-Based Questions

These questions are all designed to give you some extra practice on the topics in this book.

Money

1) Convert:

   a) £3.15 to pence.

   b) 123p to pounds.

   c) 4000p to pounds.

   ....

2) Huw buys two tins of tomatoes for 45p per tin, and a loaf of bread for £1.45. He pays with a £20 note. How much change does he get?

   ....

   ....

3) In Sanjay's local coffee shop, a large coffee costs £4.20. There is a 25% discount for anyone who brings their own cup. What will a large coffee cost Sanjay if he brings his own cup?

   ....

4) £3400 is invested in a savings account which offers 3% per year compound interest. How much will be in the account after two years?

   ....

5) Bev buys a vase for £2 in a charity shop. She sells it for £2.80. What is her percentage profit?

   ....

6) A garage charges £63 per hour. Kim's car takes 3 hours to repair and the parts cost £229.70.

   a) What will Kim be charged for the repair?

   ....

   b) VAT at 20% is then added to the bill. What is the total, including VAT?

   ....

Topic-Based Questions

Units and Measures

1) A stock cube makes 500 ml of stock. How many cubes are needed to make 2.5 litres?

   ....

2) Alan has a recipe in ounces. Use the conversion graph to answer the questions.

   a) Alan has 54 g of chocolate chips. He needs 2 oz for his recipe. How many ounces does he have?

   ....

   b) 3 oz of sugar are needed. What is this in grams?

   ....

   Converting Masses (graph: ounces (oz) vs grams (g), 0 to 100 g, 0 to 3 oz)

3) 1 pint ≈ 0.6 litres. A barrel holds 424 pints of whiskey. Roughly how many litres is this?

   ....

4) 1 km ≈ 0.62 miles. A road sign says it is 31 miles to London. What is this in km?

   ....

5) Sarah completes a 5 km run in 24 minutes. What is her speed in km/h? (speed = distance ÷ time)

   ....

6) The density of silver is 10.5 g/cm³. A silver spoon weighs 94.5 g. What is its volume? (volume = mass ÷ density)

   ....

Topic-Based Questions

Angles and Coordinates

1) Tick the correct statements. All angles...

   ...in a parallelogram add up to 360°. ☐   ...in an isosceles triangle are different. ☐

   ...in an equilateral triangle are 60°. ☐   ...in a quadrilateral are 90° or smaller. ☐

2) Find the missing angle in these shapes.

   a) 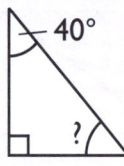   b) 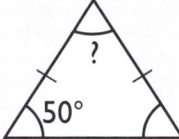   c) 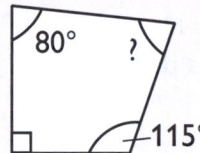   d)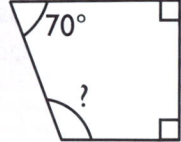

   ....

3) Two corners of a square have been plotted on the grid.

   Plot the remaining corners, and label them C and D.
   Then give the coordinates of each corner.

   A = ...   B = ...

   C = ...   D = ...

   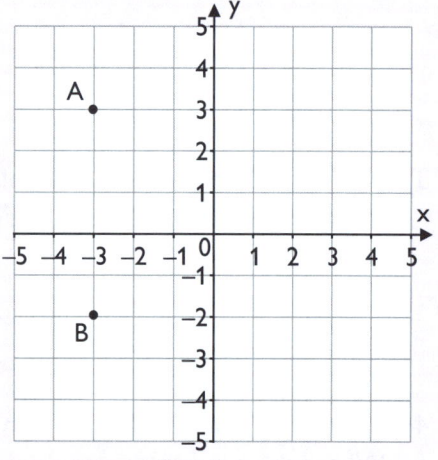

4) Find the size of angles A, B and C in this parallelogram.

   ....

5) Points P and Q are two corners of a right-angled triangle, PQR.

   • the right angle is at point Q
   • the triangle has an area of 14 cm²
   • each grid square is 1 cm²

   What are the coordinates of R?

   R = ...

   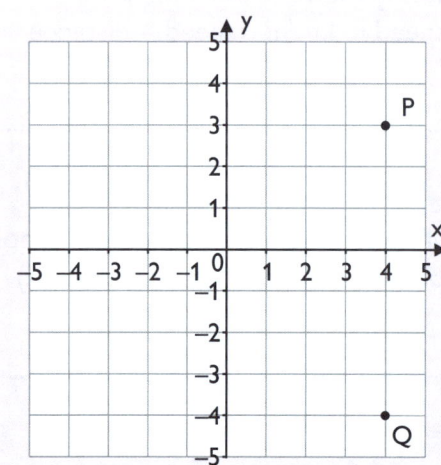

Topic-Based Questions

Scale Drawings

1) Complete the missing values in this table.

	Map A	Map B	Map C
Scale	1 cm = 50 km	1 cm = ... km	1 : 10 000
Distance on map	2.5 cm	3.1 cm	.... cm
Real-life distance	.... km	6.2 km	4 km

2) A scale drawing of a garden is shown on the right. The scale is 1 : 200.

   a) Give the real-life diameter (in m) of the pond.

   ....

   b) Give the real-life dimensions (in m) of the patio.

   ....

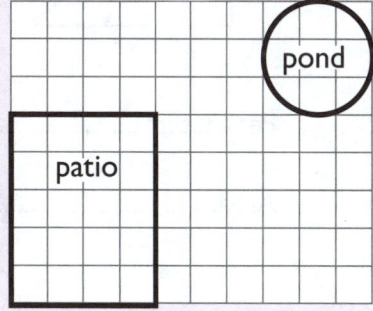

   c) Draw a flower bed on the plan, with a length of 4 m and a width of 2 m.

3) Liam has sketched the side elevation of a church, labelling the dimensions. Draw an accurate scale drawing of the elevation, using the scale 1 cm : 10 m.

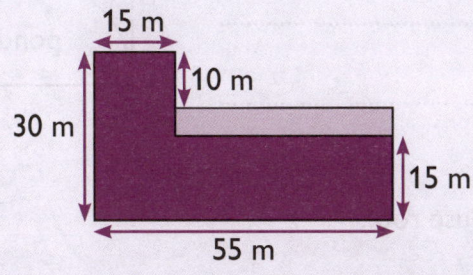
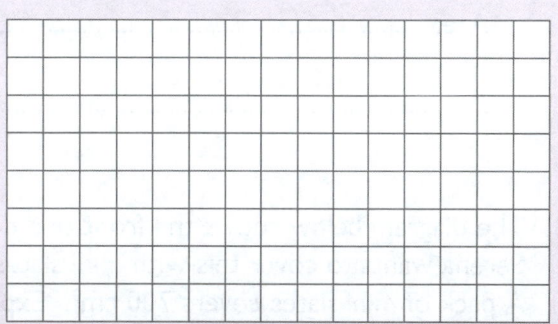

4) Dimple Island is 24 km wide. Measure its width on the map to work out the scale factor. Write your answer as a ratio.

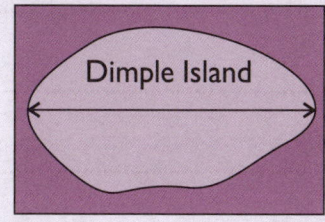

....

Topic-Based Questions

Perimeter and Area

See p.36-39 for area formulas.

1) Calculate the perimeter and area of these shapes. Use π = 3.14.

   a)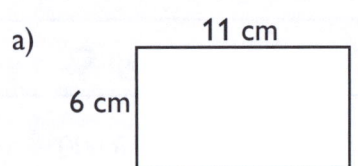

   Perimeter: ....

   Area: ....

   b)

   Perimeter: ....

   Area: ....

   c)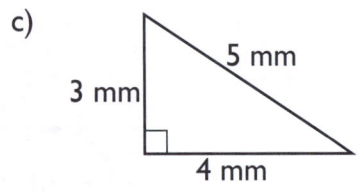

   Perimeter: ....

   Area: ....

   d)

   Perimeter: ....

   Area: ....

2) The diagram shows a semicircular pond in a square garden.
   Calculate the perimeter and area of the gravel. Use π = 3.14.

   Perimeter: ....

   ....

   Area: ....

   ....

   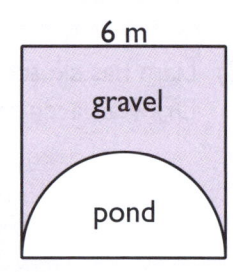

3) The diagram below shows the front of a dolls' house roof.
   Serena wants to cover this with mini slates.
   A pack of mini slates covers 700 cm². Explain how many packs she should order.

   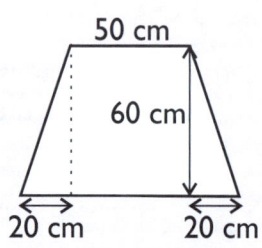

Topic-Based Questions

Nets, Plans and Elevations

1) Name the 3D shape from its net.

   a) 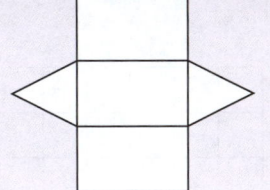   b) 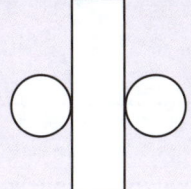   c)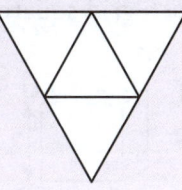

   ....

   ....

2) For each 3D shape, sketch its plan view and front elevation.

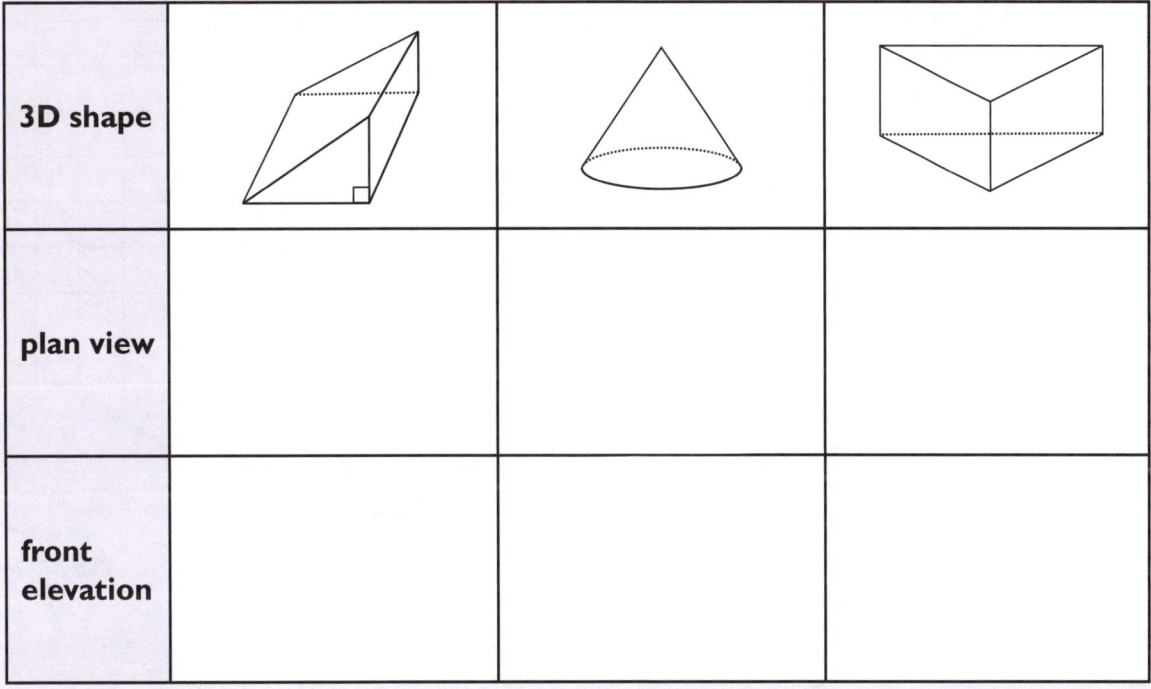

3) Draw the plan view and front and side elevations of the shape below.
   The shape is made from identical cubes with side lengths of 1 cm.

   plan view   front elevation   side elevation   plan

   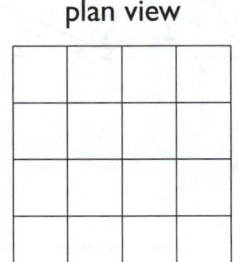 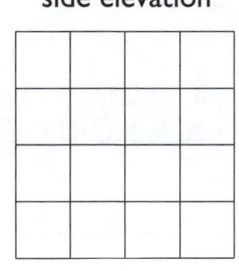 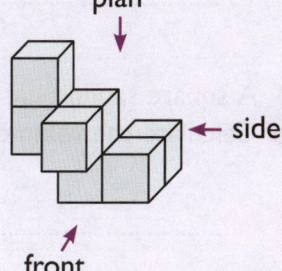

   Each grid square = 1 cm².

Topic-Based Questions

Surface Area and Volume

1) Calculate the surface area of each shape. Then draw a net for the shape.
   Each grid square = 1 cm².

   a)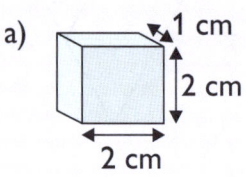

   ....

   ....

   ....

   ....

   ....

   b)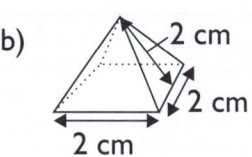

   ....

   ....

   ....

   ....

   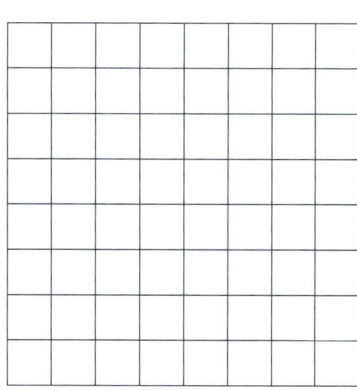

2) The formula for the surface area of cube is $6a^2$, where a is the side length.
   Work out the surface area of a cube with a side length of 5 cm.

   ....

3) Calculate the volume of the tent on the right.

   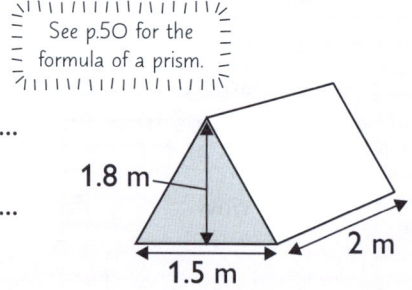

   ....

   ....

4) A square sandpit has side lengths of 2 m. Its height is 50 cm.
   Calculate the volume of sand needed to fill the sandpit.

   ....

   ....

Mixed Practice

Just like in the exam, you need to figure out how to tackle each of these questions. Off you go...

Section A   *Don't use a calculator for Section A.*

1) Corners A and B of triangle ABC have been plotted on the grid below.

   a) Plot corner C at (–3, –2). Draw triangle ABC.

   b) Write down the coordinates of point B.

   ....

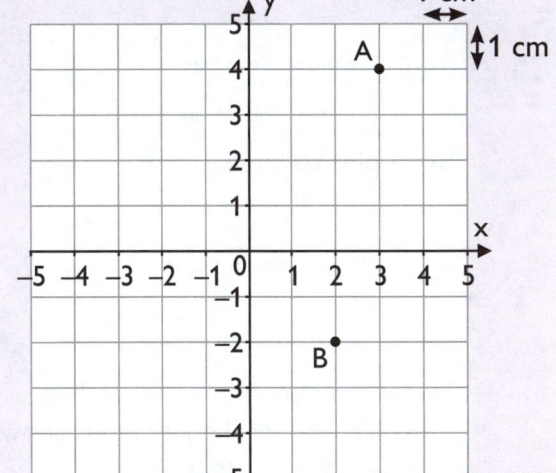

   c) Calculate the area of triangle ABC.

   ....

   ....

   d) Two of the angles in the triangle are 36° and 99°. Calculate the size of the third angle.

   ....

2) A warehouse has some shipping containers. Each container is a cuboid with dimensions of 4 m × 2 m × 2 m.

   a) Draw a net of a container on the grid using a scale of 1 : 200.

   b) Some shipping containers are stacked as shown below.

   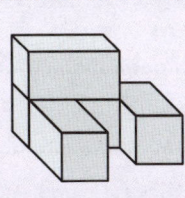

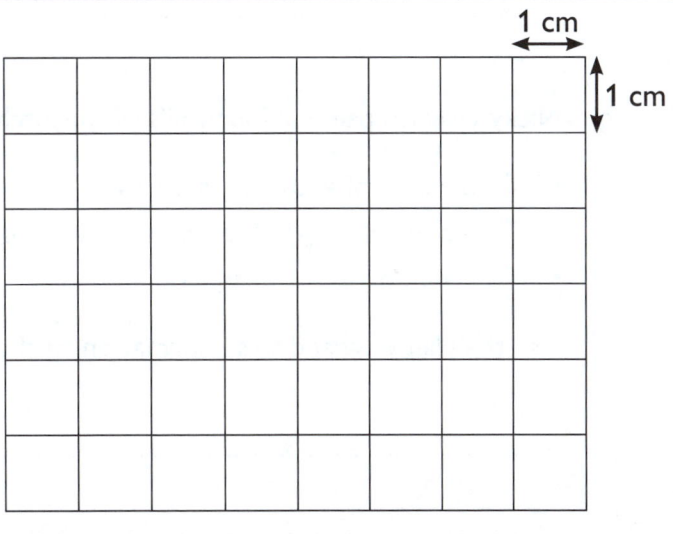

   Tick the correct plan view of the containers.

   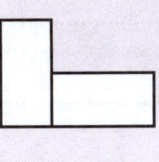   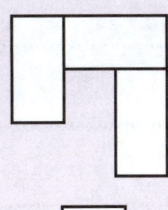   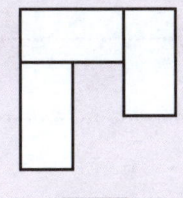   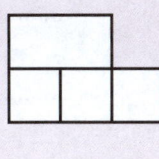

         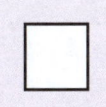   ☐

Mixed Practice

3) The graph below shows the conversion between pints and litres.
   Use the graph to convert:

   a) 2 litres to pints.

   ....

   b) 1 pint to litres.

   ....

4) Nicky is redecorating her kitchen.
   The plan view of the kitchen is shown on the right.

   a) She wants to tile the floor with square tiles.
      She chooses tiles which each cover 0.25 m².

      How many tiles does she need to cover the floor?

      ....

      ....

   b) Nicky will also paint all four walls of the kitchen. 1 tin of paint covers 13 m².

      • The height of each wall is 2.5 m.
      • The door has a width of 0.8 m and a height of 2 m.
      • The window is a 1 m square.

      Use the plan view and this information to show that Nicky should buy 3 tins of paint.

      ....

      ....

      ....

      ....

      ....

Mixed Practice

Section B

You can use a calculator for Section B.

1) The ticket prices for a cinema are shown on the right.

Adult	£9.30
Child	£5.80
Senior	£6.50
Family*	£27.80

*2 adults and up to 3 children

a) Margaret is going to the cinema with a friend and her 3 children. How much will Margaret save if she buys a family ticket rather than 2 adult and 3 child tickets?

....

....

....

b) Ismail is going to the cinema with his family. They need 1 senior ticket, 3 adult tickets and 1 child ticket. He has a 25% off voucher. How much will the tickets cost Ismail?

....

....

....

c) The cinema buys 10 kg of popcorn for £12.
It then sells 250 g servings of popcorn for £3 each.

Calculate the percentage profit the cinema makes per serving. Show your working.

....

....

....

d) A serving of popcorn is served in a cuboid-shaped box with a volume of 1500 cm³.
The box has a square base with 10 cm sides.

What is the height of the box?

....

....

Mixed Practice

2) Here is a scale drawing of Faryal's garden. The scale is 1 : 100.

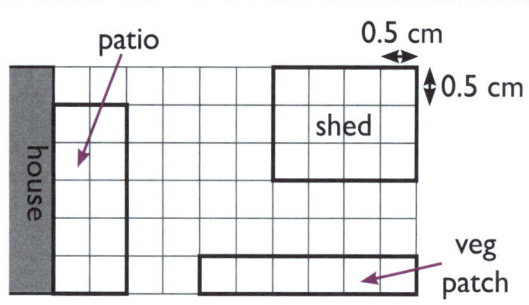

a) Complete the table.

Feature	Real-life dimensions (cm)
Shed	....
Patio	....
Veg patch	....

b) Faryal wants to sow grass seeds on the area **not** covered by the shed, patio or veg patch. Grass seed comes in three sizes of box:

Size	Small	Medium	Large
Maximum area	100 000 cm²	400 000 cm²	800 000 cm²

What is the smallest box Faryal can buy to have enough seed? Show your working.

....

....

....

....

c) Faryal needs to add a fence to the sides of the garden that aren't shared with her house. What length of fencing does Faryal need? Give your answer in metres.

....

....

d) Wire fencing is sold in 6-foot lengths which cost £32 each. Estimate how much it will cost for Faryal to fence her garden. 1 metre ≈ 3.28 feet.

Assume the fencing can go round corners.

....

....

Mixed Practice

3) A park ranger is making a circular pond with a diameter of 1.2 m and a depth of 0.3 m.

   a) The ranger needs to buy lining material to cover the inside surface of the pond. Find the area they need to cover. Use π = 3.14. *(This includes the bottom of the pond and the curved wall.)*

   ....

   ....

   b) What is the volume of the pond? Use π = 3.14. Give your answer to 2 dp.

   ....

   ....

4) Find the weight of compost needed to fill the triangular prism-shaped planter below. Compost has a density of 1.5 tonnes/m³.

   80 cm
   1.5 m
   50 cm

   ....

   ....

5) Ruth puts £500 into SuperBank's savings account.

   > 5% interest for the first year.
   > 3% compound interest per year after that.

   To the nearest 1p, how much will she have in total after:

   a) 2 years?   b) 3 years?

   ....

   ....

Mixed Practice

6) Hamza needs a new phone. He is choosing between these options:

   Deal 1:
   £30 initial payment,
   then £48/month for 2 years

   Deal 2:
   Buy phone for £744,
   then £15/month for 2 years

   Which deal will be cheaper for Hamza over 2 years? Show your working.

   ....

   ....

7) Suze sets off on a 20.8 mile charity walk at 8 am. She finishes the walk at 2:30 pm.

   a) Calculate Suze's average speed in mph.

   ....

   ....

   b) Estimate the length of the charity walk in km. 1 mile ≈ 1.6 km.

   ....

   c) Part of the walk goes along a beach between South Pier and North Pier, as marked on the map. The map uses a scale of 1 : 25 000. What is the real distance between the two piers?

   You need to measure the distance marked using a ruler.

   ....

   ....

   ....

   d) Suze's employer promised to increase the sponsor money Suze raised by 15%. She raised £472. What will her total be after her employer makes their contribution?

   ....

   ....

Mixed Practice

8) Mark works at a supermarket earning £15.60 per hour.
He works 5 six-hour shifts per week for 40 weeks each year.

a) How much does Mark earn each year?

....

....

b) Mark pays 20% tax on his annual earnings above £12 570. ← He doesn't pay any tax on earnings below this amount.
How much tax does he pay each year?

....

....

c) After other deductions from his pay, Mark takes home £1380 per month.
He has the following monthly outgoings:

Food/bills	Toiletries	Petrol	Going out	Mobile phone	Clothes
£380	£15	£132	£265	£27	£125

How much money does he have left over each month?

....

....

d) Mark plans to save the money he has left over towards a house deposit.
He needs a 5% deposit for a house costing £250 000.

How many whole months will he need to save for the deposit with his current budget?

....

....

....

Notes

Individual Learning Plan

After each lesson or topic, use the table below to record your progress. Then you and your teacher can identify what you still don't feel confident with, why you found it difficult and what you can do to improve.

1. What I Can Do Now	2. What I Found Hard
Example: Convert between units	Making scale drawings

Individual Learning Plan

Individual Learning Plan

If you want more space to write your plan, go to: cgpbooks.co.uk/fs-maths
or scan the QR code in the header to find a printable PDF of this table.

3. What I Need To Improve On	4. What I Will Do To Improve
Working with a scale given as a ratio	Always check that real-life distances make sense

CGP

www.cgpbooks.co.uk

Name ....

Functional Skills
Maths: Data Handling
Level 2

Course Booklet

Answers available online

CGP Books — The Choice of Champions!

He knows it.
You know it.
Everyone knows it ☺

cgpbooks.co.uk

Contents

✓ Use the tick boxes to check off the topics you've completed.

About This Booklet .... 1 ☐
Knowledge Organiser .... 2 ☐

Section One — Averages and Range

Median and Mode .... 6 ☐
Calculate the median and mode of a set of quantities.

Mean and Range .... 8 ☐
Calculate the mean and range.

Using Averages and Range .... 10 ☐
Use the mean, median, mode and range
to compare two sets of data.

Grouped Frequency Tables .... 12 ☐
Estimate the mean of a grouped frequency
distribution from discrete data.

Section Two — Probability

Expressing Probability .... 14 ☐
Express probabilities as fractions, decimals and percentages.

Calculating Probability .... 16 ☐
Work out probabilities, including combined events.

Probability Trees .... 18 ☐
Work out the probability of combined events using diagrams.

Two-Way Tables .... 20 ☐
Work out the probability of combined events using tables.

Sample Space Diagrams .... 22 ☐
Work out the probability of combined events using tables.

Section Three — Scatter Diagrams

Scatter Diagrams .... 24 ☐
Draw and interpret scatter diagrams and
recognise positive and negative correlation.

Topic-Based Questions

Averages and Range .... 28 ☐
Grouped Frequency Tables .... 30 ☐
Probability .... 31 ☐
Probability from Diagrams and Tables .... 32 ☐
Scatter Diagrams .... 34 ☐

Mixed Practice

Section A .... 35 ☐
Section B .... 37 ☐

Individual Learning Plan .... 42 ☐

Unlock your Digital Extras

To get your free digital extras, go to **cgpbooks.co.uk/fs-maths** or scan the QR code below.

This will take you to:
- An answer booklet
- More Individual Learning Plan pages
- A Knowledge Retriever

Published by CGP

Written by Angela Turner

Reviewer: Shanti O'Hea Francis

Editors: Liam Dyer, Sharon Keeley-Holden and Chris Lindle.

With thanks to Glenn Rogers for the proofreading.
With thanks to Beth Linnane for the copyright research.

Specification points in Contents contain public sector information licensed under the Open Government Licence v3.0. https://www.nationalarchives.gov.uk/doc/open-government-licence/version/3/

ISBN: 978 1 83774 210 3
Printed by Elanders Ltd, Newcastle upon Tyne.
Graphics from Corel®

Text, design, layout and original illustrations © Coordination Group Publications Ltd (CGP) 2025 All rights reserved.

Photocopying this book is not permitted, even if you have a CLA licence.
Extra copies are available from CGP with next day delivery • 0800 1712 712 • www.cgpbooks.co.uk

About This Booklet

This course booklet supports your learning of the 'Handling information and data' content area of the Level 2 qualification.

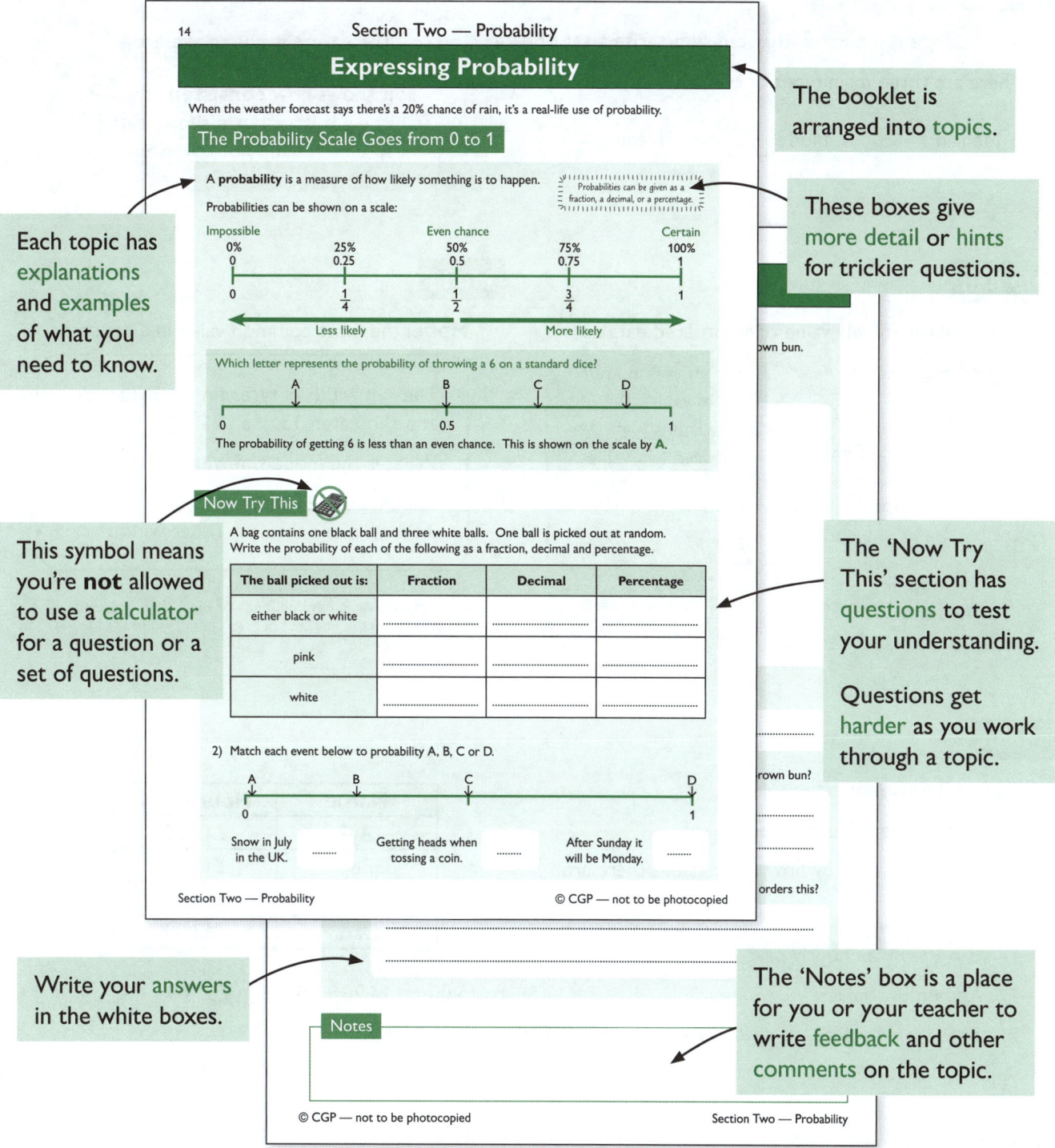

The booklet is arranged into topics.

These boxes give more detail or hints for trickier questions.

Each topic has explanations and examples of what you need to know.

This symbol means you're **not** allowed to use a calculator for a question or a set of questions.

The 'Now Try This' section has questions to test your understanding.

Questions get harder as you work through a topic.

Write your answers in the white boxes.

The 'Notes' box is a place for you or your teacher to write feedback and other comments on the topic.

At the end of the booklet, you'll find:

- **Topic-Based Questions**: more practice, split into **topics**.
- **Mixed Practice**: questions that can test you on **any** topic from the booklet — you'll need to use **more than one skill** to answer some of these.
- **Individual Learning Plan**: to track your progress towards your **learning goals**.

Knowledge Organiser

There's plenty to learn when it comes to Data Handling — here are the key facts that you need.

Averages and Range

An **average** is a number that can summarise a set of data.

There are three main types of average:

- Median
- Mode
- Mean

The **range** is not an average.

It shows how **consistent** the data is, e.g. a large range shows data is spread out and not consistent.

Median

Median: the middle value of an ordered data set.

To find the median:
1) Order the data.
2) Find the middle value.

For an even number of values, the median is halfway between two values.

Find the median of 12, 10, 17, 16.
1) Order the data: 10, 12, 16, 17
2) The middle value is between 12 and 16.
   The median is (12 + 16) ÷ 2 = **14**

Mode

Mode: the most common value in a data set.

The rim width of tyres (in mm) in stock at a shop are: 13, 15, 21, 21, 15, 21

What is the mode rim width?

The mode is **21** mm as it appears 3 times, more than any other width.

A data set can have no mode or more than one mode.

Mean

To find the **mean**:
1) Add up the values in the data set.
2) Divide the total by how many values there are.

The table shows the hourly pay for some workers. What is the mean hourly pay?

Name	Hourly pay
Ava	£12.50
Ben	£15.00
Caz	£14.20
Dara	£13.90

1) Add up the values: £12.50 + £15.00 + £14.20 + £13.90 = £55.60
2) There are 4 values, so divide by 4: £55.60 ÷ 4 = **£13.90**

Range

To find the **range**, subtract the **smallest value** from the **largest value**.

A comedy film received the following review scores out of 10: 8   7.5   9   9.5   9   8.5   8
Work out the range of review scores.

9.5 is the largest score and 7.5 is the smallest score.
So the range is 9.5 − 7.5 = **2**

The range is small, which shows the review scores are consistent.

Knowledge Organiser

Comparing Data Sets

Use averages and the ranges of two data sets to draw conclusions about them.

Mo and Yuri are plumbers. The table below shows the number of repairs they made over 5 days.

	M	T	W	T	F
Mo	3	5	4	2	0
Yuri	2	4	3	2	1

Mo
Median: 3
Mean: 2.8
Range: 5

Yuri
Median: 2
Mean: 2.4
Range: 3

- Mo made more repairs **on average**.
  He had a higher median and mean.

- Yuri made a **more consistent** number of repairs.
  She had a lower range.

Grouped Frequency Tables

In grouped frequency tables, individual data values are **unknown**. So the mean must be estimated:

Estimated mean = (total 'frequency × midpoint') ÷ (total frequency)

E.g. This grouped frequency table shows the heights of 20 women, measured to the nearest cm. Estimate the mean height of the women.

Height (cm)	Frequency	Midpoint	Frequency × midpoint
152 to 160	10	156	1560
161 to 169	8	165	1320
170 to 178	2	174	348
Total	20		3228

You often need to draw the right-hand two columns.

10 × 156 = 1560

Total 'frequency'
Total 'frequency × midpoint'

Estimated mean height
= 3228 ÷ 20 = **161.4 cm**

Probability Scale

Probability is how likely something is to happen. It can be shown on a scale:

Probabilities can be shown as a percentage, decimal or fraction.

Impossible — 0% / 0 / 0
25% / 0.25 / $\frac{1}{4}$
Even chance — 50% / 0.5 / $\frac{1}{2}$
75% / 0.75 / $\frac{3}{4}$
Certain — 100% / 1 / 1

Less likely ← → More likely

Knowledge Organiser

Calculating Probability

$$\text{Probability} = \frac{\text{Number of ways for something to happen}}{\text{Total number of possible outcomes}}$$

What is the probability of the spinner landing on A?

There are 3 sections labelled A, and 8 sections in total.

So the probability of landing on A = $\frac{3}{8}$

Multiple Events

Multiply probabilities to find the probability that two separate events both happen.

The probability of a weighted coin landing on heads is 0.2.

What is the probability that it lands on heads twice in a row?

0.2 × 0.2 = **0.04**

Events Not Happening

Probability an event **won't** happen = 1 − probability the event will happen

The probability that a tomato plant grows is 0.75. What is the probability that it doesn't grow? → 1 − 0.75 = **0.25**

If you're given the probability as a percentage, change 1 in the formula to 100%.

Tree Diagrams

Tree diagrams show all outcomes for two or more events:
- Each group of branches always adds up to **1**.
- **Multiply** along the branches to find the combined probabilities.

Rewrite the probabilities as decimals to make multiplying easier.

Chris buys a 'Lucky Blue' scratchcard and a 'Jackpot Red' scratchcard.
- 'Lucky Blue' cards offer a 10% chance of winning a prize.
- 'Jackpot Red' cards offer a 20% chance of winning a prize.

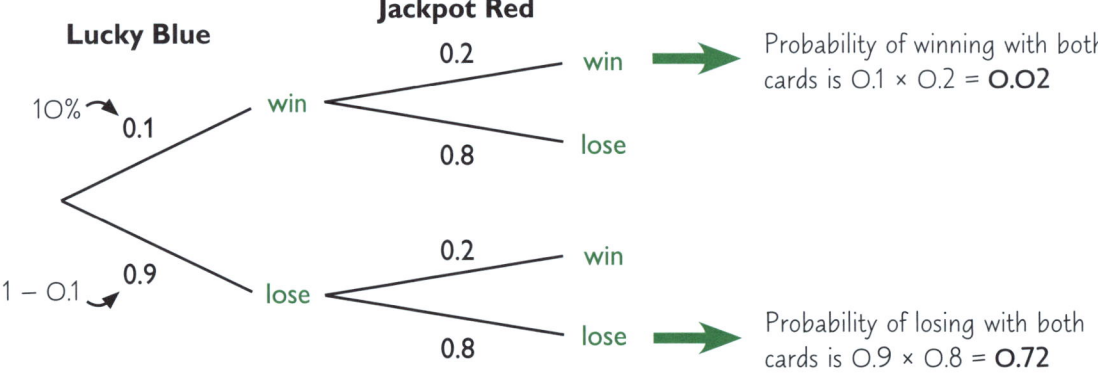

Probability of winning with both cards is 0.1 × 0.2 = **0.02**

Probability of losing with both cards is 0.9 × 0.8 = **0.72**

Knowledge Organiser

Two-Way Tables

Two-way tables show data in an organised way.

1) Add and subtract to find any missing values in the table.
2) Use the data to find probabilities:

The table shows two villages and the number of working and non-working adults from each village.

Find the probability that a randomly chosen adult from Dinby is a working adult.

65 out of 100 adults are working = $\frac{65}{100}$ or $\frac{13}{20}$

	Working	Non-working	Total
Caston	105	32	137
Dinby	(65)	35	(100)
Total	170	67	237

Sample Space Diagrams

A **sample space diagram** shows all possible outcomes of an event.

E.g. A standard coin is tossed two times.

Heads = H
Tails = T

		second toss	
		H	T
first toss	H	HH	HT
	T	TH	TT

There are 4 possible outcomes:

HH, HT, TH, TT

The probability of each outcome is $\frac{1}{4}$ or 0.25.

Scatter Diagrams

A **scatter diagram** can show a correlation between two things.

positive correlation — If one thing increases, so does the other.

negative correlation — If one thing increases, the other decreases.

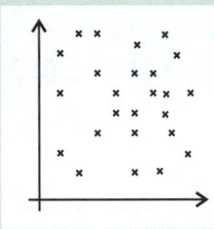

no correlation

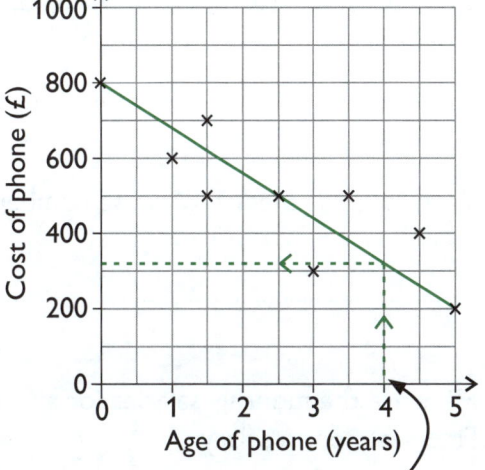

Line of best fit: a straight line roughly through the middle of all the points.

Cost of phone (£) vs age of phone (years)

Use a line of best fit to **predict values**.
E.g. a 4-year-old phone is likely to be about £320.

Section One — Averages and Range

Median and Mode

The median and mode are types of average. They can summarise a set of data.

The Median is the Middle Value of an Ordered Data Set

To find the **median**, put the values in **order** and find the **middle** value.

The ages of people on a cookery course are: 20, 23, 34, 21, 34, 46, 32, 22, 25, 40, 29
Find the median age.

1) Order the data: 20, 21, 22, 23, 25, 29, 32, 34, 34, 40, 46
2) Find the middle value:

Cross off the values from the data set as you order them.

Count in the same number of values from each end. The median is **29**.

For a data set with an **even** number of values, there are **two** middle values. The median is exactly halfway between these values.

The 25-year-old leaves the cookery course above. Find the new median age.

1) Order the data: 20, 21, 22, 23, 29, 32, 34, 34, 40, 46
2) Find the two middle values:
3) Add the middle values together and divide by 2:   The median is (29 + 32) ÷ 2 = 61 ÷ 2 = **30.5**

Now Try This

1) Find the median of:
   12, 15, 2, 23, 21, 8, 11

   ....

2) The shoe sizes of the members of a bowling team are:
   8, 5, 2, 5, 6, 10, 8, 3, 5, 7, 6, 5, 4. Find the median shoe size.

   ....

3) Work out the median of these numbers: 2.2, 3.4, 9.8, 6.1, 7.5, 3.4, 5.9, 3.4, 2.3, 9.8

   ....

4) Here are the monthly salaries for a firm: £2820, £2700, £1941, £4500, £2010, £3200.
   Find the median salary.

   ....

Median and Mode

The Mode is the Most Common Value

The **mode** is the value that appears **most** in a data set.
A data set can have no mode, or more than one mode.

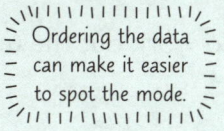
Ordering the data can make it easier to spot the mode.

The scores in a maths test are: 8, 7, 1, 2, 4, 9, 3, 9, 8, 6, 5, 9
Find the mode of the scores.

9 appears more than any other value, so the mode is **9**.

Now Try This

1) Find the mode of: 23, 26, 21, 22, 22, 25, 20, 23, 22, 26, 22 ....

2) A dentist records the number of fillings of his patients one day.
They are: 3, 0, 0, 4, 2, 6, 1, 0. What is the mode of the numbers of fillings?

   ....

3) The table shows the ice cream flavours sold one day.
Which flavour is the mode?

vanilla	chocolate	toffee	mint	coffee
43	26	14	36	18

   ....

4) The total numbers of medals won by Great Britain at each Olympic Games between 1988 and 2024 was: 24, 20, 15, 28, 30, 51, 65, 67, 64, 65

   a) What was the median number of medals?

   ....

   b) What was the mode of the numbers of medals? ....

Notes

Mean and Range

Just one more type of average to get to grips with — the mean. Then the range, which isn't an average.

Find the Mean by Adding Then Dividing

To work out the mean:
1) **Add up** the values in the data set.
2) **Divide** the total by how many values there are.

5 drivers were caught speeding. Their speeds in mph were: 37, 42, 38, 40, 39. Find the mean speed.

1) Add up the values: 37 + 42 + 38 + 40 + 39 = 196
2) There are 5 values, so divide by 5:   The mean is 196 ÷ 5 = **39.2 mph**

Now Try This

1) Find the mean for each set of data:

   a) 22, 25, 11, 22, 20, 20

   ....

   b) 0.6, 0.2, 0.9. 1.0, 0.7

   ....

   c) 289, 653, 267, 451

   ....

2) The heights of 5 sunflowers are: 395 cm, 380 cm, 330 cm, 234 cm, 229 cm. Find the mean height.

   ....

3) Lois has 8 textbooks. Two of them have 150 pages. One has 94 pages. The rest have 110. What is the mean number of pages?

   ....

   ....

Mean and Range

The Range is the Gap Between the Biggest and Smallest

To find the **range**, subtract the **smallest** value from the **largest**.

> Sam has grown 5 pumpkins. Their weights, in kilograms, are: 2.6, 3.7, 3.1, 4.2, 2.9
> What is the range of the weights?
>
> Range = largest value − smallest value = 4.2 − 2.6 = **1.6 kg**

Now Try This

1) Find the range of each set of data:

   a) 4, 7, 2, 3, 5

   b) 4.2, 7.4, 9.1, 4.2, 6.0, 2.5

   c) 608, 256, 786, 563

   d) 14, 568, 21

2) Polly sells used cars. The prices of her current used cars are: £2295, £3195, £5625, £2395. Find the range of the prices.

3) 4 teams compete in a crate-stacking activity. The range of the numbers of crates stacked is 7. The winning team stack 20 crates. What was the fewest crates stacked by a team?

4) A dog had 6 litters of puppies. The range of the numbers of puppies in a litter is 8. The numbers of puppies in 5 of these litters are: 3, 5, 4, 7, 3. How many puppies were in the sixth litter?

Notes

Using Averages and Range

You can use averages (median, mode and mean) and range to compare sets of data.

Averages and Range Help You Draw Conclusions

An Average is a Typical Value of a Data Set

You can compare two averages to draw conclusions.

Ali is comparing two restaurants using their 5 most recent online ratings.

Which restaurant has the better reviews?

Restaurant	Ratings				
Pink Dog	4	5	1	2	5
Flibber	3	3	3	3	4

Find the **mean** of each set of ratings:

Pink Dog = (4 + 5 + 1 + 2 + 5) ÷ 5 = 3.4
Flibber = (3 + 3 + 3 + 3 + 4) ÷ 5 = 3.2

From these means, **Pink Dog** has the better reviews.

Using the mode or median would have drawn the same conclusion.

The Range Shows How Consistent Data Is

A large range means the data is very spread out — it is **not consistent**.
A small range means the values are all quite similar — the data is **consistent**.

Does Pink Dog or Flibber have more consistent ratings?

Find the **range** for each data set: Pink Dog = 5 – 1 = 4   Flibber = 4 – 3 = 1

Flibber has more consistent ratings.

Now Try This

1) Kim and Bob are dog walkers. The lengths of their walks, in hours, for each day this week are shown in the table.

	Mon	Tue	Wed	Thur	Fri	Sat	Sun
Kim	1.5	2	3.5	2.5	4	5.5	2
Bob	0.5	3.5	3	1	4.5	6.5	4.5

a) Find the **range** of the lengths of walks taken by each dog walker.

....

b) Which dog walker has the **more consistent** length of walks? Explain your answer.

....

....

Section One — Averages and Range

Using Averages and Range

2) Ali and Giles shear 6 sheep each. Ali's times in seconds are: 120, 135, 127, 152, 147, 132.
Giles' times in seconds are: 133, 138, 131, 145, 129, 140.

a) Find the **median** and **mean** time for each sheep shearer.

	Median	Mean
Ali	....	....
Giles	....	....

b) Ali thinks he was, on average, a faster shearer than Giles. Is he correct? Explain why.

....

....

3) The table shows the number of times two delivery apps were used from Friday to Sunday.

	Friday	Saturday	Sunday
Foodie	150	288	195
Fasteat	188	206	122

a) Find the **mean**, **median** and **range** of the number of uses of each app.

	Mean	Median	Range
Foodie	....	....	....
Fasteat	....	....	....

b) Give **two** conclusions based on your results.

....

....

....

Notes

Grouped Frequency Tables

Grouped data is data that's organised into groups to make it easier to manage.

You Estimate the Mean for Grouped Data

Individual data values in a grouped frequency table are unknown, so you can't find the exact mean.

To **estimate the mean**:

1) Work out the **midpoint** of each group.
2) Work out **frequency × midpoint** for each group.
3) Work out the **total frequency** and the total '**frequency × midpoint**'.
4) Use the formula: Estimated mean = (Total 'frequency × midpoint') ÷ (Total frequency)

The grouped frequency table below shows the test scores for some students. Estimate the mean mark.

There are 5 marks in each group. 4 students got between 0 and 4 marks.

This is the number of students in the class.

Number of Marks	Frequency	Midpoint	Frequency × Midpoint
0 to 4	4	2	8
5 to 9	6	7	42
10 to 14	11	12	132
15 to 19	14	17	238
Total	35		420

You may need to draw these 2 columns.

2 is halfway between 0 and 4.

11 × 12 = 132

Estimated mean mark = 420 ÷ 35 = **12**

Now Try This

1) The data below shows the number of times each member visited a gym during February. Complete the table and then estimate the mean number of visits.

Number of visits	Frequency	Midpoint	Frequency × Midpoint
0 to 6	8		
7 to 13	16		
14 to 20	26		
21 to 27	32		
Total			

Estimated mean number of visits: ....

Grouped Frequency Tables

2) The table below shows the number of online reviews Martin wrote per day in June. Complete the table and then estimate the mean number of reviews he wrote per day.

Number of reviews per day	Frequency	Midpoint	Frequency × Midpoint
1 – 10	8	....	....
11 – 20	3	....	....
21 – 30	12	....	....
31 – 40	7	....	....
Total	....		....

Estimated mean number of reviews: ....

3) A newspaper article says that the mean monthly rent of a room in Penham is less than £400. The rental costs (to the nearest pound) of the available rooms in Penham are recorded below. Complete the table and find an estimate to support the newspaper article.

Rent per month (£)	Frequency		
		....	....
201 – 300	3	....	....
301 – 400	12	....	....
401 – 500	8	....	....
501 – 600	2	....	....
Total	....		....

....

....

Notes

Section Two — Probability

Expressing Probability

When the weather forecast says there's a 20% chance of rain, it's a real-life use of probability.

The Probability Scale Goes from 0 to 1

A **probability** is a measure of how likely something is to happen.

Probabilities can be given as a fraction, a decimal, or a percentage.

Probabilities can be shown on a scale:

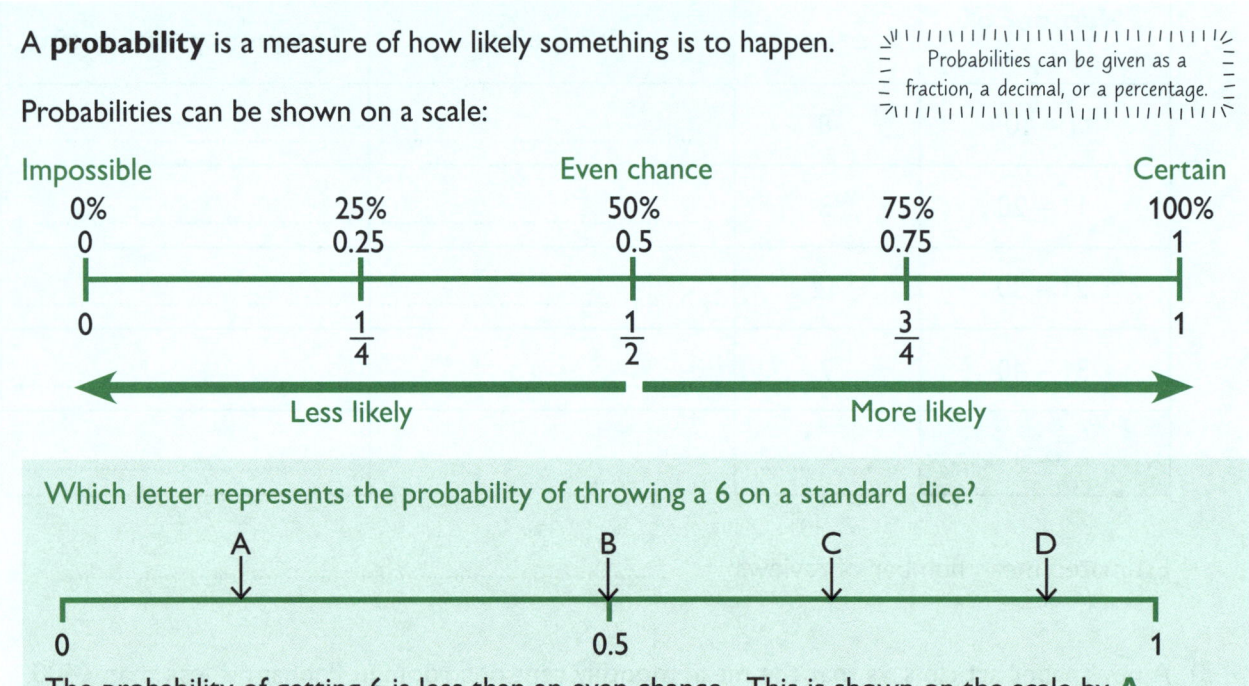

Which letter represents the probability of throwing a 6 on a standard dice?

The probability of getting 6 is less than an even chance. This is shown on the scale by **A**.

Now Try This

1) A bag contains one black ball and three white balls. One ball is picked out at random. Write the probability of each of the following as a fraction, decimal and percentage.

The ball picked out is:	Fraction	Decimal	Percentage
either black or white			
pink			
white			

2) Match each event below to probability A, B, C or D.

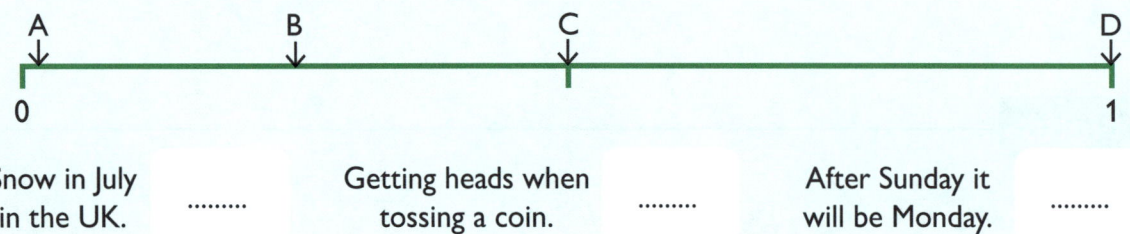

Snow in July in the UK. ....   Getting heads when tossing a coin. ....   After Sunday it will be Monday. ....

Expressing Probability

Divide to Find the Probability of Something Happening

Work out the probability of something happening using this formula:

$$\text{Probability} = \frac{\text{Number of ways for something to happen}}{\text{Total number of possible outcomes}}$$

An 'outcome' is just one thing that could happen.

A bag contains 3 red jelly beans, 2 white jelly beans and 5 purple jelly beans.
What is the probability that a red jelly bean is selected at random?
Give your answer as a percentage.

Number of ways that a red jelly bean could be selected = 3
Total number of possible outcomes = total number of jelly beans = 3 + 2 + 5 = 10

Probability = $\frac{3}{10}$ As a percentage: 3 ÷ 10 × 100 = **30%**

Now Try This

1) Write down the probability of rolling an even number on a standard dice.
Give your answer as a decimal.

   ....

2) 5 out of 10 000 bags of crisps contain a prize. Sue buys a random bag.
What is the probability that she'll find a prize inside? Give your answer as a percentage.

   ....

3) A game show studio contains 240 audience seats. There is a giant key under 4 of the seats.
What is the probability that an audience member, seated at random, will find a key under
their seat? Give your answer as a fraction in its simplest form.

   ....

4) Numbers in a game of bingo go from 1 to 90. What is the probability that the first number
called will **not** end in 0 or 5? Give your answer as a fraction in its simplest form.

   ....

Notes

Calculating Probability

The previous pages introduced you to the idea of probability. Time to step things up a notch.

Finding a Probability May Involve Subtracting or Multiplying

Subtract to Find the Probability of Something Not Happening

Use this formula to find the probability of something not happening.

Probability that an event won't happen = 1 − probability that the event will happen

The probability that Dan's train is cancelled is $\frac{1}{3}$.
What is the probability that his train isn't cancelled?

Probability that train isn't cancelled = 1 − probability that train is cancelled = $1 - \frac{1}{3} = \frac{2}{3}$

Multiply to Find the Probability of Two Things Happening

To find the probability of two separate things **both** happening, multiply the individual probabilities.

Mike tosses two fair coins. What is the probability of getting two heads?

Probability of heads on one coin = 0.5

Probability of getting heads twice = 0.5 × 0.5 = **0.25**

These coin tosses are called 'independent' events. This is because the outcome of one coin toss doesn't affect the outcome of the other.

Now Try This

1) There are 33 pies on a tray. 13 are cheese, 14 are steak and the rest are chicken.

   a) What is the probability that a randomly selected pie will be cheese?

   ....

   b) What is the probability that a randomly selected pie will **not** be cheese?

   ....

2) The spinner shown is spun twice. What is the probability of getting:

   a) two fours? b) no fours?

   ....

Section Two — Probability

Calculating Probability

3) There is a 20% probability of rain today.
   The probability that Adam will remember to take his umbrella on any day is 0.6.

   a) What is the probability that it won't rain today?

   ....

   b) What is the probability that Adam will forget his umbrella today?

   ....

   c) What is the probability that it rains and he takes his umbrella?
   Give your answer as a decimal.
   Convert the percentage to a decimal before you multiply.

   ....

4) A toy company sells 'blind bags' that contain one of four different animals.
   The probability a bag contains a sloth is 0.25, a llama is 0.44 and a golden unicorn is 0.01.

   a) What is the probability that a randomly chosen bag won't contain a golden unicorn?

   ....

   b) What is the probability that three randomly chosen bags will all contain llamas?
   Give your answer as a decimal to 3 dp.

   ....

   c) A panda is the only other animal in the bags.
   What is the probability that a randomly chosen bag contains a panda?

   ....

Notes

Probability Trees

Probabilities of multiple events can get complicated. That's where probability trees come in.

Use a Tree Diagram for Combined Events

Probability tree diagrams show all the outcomes when there are two or more events. Each group of branches always adds up to 1.

Xavier has a weighted coin. The probability of getting heads is 0.8. Calculate the probability of getting a head, then a tail, when the coin is tossed twice.

1) Draw a set of branches for each event (each coin toss).

H and T are used as shorthand for heads and tails.

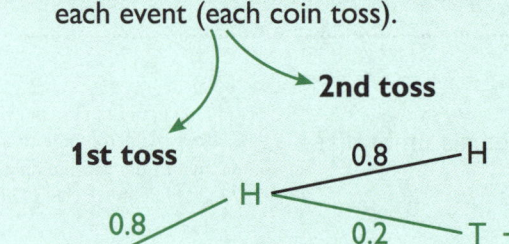

2) Multiply along the branches with the correct outcomes to get the combined probability.

$0.8 \times 0.2 = \mathbf{0.16}$

The probability of getting a head then a tail is **0.16**.

Now Try This

1) David has 1 plain shirt and 7 striped shirts. He has 3 blue pairs of jeans and 2 grey pairs. He chooses his shirt and jeans randomly each day.

a) Complete the probability tree diagram on the right.

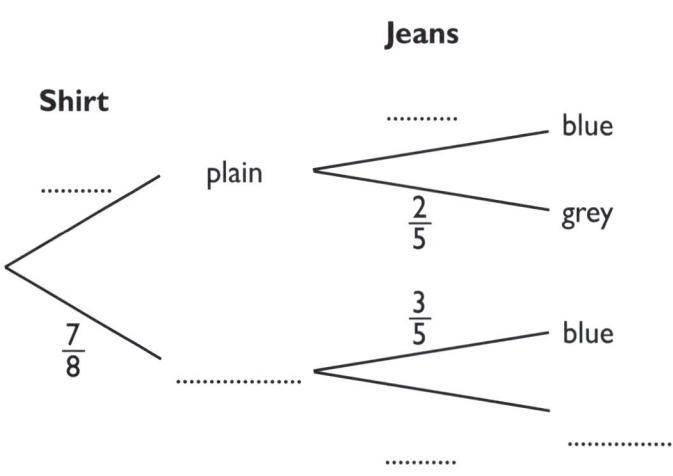

b) What is the probability that David selects a plain shirt with grey jeans?

You can multiply the fractions, or convert them to decimals first.

....

Probability Trees

2) Jo sells only bacon buns or sausage buns. A customer can choose a white or brown bun. The probability that a customer will choose a white bun is 0.6.

   a) Complete the probability tree diagram below.

   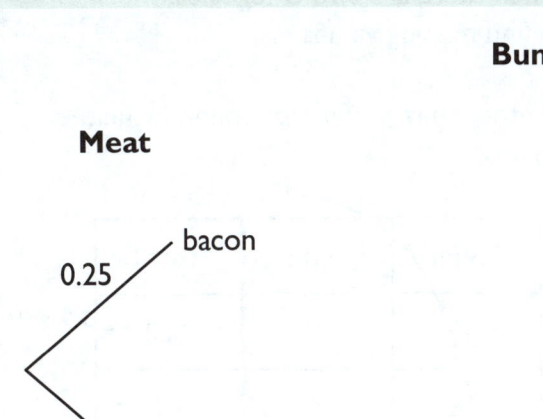

   b) What is the probability that a customer will choose bacon on a brown bun?

   ....

   c) Is a customer more likely to choose bacon on a white bun or sausage on a brown bun?

   ....
   ....

   d) Which combination is most popular? What is the probability that someone orders this?

   ....
   ....

Notes

Two-Way Tables

Two-way tables are ones that you read both horizontally and vertically.

Two-Way Tables are a Type of Frequency Table

Two-way tables are used to organise data when there are two categories.
You need to use addition and subtraction to find missing values.

200 people were asked for their age and whether they prefer tea, coffee or neither.
The table below shows the results of the survey.

a) Complete the table.

	Tea	Coffee	Neither	Total
Under 30	35	**55**	30	120
30 or over	40	36	4	**80**
Total	75	**91**	34	200

35 people aged under 30 said they prefer tea.
120 – 35 – 30
120 people aged under 30 were surveyed.
200 – 120
55 + 36

b) A person aged 30 or over is chosen at random.
What is the probability that they prefer neither tea or coffee?

4 out of 80 people aged 30 or over preferred neither. So the probability is $\frac{4}{80} = \frac{1}{20}$

Now Try This

1) The employees of GCP Food Ltd are asked whether they are coming to the Christmas party.
The table shows their responses.

	Coming to party	Not coming to party	Total
Male	42	....	60
Female	....	21	....
Total	49	....	....

a) Complete the table.

b) What is the probability that an employee chosen at random will be male?
Give your answer as a fraction in its simplest form.

....

c) What is the probability that a randomly-chosen employee who is coming to the party is female? Give your answer as a fraction in its simplest form.

....

Section Two — Probability

Two-Way Tables

2) At an activity centre, guests choose one outdoor activity and one indoor activity. The table shows the activities a group of guests chose one day.

a) Complete the table below.

		Outdoor activity			
		Climbing	Kayaking	Zip wire	**Total**
Indoor activity	Escape room	6	....	8	18
	Axe throwing	4	1	4	....
	Pottery	....	....	....	....
	Total	15	....	34	60

b) A guest is selected at random. What is the probability that they chose kayaking and axe throwing?

Give each answer as a fraction in its simplest form.

....

c) A guest is selected at random. What is the probability that they chose zip wire?

....

d) A guest who chose climbing is selected at random. What is the probability that they also chose pottery?

....

e) A guest is selected at random. What is the probability that they chose **either** escape room or axe throwing?

....

Notes

Section Two — Probability

Sample Space Diagrams

Now for another type of table you can use for finding probabilities.

Sample Space Diagrams Show All Possible Outcomes

A sample space diagram can be a **list** or a **two-way table** showing all possible outcomes.

The two spinners shown on the right are spun.
The numbers they land on are added together.

a) Make a sample space diagram showing all possible outcomes.

b) What is the probability that the result is 7?

A 1 on the first spinner and a 4 on the second spinner results in an outcome of 5.

You could also have made a list of these 9 outcomes.

	second spinner		
first spinner	4	5	6
1	5	6	7
2	6	7	8
3	7	8	9

There are 9 possible outcomes.

3 of these are '7'.

So the probability is $\frac{3}{9} = \frac{1}{3}$

Now Try This

1) Two coins are tossed.

a) Complete the sample space diagram on the right.

b) What is the probability of getting 2 heads? Give your answer as a fraction.

....

c) What is the probability of getting a head and a tail? Give your answer as a decimal.

H = heads, T = tails

		second coin	
		H	T
first coin	H	HH	....
	T	....	....

....

2) Aisha rolls a normal 6-sided dice and tosses a coin.

a) Complete the sample space diagram.

b) What is the probability of getting a head and an odd number? Give your answer as a decimal.

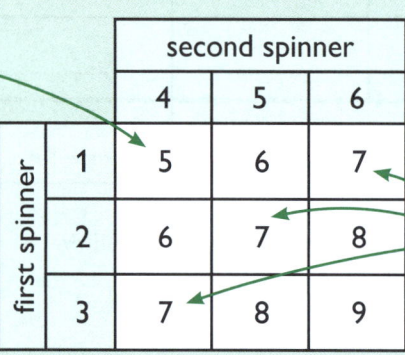

....

Sample Space Diagrams

3) Two four-sided dice, each numbered 1, 2, 3, 4, are rolled. The numbers they land on are multiplied together.

		second dice			
		1	2	3	4
first dice	1	....	....	....	....
	2	....	....	....	8
	3	....	6	9	....
	4	....	....	12	....

a) Complete the sample space diagram on the right.

b) What is the probability that the result is 4? Give your answer as a fraction.

....

c) What is the probability that the result is greater than 10? Give your answer as a fraction.

....

d) What is the probability that the result is odd? Give your answer as a decimal.

....

4) At a wedding, guests must choose from lamb (L), beef (B) or salad (S) for the main course. For dessert, they must choose between trifle (T) and cake (C).

a) Complete the sample space diagram.

		Main course		
		....	....	....
Dessert	....			
	....			

b) Abdullah says that the probability of a guest choosing salad and cake is $\frac{1}{6}$. Is he correct? Explain your answer.

....

....

Notes

Scatter Diagrams

Scatter diagrams can show if there are any patterns in your data. Neat.

Look for Correlation in a Scatter Diagram

A scatter diagram shows the relationship (**correlation**) between two things.

Positive correlation
If one thing increases, so does the other.

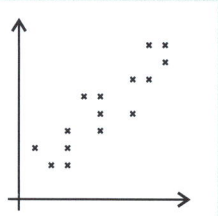

E.g. ice cream sales increase when temperatures rise.

Negative correlation
If one thing increases, the other decreases.

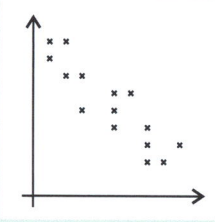

E.g. heating costs decrease when temperatures rise.

No correlation
If one thing increases, the other one is not affected.

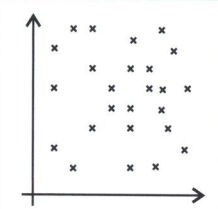

E.g. increasing shoe size of adults doesn't affect intelligence.

A **line of best fit** is a straight line through the middle of the points. You can use a line of best fit to **predict** values.

There should be about the same number of points on either side of the line of best fit.

The scatter diagram shows ages of a company's cars against their mileage. Predict the mileage of a 4-year-old car.

1) Read up from 4 on the 'Age' axis to the line of best fit.
2) Read across to the 'Mileage' axis.

So the predicted mileage of a 4-year-old car is **40 000 miles**.

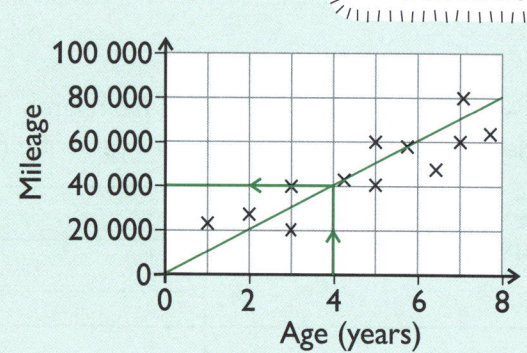

Now Try This

1) Draw lines to match each scatter diagram to the type of correlation it shows.

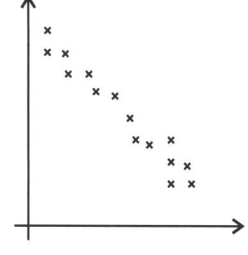

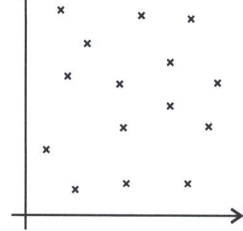

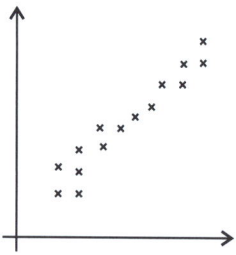

positive correlation   negative correlation   no correlation

Scatter Diagrams

2) The scatter diagram on the right shows how the number of visitors to a park changes with the peak daily temperature.

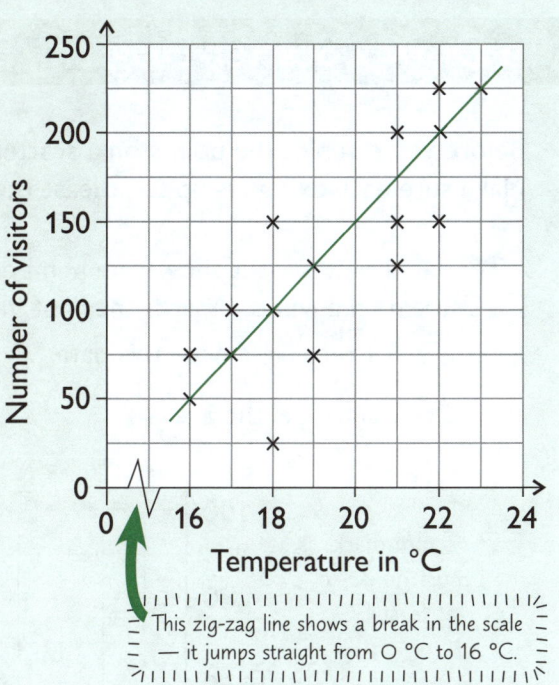

a) What type of correlation is shown between the number of visitors to the park and the temperature?

   ....

b) Predict the number of visitors to the park when the temperature is 20 °C.

   ....

3) The scatter diagram shows how cake sales in a bakery change with the price of the cake.

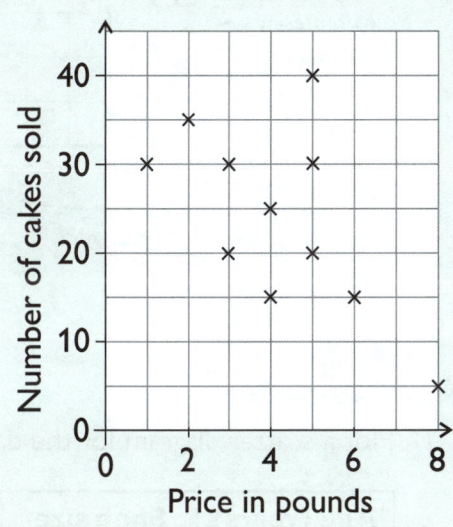

a) Draw a line of best fit on the diagram.

b) What type of correlation is shown?

   ....

c) Describe the relationship between the price of the cakes and how many are sold.

   ....
   ....
   ....

d) Predict the number of cakes that would be sold if the price was £2.   ....

Notes

Scatter Diagrams

You might be given some data and have to make your own scatter diagram from scratch.

To Draw a Scatter Diagram, Plot the Data

Before you can plot the points on a scatter diagram, you need to draw the **axes**. Make sure each axis goes up to at least the maximum data value.

The table on the right shows the number of practice papers 8 students did and the marks they got in the exam. Draw a scatter diagram for this data.

1) Draw and label the axes.

Practice papers	Exam mark
0	8
3	20
3	50
4	70
6	60
7	30
9	60
10	90

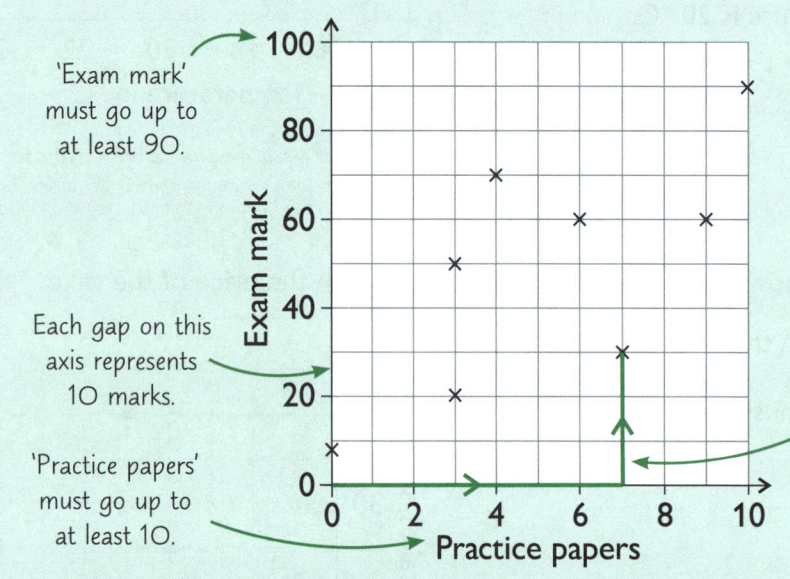

'Exam mark' must go up to at least 90.

Each gap on this axis represents 10 marks.

'Practice papers' must go up to at least 10.

2) Plot the points.

E.g. the student who did 7 practice papers got an exam mark of 30. So go across to 7 on the 'Practice papers' axis, then up to 30 on the 'Exam mark' axis.

Now Try This

1) Plot a scatter diagram for the data below. Add a line of best fit.

Age (years)	Shoe size
0.5	3
1	3
2	6
4	8
4	10
5.5	11
5.5	12
6	11

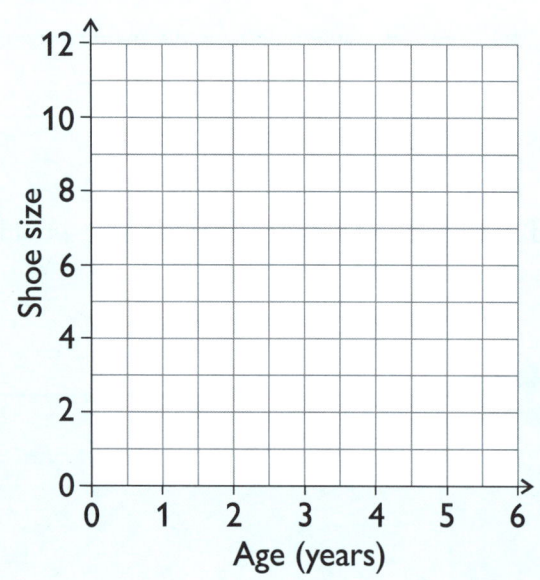

Section Three — Scatter Diagrams

Scatter Diagrams

2) The table on the right shows the rainfall and a shop's charcoal sales on 10 days in August.

Rainfall (mm)	Charcoal sales (bags)
0	100
0	70
5	90
5	50
10	40
15	20
20	20
20	0
25	10
25	0

a) Label each axis with a suitable scale. Then plot the points.

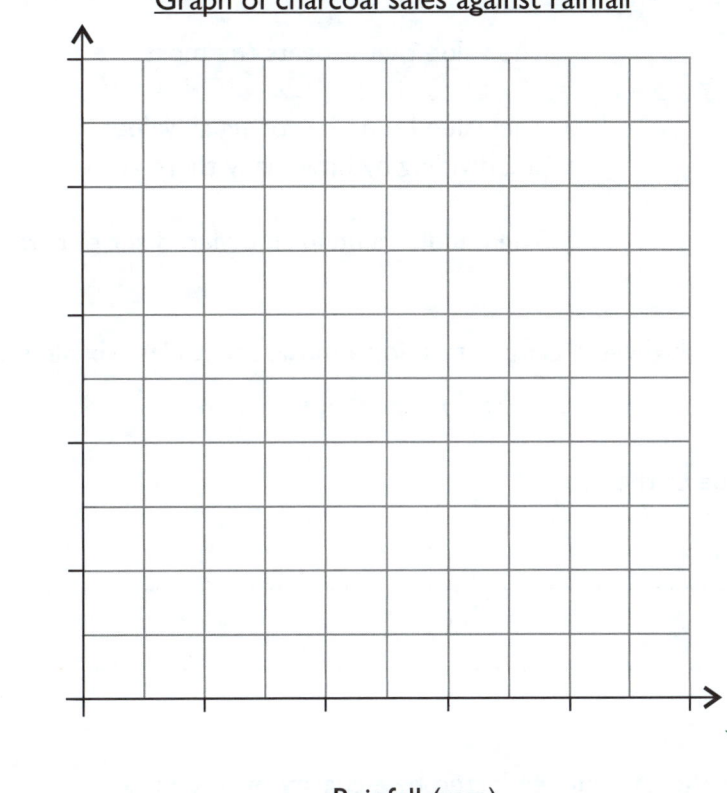

Graph of charcoal sales against rainfall

Charcoal sales (bags)

Rainfall (mm)

Decide what value each scale must go up to, then work out what each gap must represent.

b) Draw a line of best fit on the scatter diagram.

c) Predict the rainfall on a day when 30 bags of charcoal were sold.

....

d) Predict the charcoal sales on a day with 2.5 mm of rainfall.

....

Notes

Topic-Based Questions

These questions are all designed to give you some extra practice on the topics in this book.

Averages and Range

1) Draw lines to match each word to its correct description.

    Range — The highest value minus the lowest value.

    Mean — The value that repeats the most.

    Median — The value found by adding all values and dividing by how many there are.

    Mode — The middle value in an ordered set of data.

2) The list below shows the highest chart position for a music artist's last six albums.

    2   3   2   5   7   11

    Find the mean and mode of the data.

    Mean: ....

    Mode: ....

3) The table below shows the amounts collected by a charity over a week.

Mon	Tue	Weds	Thurs	Fri	Sat	Sun
£36	£75	£21	£89	£94	£12	£44

    a) Calculate the mean amount of money collected by the charity per day.

    ....

    b) Calculate the range.

    ....

4) Zainab has this list of 7 numbers: 3.2   4.6   7.6   5.1   9.0   2.5   8.7
    She adds another number to the list. The mean is now 6. What number does she add?

    ....

Topic-Based Questions

5) Polina wants to ask Archie or Bilal to join her pub quiz team.
The number of questions they've answered correctly in past quizzes is shown below.

Archie: 6 4 1 4 8 1 10 5 9 8 6 4   Bilal: 6 7 4 5 3 4 4 5 4 6

a) Who should Polina ask to join her team? Give a reason for your answer.

....

....

b) Who is more consistent with the number of correct answers they give?
Give a reason for your answer.

....

....

6) Two football players recorded the number of minutes they played across eight games.

Jan	43	34	7	75	41	42	39	40
Orla	35	40	41	87	45	40	40	38

Round each mean to 1 dp.

a) Find the median and the mean for the number of minutes played by Jan.

Median: ....

Mean: ....

b) Find the median and the mean for the number of minutes played by Orla.

Median: ....

Mean: ....

c) Give a conclusion based on your results from parts a) and b).

....

....

Topic-Based Questions

Grouped Frequency Tables

1) Claudia records the number of students in her college class on different days. Estimate the mean number of students in her class each day.

No. of students	Frequency	Midpoint	Frequency × Midpoint
14 to 16	4	....	....
17 to 19	6	....	....
20 to 22	6	....	....
23 to 25	14	....	....
Total	....		....

Estimated mean number of students: ....

2) Levy is a takeaway delivery driver. His mean delivery time last week was 15 minutes. The times for the deliveries he made this week are recorded in the table.

Delivery time (nearest minute)	Frequency		
		....	....
5 to 8	16	....	....
9 to 12	38	....	....
13 to 16	44	....	....
17 to 20	62	....	....
Total	....		....

Suggest whether Levy's average delivery time this week has improved from last week. Show your working.

....

....

....

Topic-Based Questions

Probability

1) Look at the spinner on the right.
   Write a number to make each statement correct.

   It is **unlikely** the spinner will land on ....

   It is **impossible** that the spinner will land on ....

   There is a $\frac{1}{2}$ chance that the spinner will land on ....

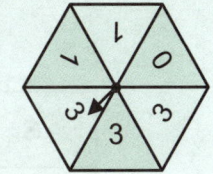

2) A flower bouquet has five different types of flower.
   The table shows the probabilities of picking each type of flower at random.

Rose	Tulip	Daisy	Carnation	Lily
0.05	0.25	?	0.2	0.1

   a) What is the probability of picking a daisy? Give your answer as a decimal.

   ....

   b) What is the probability of picking a tulip?
      Give your answer as a fraction in its simplest form.

   ....

3) A factory produces 250 car batteries. A quality check finds that 5 batteries are faulty.
   What is the probability that a car battery picked at random is **not** faulty?
   Give your answer as a percentage.

   ....

4) Emma has a fair coin. She tosses it three times.
   What is the probability that she gets three tails in a row?

   ....

   ....

Topic-Based Questions

Probability from Diagrams and Tables

1) Pepe has 3 cards with a letter (**S, K, Y**) and 4 cards with a number (**2, 3, 5, 7**).
   He chooses a random letter card, then a random number card.

   a) Complete the table to show the combinations of cards he could choose.

	2	3	5	7
S				
K				
Y				

   b) What is the probability that he chooses a letter 'S' and an even number?

   ....

   c) What is the probability that he **doesn't** choose the letter 'Y'?

   ....

2) 280 people visited Barning Zoo on Monday.
   The table below shows information about the visitors.

   a) Complete the table.

	Adult Man	Adult Woman	Child	Total
Morning	31	....	86	173
Afternoon	....	21	37	....
Total	80	77	....	280

   b) What is the probability that a visitor on Monday was an adult man?

   ....

   c) What is the probability that a visitor on Monday afternoon was a child?

   ....

Topic-Based Questions

3) A college offers 3 courses: Business, Sport and Childcare.
   496 people applied to study at the college:
   - 187 people applied for 'Business'. Of those, 123 people were accepted.
   - 203 people applied for 'Sport'. Of those, 145 people were accepted.
   - 106 people applied for 'Childcare'. Of those, 69 people were accepted.

   a) Draw a two-way table to show this information.

	....	....	....	**Total**
....				....
....				....
Total	....	....	....	496

   b) A person accepted into the college is chosen at random.
      What is the probability that they are studying 'Sport'?

      ....

4) Violet chooses a book to borrow at random from the library.

   The probability that the book is a hardback is 0.6.
   The probability that she's read the book before is 0.3, whether it's a hardback or a paperback.

   a) Complete the tree diagram.

   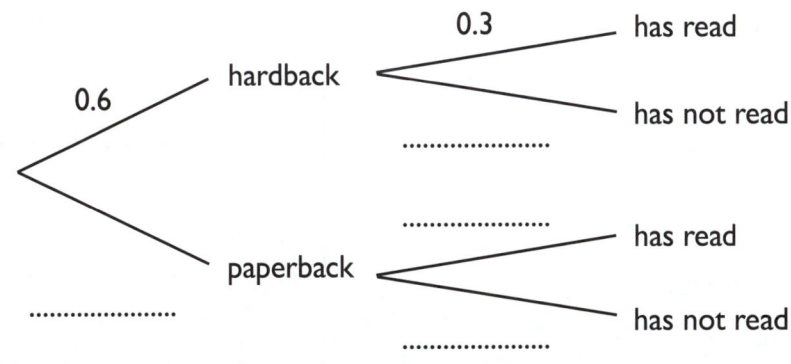

   b) What is the probability that she chooses a hardback book and has read it?

   ....
   ....

Topic-Based Questions

Scatter Diagrams

1) This scatter diagram shows the weight of some vans and their fuel mileage (in mpg).

   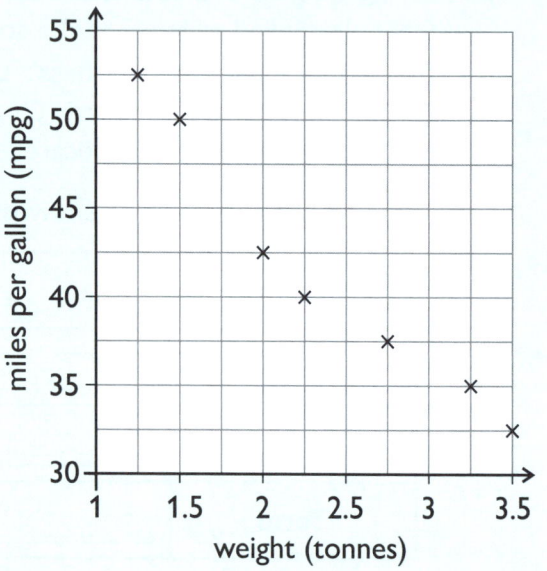

   a) What type of correlation is shown?

   ....

   b) Draw a line of best fit on the diagram.

   c) Use your line of best fit to predict the weight of a van with a fuel mileage of 45 mpg.

   ....

2) The table below shows the temperature at midday on a beach for some days in September and the number of surfers on those days.

Temperature (°C)	12.5	15	10	22.5	20	27.5	30
Number of surfers	8	16	0	24	20	32	40

   a) Draw a scatter diagram on the right to show the information above.

   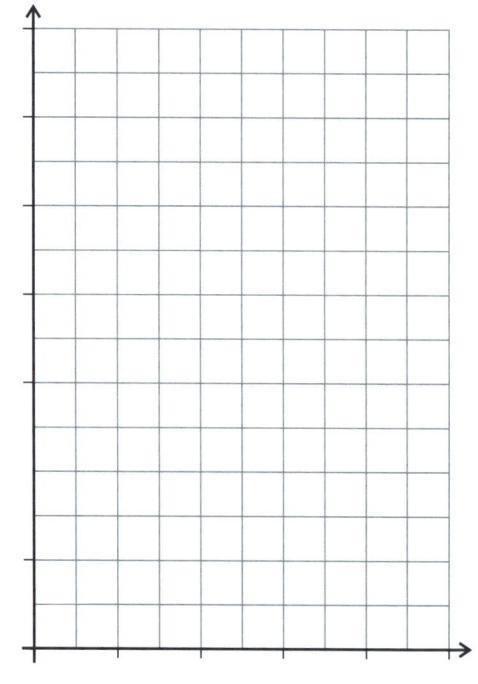

   b) Describe the relationship shown on the scatter diagram.

   ....

   ....

   ....

   c) Use the diagram to estimate the temperature when there were 15 surfers.

   ....

   ....

Mixed Practice

Have a go at these questions — they'll test you on all the stuff you've seen on Data Handling.

Section A   *Don't use a calculator for Section A.*

1) A dice, numbered 1 to 6, is rolled.

   a) What is the probability of rolling a number greater than 3? Tick (✓) your answer.

   25% ☐   50% ☐   100% ☐   10% ☐

   b) What is the probability of rolling a multiple of 3? Give your answer as a fraction.

   ....

   c) What is the probability of rolling an odd number? Give your answer as a decimal.

   ....

2) Complete the statements below about this set of numbers:

   The median is: ....   The mode is: ....

   The mean is: ....   The range is: ....

3) A train has 4 carriages. A passenger is chosen at random.
   The table shows the probability that they are in a certain carriage.

Carriage A	Carriage B	Carriage C	Carriage D
0.25	0.4		0.2

   a) Complete the table.

   b) There are 200 passengers in total.
      Show that there are 80 passengers in carriage B.

   ....

   ....

Mixed Practice

4) An online dating business wants to see if there is a correlation between the ages of users of their app and the numbers of matches they had this year.

The scatter diagram below shows the data they collected from 10 users.

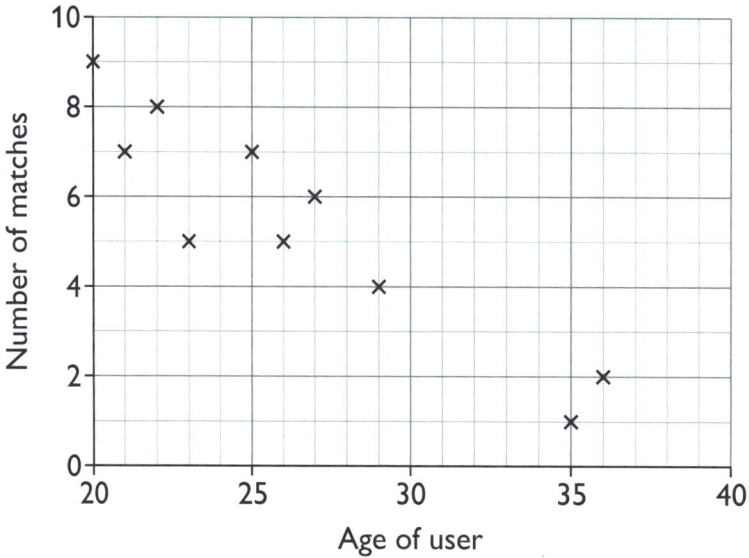

a) Draw a line of best fit on the scatter diagram.

b) What type of correlation is shown by the scatter diagram?

....

c) Describe the relationship between the age of a user and the number of matches.

....

....

d) Use your line of best fit to estimate the age of a user who had 3 matches this year.

....

e) What was the median age of the 10 users? Show how you know.

....

....

Mixed Practice

Section B

You can use a calculator for Section B.

1) Mario owns a coffee shop. He sells different types of coffee in jars.

   a) The weights of 7 different jars of coffee are shown in the table.

Weight (g)	375	450	200	250	300	480	220

   Show that the median weight of a jar of coffee is less than the mean weight.

   ....

   ....

   ....

   b) A customer chooses one of the 7 jars of coffee at random.
      Work out the probability that it weighs more than 350 g. Give your answer as a fraction.

   ....

2) A 3-sided spinner has a different shape on each face:

   The spinner is spun twice.
   The number of sides on each shape landed on are added together.

   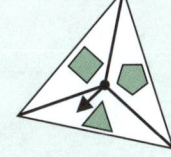

   a) Complete the sample space diagram below.

		second spin		
first spin	3 sides			
	4 sides			
	5 sides			

   b) Work out the probability that the total number of sides is 7.

   ....

   ....

Mixed Practice

3) Barsha asked 50 men and 150 women which type of film they prefer from four options: *Horror, Drama, Action* or *Comedy*.

- 42 of the people who prefer horror films are women.
- 72 people prefer drama films. One quarter of them are men.
- 20% of men and 20% of women prefer action films.

	Horror	Drama	Action	Comedy	**Total**
Men	14				50
Women					150
Total					200

a) Complete the table above.

b) A man is chosen at random. What is the probability that they prefer horror films?

....

Give your answers to parts b) and c) as simplified fractions.

c) A person who prefers comedy is chosen at random. What is the probability that they are a woman?

....

4) The table shows two broadband companies and the broadband speeds (in Mbps) provided to different households.

BroadZap	28	32	25	27	30
Qwik-Net	26	20	40	42	27

a) Other than the mode, compare **two** different averages for these data sets.

....

....

....

b) Which company provides a more consistent broadband speed? Explain how you know.

....

....

Mixed Practice

5) Last month, the mean number of birds visiting Tara's garden each day on her lunch break (1-2 pm) was 5.5. She puts bird feeders out to see if this affects the number of visiting birds. She makes a table of the birds that visit each day this month.

Number of birds	Frequency	Midpoint	Freq. × Midpoint
1 – 2	5		
3 – 4	10		
5 – 6	3		
7 – 8	7		
9 – 10	5		
Total	**30**		

You'll need to fill in the rest of the table to answer the question.

Suggest whether the bird feeders increased the number of visiting birds. Explain your answer.

....

....

6) Diya records the number of members of some gyms and their membership cost.

Number of members	Membership cost per month (£)
275	15
900	35
800	30
400	20
1000	40

a) Plot the points on the scatter diagram.

b) Estimate the number of members for a gym with a £25 membership cost.

....

....

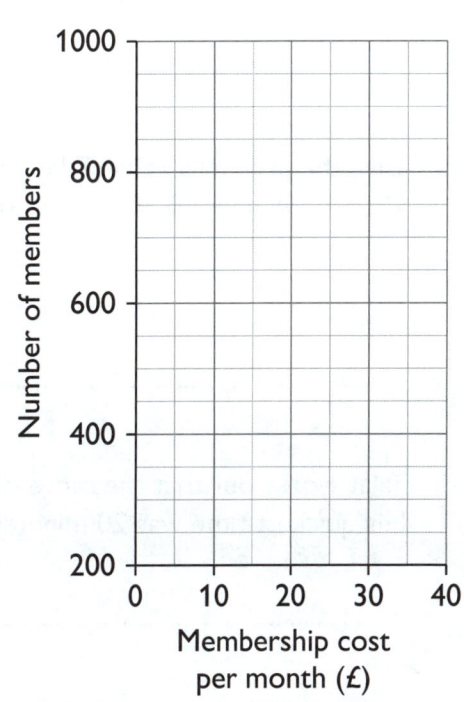

Mixed Practice

7) Talat works as a cleaner. He always cleans a kitchen first, then a bathroom.

   - The probability he cleans a kitchen in less than an hour is 0.6
   - The probability he cleans a bathroom in less than an hour is 0.8

   a) Circle the letter on the probability scale below that shows how likely it is that he cleans a kitchen in less than an hour.

   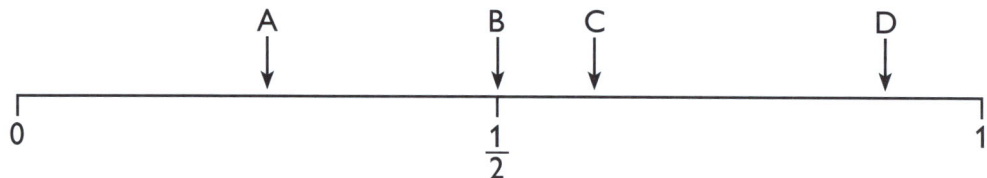

   b) Complete the tree diagram to show the information above.

   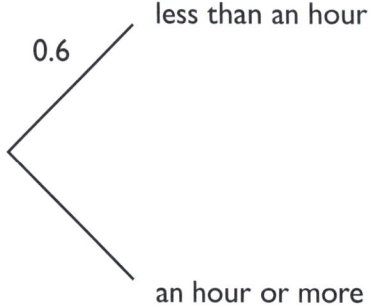

   c) Give the probability that Talat would take less than an hour to clean a kitchen, then less than an hour to clean a bathroom. Show your working.

   ....

   ....

   d) Talat works out that the range of times he took to clean a bathroom was 80 minutes. His quickest time was 20 minutes. What was the longest time taken?

   ....

   ....

Mixed Practice

8) Ada makes videos about beauty products. Each video has an advert at the start. For each video, the probability that a viewer clicks on an advert is $\frac{1}{10}$.

a) What is the probability that a viewer **doesn't** click on an advert in a video? Give your answer as a percentage.

....

....

b) The video platform pays Ada £2 for every 1000 views of a video. The table shows the number of views her videos have had in the last 6 months.

No. of views (x)	Frequency	....	....
1000 ≤ x < 2000	6	....	....
2000 ≤ x < 3000	8	....	....
3000 ≤ x < 4000	3	....	....
4000 ≤ x < 5000	10	....	....
Total	27		....

≤ means less than or equal to, and < means less than.

Ada thinks she made £6 per video on average in the last 6 months. Suggest whether Ada is correct. Explain your answer.

Estimate the mean number of views per video and work out how much money this would earn Ada.

....

....

....

Notes

Individual Learning Plan

After each lesson or topic, use the table below to record your progress. Then you and your teacher can identify what you still don't feel confident with, why you found it difficult and what you can do to improve.

1. What I Can Do Now	2. What I Found Hard
Example: Find easy probabilities	Finding probabilities of combined events

Individual Learning Plan © CGP — not to be photocopied

Individual Learning Plan

If you want more space to write your plan, go to: cgpbooks.co.uk/fs-maths
or scan the QR code in the header to find a printable PDF of this table.

3. What I Need To Improve On	4. What I Will Do To Improve
Making accurate probability trees	Always check the pairs of branches add up to 1

CGP

www.cgpbooks.co.uk

Name ....

Functional Skills
Maths: Mixed Practice
Level 2

Course Booklet

Answers available online

CGP Books — The Choice of Champions!

He knows it.
You know it.
Everyone knows it ☺

cgpbooks.co.uk

Contents

✓ Use the tick boxes to check off the topics you've completed.

Assessment Advice

About the Test...2 ☐
What is the Question Asking?..........................4 ☐
What Maths is Needed?....................................6 ☐

Mixed Practice

Mixed Practice 1...8 ☐
Mixed Practice 2...10 ☐
Mixed Practice 3...12 ☐
Mixed Practice 4...14 ☐
Mixed Practice 5...16 ☐
Mixed Practice 6...18 ☐
Mixed Practice 7...20 ☐
Mixed Practice 8...22 ☐
Mixed Practice 9...24 ☐
Mixed Practice 10...26 ☐

Gaps and Revision Tracker.............................28 ☐

Unlock your Digital Extras

To get your free digital extras, go to cgpbooks.co.uk/fs-maths or scan the QR code below.

← This will take you to:
- An answer booklet
- More Individual Learning Plan pages

Published by CGP

Reviewer: Linda Walker

Editors: Liam Dyer, Sharon Keeley-Holden and Duncan Lindsay.

With thanks to Glenn Rogers for the proofreading.
With thanks to Beth Linnane for the copyright research.

ISBN: 978 1 83774 210 3
Printed by Elanders Ltd, Newcastle upon Tyne.
Graphics from Corel®

Text, design, layout and original illustrations © Coordination Group Publications Ltd (CGP) 2025 All rights reserved.

Photocopying this book is not permitted, even if you have a CLA licence.
Extra copies are available from CGP with next day delivery • 0800 1712 712 • www.cgpbooks.co.uk

About the Test

For Level 2 Maths, you'll sit a test to show what you can do. Here's all the info you need.

The basics...

The time to complete the test is between 1 hour 45 minutes and 2 hours 30 minutes.

You might take this test on a **computer** (on screen) or on **paper**.

The test will have **two sections** (or papers):
- Section 1 is worth 25% of the total marks. A calculator is **not** allowed.
- Section 2 is worth 75% of the total marks. A calculator **is** allowed.

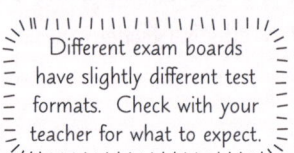
Different exam boards have slightly different test formats. Check with your teacher for what to expect.

There may be an on-screen calculator and other special tools for on-screen testing.

The **front cover** of each section tells you what you're allowed to use for that part of the test, as well as other important details, e.g. what value of π to use.

What does the test cover?

The test covers **three content areas**:

1) Using numbers and the number system
2) Using measures, shape and space
3) Handling information and data

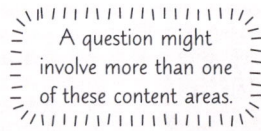
A question might involve more than one of these content areas.

There are **two types** of question:

- 25% of the questions will **tell you** what maths to do, without giving you a context. For example:

  Calculate $2\frac{8}{9} - 1\frac{1}{3}$ **[1 mark]**

- 75% of the questions will involve **problem-solving**. You'll need to decide what maths you need to use. These questions often have a **real-life context**.

See pages 4-7 for some top tips for tackling these types of problems.

Notes

Jot down info about the test you're going to be sitting here.

About the Test

Read the Question Carefully

Here are some examples of things to watch out for.

> Two smartphones are discounted.
>
> Phone A: price decreased from £998 to £798.40
> Phone B: price decreased from £500 to £325
>
> Which phone has the bigger **percentage** decrease in price?
> You **must** show your working. **[4 marks]**

- You're asked 'which phone...?', so your answer needs to state 'Phone A' or 'Phone B'.
- If you don't show your working, you can't get full marks. So write down each step you do.
- Key words may be in bold to draw your attention to them.
- This question's worth 4 marks, so getting the answer will take a few steps.

Check your Answers

This is really, really important. Checking your answers helps you to spot mistakes you've made. Here are three **quick checks** you can do:

For some exam boards, you get marks if the examiner can see evidence that you've checked your work.

Check your answer seems **sensible**.
Using **estimation** is a good way to do this:

> A garage bill was £1486, including VAT at 20%.
> What was the bill before VAT was added? **[1 mark]**

So, after punching the numbers into your calculator, you get £1188.80.
Is it sensible? The price **before** VAT should be a bit lower than £1486 — and it is.
Using estimation: Round £1486 to £1500 → 10% of £1500 = £150, so 20% = £300
£1500 − £300 = £1200. Our answer is pretty close — great.

Use a **reverse calculation**:

> A wine cellar contains 37 bottles. Each bottle holds 750 ml.
> Work out the total volume of wine. **[1 mark]**

You work this out by doing 37 × 750 = 27 750 ml.
A reverse calculation to check could be 27 750 ÷ 750 = 37.

Look back at the question to check your answer is in the **right format**.

> Express 16 out of 20 as a fraction in its simplest form. **[1 mark]**

Simple, you say: $\frac{16}{20}$. But the question wants the fraction in its **simplest form**: $\frac{4}{5}$.

What is the Question Asking?

To answer a question, you need to figure out what it's asking. That's what these pages are about.

Pick Out the Important Details

Word problems have a lot of **information** to get your head around.
Before you jump in, be sure to:

- Read the question carefully and make sure you **understand** all the information.

- Identify **what** the question is asking. It'll usually tell you this at the end.

- Read through the question a second time, **underlining** or **highlighting** key details.

Look for numbers. The number of ducks is probably going to be important (well, it is a maths question).

This question is about a duck race. You don't need to know anything about duck races to answer the question.

This bit tells you there are only pink, red and blue ducks in the race.

There are <u>310 ducks</u> in a charity duck race. <u>220 are pink</u>, <u>45 are red</u> and the rest are blue. Calculate the <u>percentage</u> of ducks that are <u>blue</u>. Give your answer to <u>2 decimal places</u>.

This sentence tells you what you need to work out. The word 'percentage' is important. It's easy to miss it and answer with the number of blue ducks.

This suggests you're going to work with lots of decimal places. You need to round your answer at the end for full marks.

Now Try This

1) a) Underline the important parts of this question.

   Jo is planning to paint her fence. It is 25 metres long and 180 cm high.
   The paint comes in 2.5 litre cans and 1 litre covers 5 m².
   Each can costs £10.99. How many cans must she buy to have enough?

   b) Which of the following could be the correct answer to this question?
      Explain your choice. You don't need to work the answer out.

   45 m² ☐   9 litres ☐   4 cans ☐   3.6 cans ☐

   Explanation: ....
   ....

   c) Write down some information from the question that doesn't affect the answer.

   ....

Assessment Advice © CGP — not to be photocopied

What is the Question Asking?

Picture the Problem

Drawing **diagrams** can help you work out what you need to do to answer a word problem. Your drawing doesn't need to be neat, but it should make things **clearer to you**.

> Fiona is going on holiday by ferry. She must drive 8000 metres from her house to the port. The ferry crossing is 728 km, then it is 50 miles to her campsite.
> How far will she travel in total? Give your answer in km. 1 mile ≈ 1.6 km.

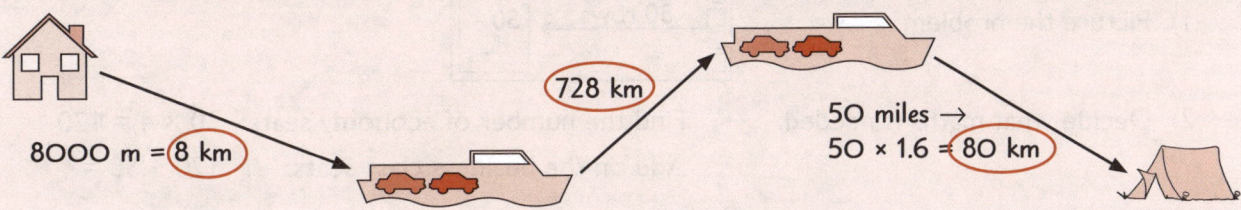

8000 m = (8 km)   728 km   50 miles →
                              50 × 1.6 = 80 km

You'd then add up all the distances in km to get the answer.

Now Try This

1) For the paint question on the previous page, draw a diagram to picture the problem.

2) Cola cans are sold in <u>packs of 6 for £5.49</u>. They are on a '<u>3 packs for the price of 2</u>' offer. Individual cans cost <u>95p each</u>, but there is a <u>20% discount</u> offer. Bob needs <u>54 cans</u>. What is the <u>cheapest</u> way for him to buy these?

   Draw a diagram that helps you picture this problem.

Notes

Assessment Advice

What Maths is Needed?

Once you know what a question is asking, you need to work out **how** to solve it.

Translate the Word Problem into Maths

You'll need to decide which **operation** (e.g. addition, multiplication etc.) you need to do. Some problems need **more than one** operation.

> An aeroplane has 30 rows of 4 seats in economy class and 50 seats in business class. How many seats is this in total?
>
> 1) Picture the problem:
>
>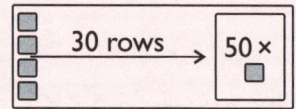
>
> 2) Decide what maths is needed:
> - Find the number of economy seats: 30 × 4 = 120
> - Add on the business class seats: 120 + 50 = **170**

It can help to choose a **letter** to stand for an unknown number.

> There are 310 ducks in a charity duck race. 220 are pink, 45 are red and the rest are blue. Calculate the percentage of ducks that are blue. Give your answer to 2 decimal places.
>
> 1) Picture the problem:
>
> 310 × 🦆
> 220 pink   ? blue → **b**
> 45 red
>
> *It's back to the duck race from page 4.*
>
> 2) Decide what maths is needed:
> - Find **b**: b = 310 − 220 − 45 = 45
> - Find 45 as a percentage of 310:
>   45 ÷ 310 × 100 = 14.5161... = **14.52%** (2 dp)

Now Try This

1) Fred cycles 14 km in 28 minutes. How long would it take him to cycle 26 km at the same speed?

   Fill in the gaps to show how to solve the problem.

   Step 1: Find time taken to cycle 1 km: .... ÷ 14 = ...

   Step 2: Find time taken to cycle 26 km: .... × .... = ...

2) Ahmed buys some pies for £2.89 each. The total cost is £14.45.
   Tick the calculation that works out the number of pies. Explain your choice.

   £14.45 − £2.89 ☐   £2.89 ÷ £14.45 ☐   £14.45 ÷ £2.89 ☐

   Explanation: ....

   ....

Assessment Advice

What Maths is Needed?

3) Sam is wallpapering a 9-metre wide wall. The wallpaper is 50 cm wide. How many strips of wallpaper will he need?

   In words, explain the calculations you would need to do to answer this question.

   ....

   ....

4) A sofa is 6 feet long. What is its length to the nearest centimetre? 1 metre ≈ 3.28 feet.

   Step 1: Find sofa length in metres: .... ÷ 3.28 = ...

   Step 2: Convert the length to cm: .... × .... = ...

5) The organisers of an event have forty-seven 750 ml bottles of champagne. How many 125 ml glasses can they fill?

   Tick the method you could follow to solve the problem.

   Do 47 + 750, then add on 125 ☐   Do 750 ÷ 47, then divide the result by 125 ☐

   Do 47 × 750, then subtract 125 ☐   Do 47 × 750, then divide the result by 125 ☐

6) Su sits a test with 42 questions. She answers every question and gets $\frac{3}{7}$ of them correct. How many questions did she get wrong?

   In words, explain the calculations you would need to do to answer this question.

   ....

   ....

   ....

Notes

Mixed Practice 1

Best get started then... have a go at these questions to test the range of your maths knowledge.

1) The table below shows the number of visitors to a cafe each week over 7 weeks.

Week	1	2	3	4	5	6	7
Number of visitors	2660	2546	2256	2681	2557	2689	2487

a) In which week did the cafe have the most visitors?

....

b) Find the median number of weekly visitors to the cafe.

....

2) Calculate:

a) 3.15 + 2.974

b) 16.54 − 5.829

c) 22.354 + 57.99

d) 49.218 − 38.593

e) 5.54 × 0.4

f) 9.864 ÷ 0.2

3) Alesha has a pot containing $8\frac{1}{2}$ litres of paint. She uses $2\frac{3}{5}$ litres to paint a wall, and $3\frac{7}{10}$ litres to paint a table. How much paint is left in the pot?

....

....

Mixed Practice 1

4) Johan is building a shelf. The diagram shows one of the brackets for the shelf.

   a) Calculate the size of angle *x*.

   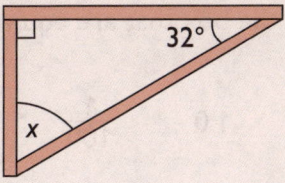

   ....

   b) The shelf is 4 feet and 10 inches long. Use the conversions 1 foot ≈ 30 centimetres and 1 inch ≈ 2.5 centimetres to convert this length into centimetres.

   ....

5) The table below shows shoe size and waist size for a group of men.

Shoe Size	10	9	11	8	13	8	12	13	10	10	9
Waist (inches)	32	32	40	38	34	36	38	32	36	40	30

   a) Complete the scatter diagram to show this data.

   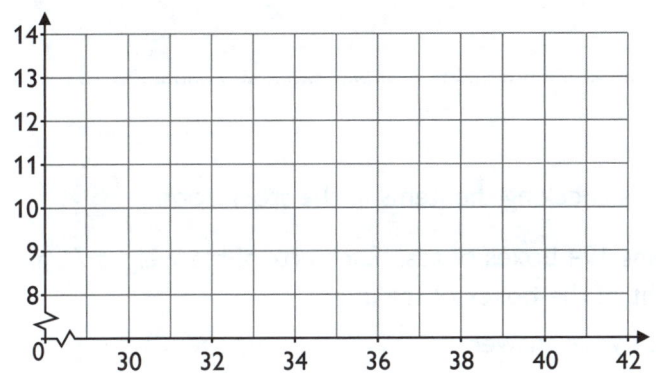

   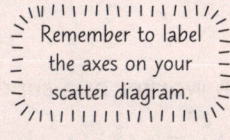
   Remember to label the axes on your scatter diagram.

   b) A student says, "The larger someone's waist size, the larger their shoe size is likely to be." Her teacher does not agree. Does the scatter diagram suggest that the student or her teacher is right? Explain your answer.

   ....

   ....

Notes

Mixed Practice 2

The more practice you do, the easier the questions will seem, so give these questions a go.

1) Circle the values in the box that are equivalent to the percentage.

   a) 10%   0.1   1.0 $\frac{1}{100}$ 0.01 $\frac{1}{10}$ 0.5 $\frac{2}{20}$

   b) 2.5% $\frac{1}{4}$ 0.25 $\frac{5}{200}$ 0.04 $\frac{1}{40}$ 0.025 $\frac{2}{20}$

2) A clothing shop is having a sale.

   a) A jacket is on sale at a price of £84. The original cost of the jacket was £120.
      What is the sale price as a fraction of the original price?
      Give your answer in its simplest form.

      ....

   b) A pair of jeans is on sale at 20% off. The original cost of the jeans was £76.
      Calculate the sale price of the jeans.

      ....

3) A worker at a supermarket is checking the items in the stock room.

   a) The stock room contains 194 boxes of tea. Each box of tea weighs 71 g.
      What is the total weight of the boxes of tea in g?
      Use estimation to check your answer.

      ....

      ....

   b) A crate contains 22 464 g of chocolate eggs. Each chocolate egg weighs 39 g.
      How many chocolate eggs are in the crate?
      Use estimation to check your answer.

      ....

      ....

Mixed Practice 2

4) The diagram on the right shows the net of a 3D shape.

   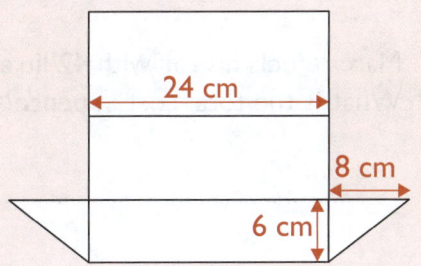

   a) What 3D shape will the net make?

   ....

   b) Calculate the volume of the 3D shape.

   ....

5) Use a calculator to work out each calculation. Give each answer to 2 decimal places.

   a) 15.55 × 0.22 − 2.17

   b) 82.75 + 16.8 × 4.23

   c) 4.51 + 9.65 ÷ 1.22 − 7.7

6) The table below shows the prices (to the nearest pound) of laptop computers sold by an electronics store.

   a) Complete the table.

Price (£)	Frequency	Midpoint	Frequency × Midpoint
101-400	14		
401-700	19		
701-1000	21		
1001-1300	16		
Total			

   b) Estimate the mean price of a laptop computer in the store. Give your answer in pounds, to the nearest penny. Show your working.

   ....

Notes

Mixed Practice 3

Another round of mixed maths questions. Make sure your answers have the right units.

1) Marc refuels his car with 42 litres of petrol. The price of petrol is 136.5p per litre. What is the total cost in pence? Write down the formula you use.

   ....

   ....

2) Angelica is running in a marathon. A scale drawing of part of her route is shown below.

   a) The real distance between points A and B is 180 m.
      What is the scale of the scale drawing as a ratio in its simplest form? Show your working.

      ....

      ....

   b) It takes Angelica 45 seconds to run from point A to point B.
      Calculate Angelica's speed between these points in m/s (metres per second).

      ....

3) A cylindrical block of ice has a volume of 1.20 m³ and a radius of 0.48 m.
   The density of ice is 917 kg/m³.

   a) Calculate the mass of the ice block.

      ....

   b) The height of the ice block is given by $h = V \div \pi r^2$,
      where V = volume of the ice block and r = radius of the ice block.
      Work out h. Give your answer in metres to 2 decimal places.

      Use the π button on your calculator, or use π = 3.14.

      ....

      ....

Mixed Practice 3

4) A snack food is advertised as containing 25% less salt than its original recipe. It now contains 0.3 g of salt.

   a) Calculate the amount of salt in the snack's original recipe.

   ....

   b) The maximum recommended daily intake of salt is 6 g.
   Express the amount of salt in the new snack recipe as a fraction of this value.

   ....

   c) A special packet of the snack food is advertised as containing 40% more than the standard packet. The standard packet contains 27 g of the snack. How much of the snack, in g, does the special packet contain?

   ....

5) The lists below show the masses of potatoes in two bags, bag A and bag B.

   Bag A: 151 g, 143 g, 143 g, 152 g, 201 g, 171 g, 143 g, 186 g, 171 g, 163 g, 194 g

   Bag B: 114 g, 191 g, 155 g, 155 g, 132 g, 144 g, 151 g, 132 g, 184 g, 196 g, 132 g

   a) Complete the table below. Give your answers to the nearest whole number.

Bag	Range (g)	Mode (g)	Median (g)	Mean (g)
A	....	....	....	....
B	....	....	....	....

   b) One of the potatoes in bag A is chosen at random.
   Calculate the probability that the chosen potato weighs more than 170 g.
   Give your answer as a percentage, to 2 decimal places.

   ....

Notes

Mixed Practice 4

Percentages, proportion, pay and probability — it's all about the Ps in this set of questions.

1) Write these proportions as percentages.

   a) 8 out of 20

   b) 112 out of 400

   c) 17 out of 68

   ....

2) A recipe requires butter, flour and water in the ratio 2 : 3 : 1.
   If 104 g of butter is used, how much flour is needed for the recipe?

   ....

3) The heights of two groups of people (group X and group Y) are measured.
   The data for group X is:
   1.74 m, 1.81 m, 1.64 m, 2.03 m, 1.88 m, 1.83 m, 1.53 m, 1.76 m, 1.68 m

   a) Complete the table below by putting the data from group X in ascending order.

Group	Smallest								Largest
X (m)	....	....	....	....	....	....	....	....	....
Y (m)	1.47	1.63	1.77	1.91	1.91	1.94	1.99	2.00	2.01

   b) Which group has more variable heights?
      Justify your answer, stating the range for each group.

      ....

      ....

   c) Which group is smaller on average? Use the median to explain your answer.

      ....

      ....

4) A worker earns £17.26 per hour. How much money do they earn if they work for 7.5 hours?

   ....

Mixed Practice

Mixed Practice 4

5) Look at the shape drawn on the grid:

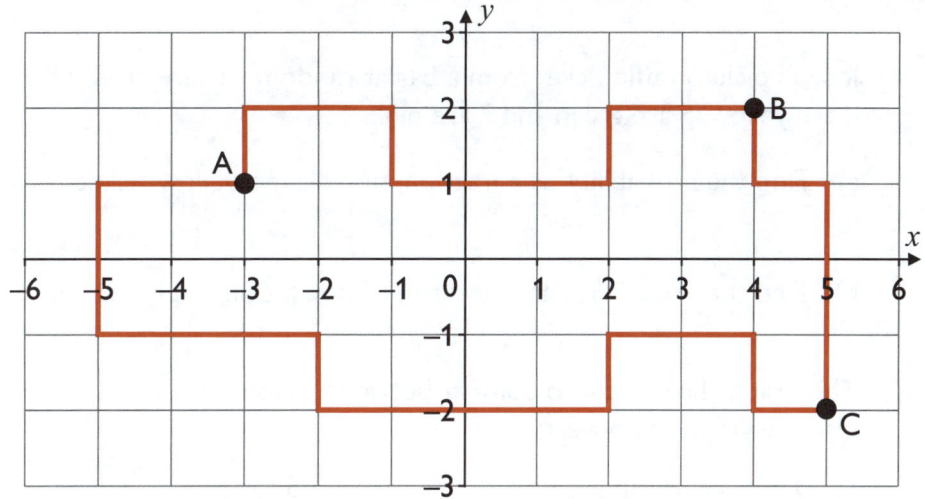

a) Give the coordinates of these points:

A (............, ...)   B (............, ...)   C (............, ...)

b) Each square on the grid is **1 centimetre** tall and **1 centimetre** wide. Work out the perimeter of the shape.

....

6) Ivan and Padma are playing a dice game. Ivan uses a 20-sided dice, marked with the numbers 1-20. Padma uses a 12-sided dice, marked with the numbers 1-12.

a) Each face of Ivan's dice is a triangle. A face is 1.4 cm wide and 1.2 cm tall. Calculate the surface area of his dice.

....

b) Ivan rolls the 20-sided dice. He scores if the face shows a multiple of 3. Padma rolls the 12-sided dice. She scores if the face shows a number more than 6. Who is more likely to score? Explain your answer.

....

....

Notes

Mixed Practice 5

You'll often have to use a few different maths skills to answer a question. Have a crack at these ones...

1) Joseph picks a raffle ticket from a bag at random. There are 20 tickets in the bag. 8 are yellow, 5 are green and 7 are pink.

   a) Find the probability, as a fraction, of picking a yellow ticket. Give your answer in its simplest form.

   ....

   b) Find the probability, as a decimal, of **not** picking a pink ticket.

   ....

2) This graph shows how to convert between gallons and litres. Use the graph to convert:

   a) 2.7 litres to gallons.

   ....

   b) 0.4 gallons to litres.

   ....

   c) 2.4 gallons to litres.

   ....

3) On a winter's night at midnight, the temperature is −8.1 °C. The next day at midday, it is 5.4 °C. Calculate the difference between these temperatures.

   ....

4) Kaitlin is given information about the angles marked in this company logo:

   • The two angles add up to 360°.

   • Angle *a* is 30° larger than a right angle.

   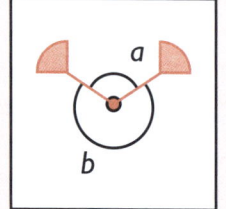

   In fact, the angles around a central point will always add up to 360°.

   Work out the size of angle *b*.

   ....

Mixed Practice 5

5) Copy out each calculation. Draw a pair of brackets to make the calculation correct.

   a) 9 + 5 × 15 = 210

   b) 11 × 5 + 3 ÷ 4 = 22

6) The scatter diagram shows the weights and heights of a group of people.

   a) What type of correlation is shown?

   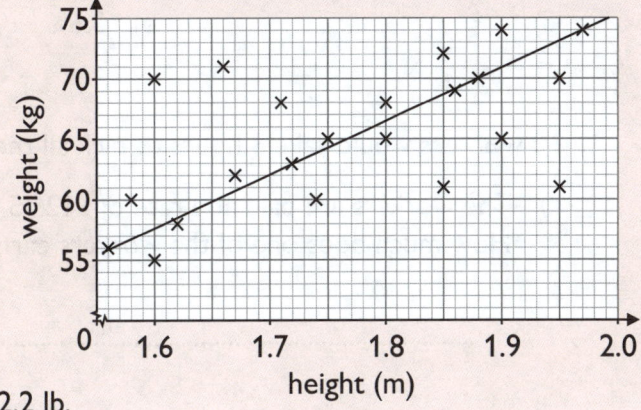

   b) Use the graph to predict the weight, to the nearest lb, of a person who is 1.7 m tall. Use the conversion 1 kg ≈ 2.2 lb.

7) A market trader offers two different boxes of laundry powder, as shown in the diagrams. Box 1 costs £5 and Box 2 costs £4.

   Which box is the better value?
   Support your answer with calculations.

   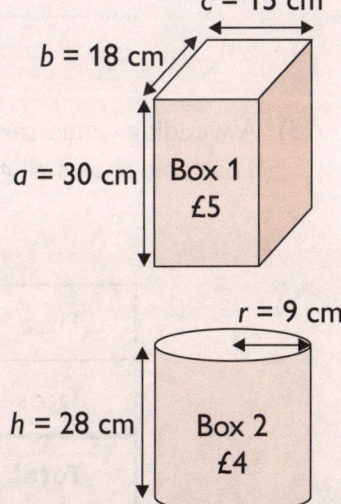

   Box 1: $a = 30$ cm, $b = 18$ cm, $c = 15$ cm — £5

   Box 2: $r = 9$ cm, $h = 28$ cm — £4

Notes

Mixed Practice 6

You're halfway through the book — you're doing great...

1) For each of the values below, write an equivalent decimal.

   a) 25% .... b) $\frac{1}{10}$ .... c) 40% ....

   d) $\frac{3}{5}$ .... e) 3.6% .... f) $\frac{12}{16}$ ....

2) 60 workers would take 3 hours to pick all the fruit in a field.

   a) The workers are paid at a rate of £12.75 per hour.
      How much does one of the workers earn in 3 hours?

      ....

      ....

   b) The fruit needs to be picked in no more than 4.5 hours.
      What is the minimum number of workers needed? *Assume all workers work at the same rate.*

      ....

      ....

3) A wedding venue serves a choice of pizza or tacos for guests in the evening.
   The table shows all guests at the wedding and their choice of food.

	Aged 40 and under	Aged over 40	**Total**
Pizza	12	20	....
Tacos	16	....	26
Total	....	....	....

   a) Complete the table.

   b) A person aged over 40 is chosen at random.
      What is the probability they chose tacos?

      ....

Mixed Practice 6

4) Tao and Rita win £112.49 and split the money in a ratio of 4 : 3. How much does Tao get?

　...

5) The diagram shows the net of a cuboid.
   It is drawn using a scale of 1 : 20.
   Each square has side length of 0.4 cm.
   Give the dimensions of the real cuboid.

   　..

   　..

   　..

   　..

   　..

6) Cillian is stacking identical cubes on top of each other to make a tower. A tower made from 15 cubes is 141 cm tall. How tall is a tower made from 27 cubes?

　...

7) Gita and Lesley are training for a race.

   a) Gita runs 153.25 metres in 31.58 seconds.
      Calculate her speed in metres per second (m/s).

      Give your answers to 2 decimal places.

   　...

   b) Lesley runs at a speed of 6.51 metres per second for 12.64 seconds.
      Work out how far she ran in metres.

   　...

Notes

Mixed Practice 7

Keep going... test the depth of your maths knowledge with this set of practice questions.

1) The lengths of vehicles in a car park are listed below.

   4.37 m, 3.86 m, 4.37 m, 4.09 m, 3.71 m, 4.31 m, 4.37 m, 4.31 m

   a) Put the values in order from shortest to longest.

   ....

   b) What is the mode and median vehicle length?

   mode: ....   median: ....

2) The diagram on the right shows the net of a 3D shape.

   a) Name the 3D shape formed by the net.

   ....

   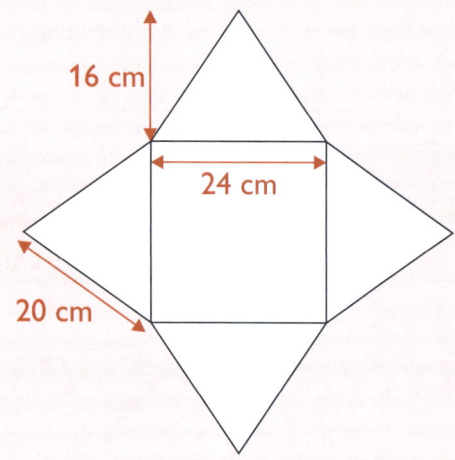

   b) Calculate the perimeter of the net.

   ....

   ....

   c) Calculate the total area of the net.

   ....

   ....

3) A factory packages drink cans in boxes of 6.
   How many boxes are needed to hold 664 524 cans?
   Use an estimation to check your answer.

   ....

   ....

Mixed Practice 7

4) All of the workers at a company are given a pay rise.

   a) Anya is given a 3.2% pay rise. Her annual salary after the pay rise is £33 122.04. Calculate her annual salary before the pay rise.

   ....

   b) Last year, Jalil's annual salary was £28 650. He receives a 6.7% pay rise. He thinks that his new annual salary is higher than Anya's new annual salary. Is Jalil correct? Show your working.

   ....

   ....

5) Dolls are sold in mystery boxes. Each box contains one of three designs of doll (A, B or C) and one of two accessories (a hat or a bag).

   The probability of getting doll B is 0.5. The probability of getting a hat is 0.2. The probability of getting doll C **and** a hat is 0.02.

   Use this information to complete the probability tree diagram below.

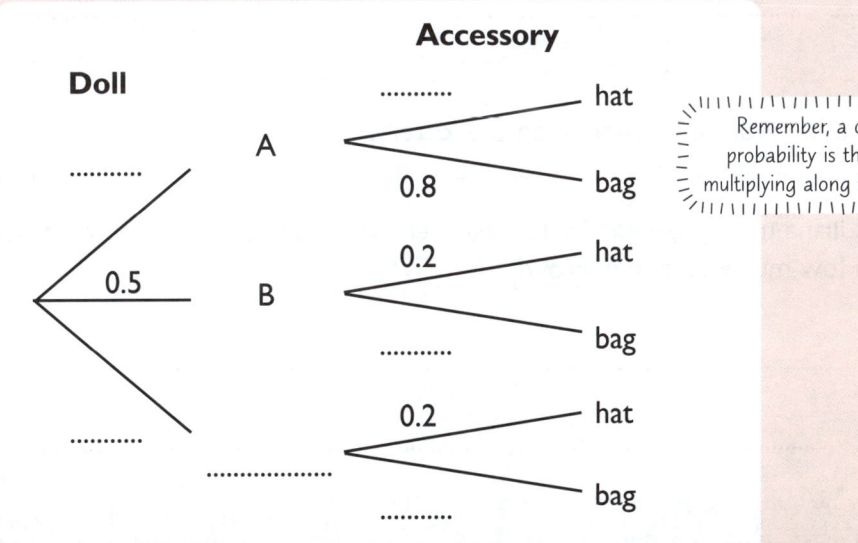

Remember, a combined probability is the result of multiplying along the branches.

Mixed Practice 8

Another set of questions on lots of different topics. That's why it's called mixed practice.

1) Plot the following points on the axes. Label each point.

   A: (4, 2)

   B: (5, −2)

   C: (−6, 1)

   D: (−7, −3)

   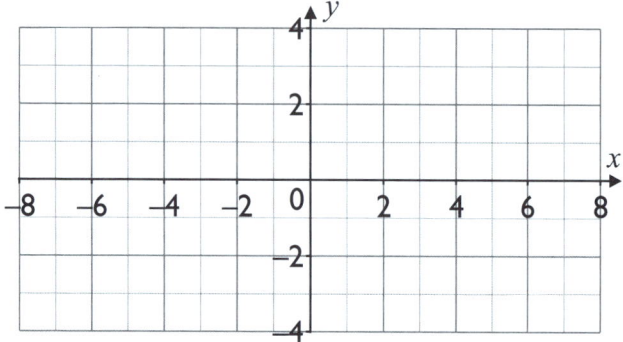

2) How long does a 5.5 kg turkey take to cook according to this formula?

   time to cook in minutes = (mass of turkey in kg × 20) + 90

   ....

3) A company renovating a bathroom charges £2893.10 without VAT. Calculate the total charge including VAT. (VAT is 20%)

   ....

   ....

4) Liliana has won some money on the lottery. She will use the money to pay back a loan, and will also put some in a savings account.

   a) Liliana must pay £655.20 to clear her loan. This is 30% more than she borrowed. How much did she borrow?

   ....

   ....

   b) Liliana puts £13 500 in a savings account. It has an annual compound interest rate of 3.8%. How much will be in the account after 3 years? Give your answer to the nearest 1p.

   ....

   ....

Mixed Practice 8

5) The data on the right shows the prices of shoes in two different shops, A and B.

Shop A	£73.95	£39.95	£49.00	£66.50	£97.00
Shop B	£41.00	£81.50	£65.00	£54.95	£75.50

a) Find the mean price and range of prices for each shop.

Shop A: ....

Shop B: ....

b) Give two conclusions based on your answer to a).

....

....

6) The sculpture below is made from one 2 m wide cube, and eleven 1 m wide cubes.

a) Draw the plan view and front elevation of the sculpture on the grids below. 1 square on the grid = 1 m in real life.

Clearly show the changes in depth on your drawings.

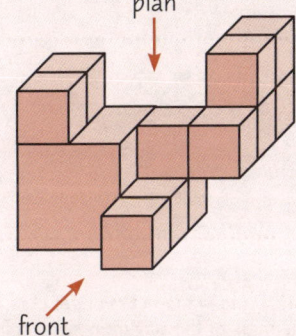

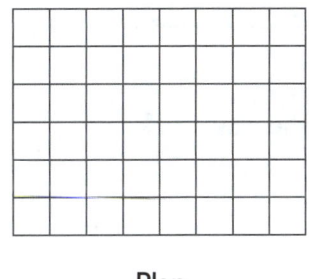
Plan

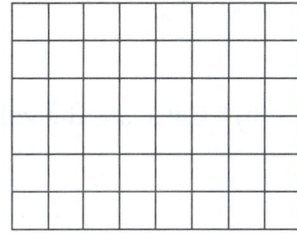
Front Elevation

b) The 2 m wide cube has a weight of 480 kg. Each 1 m wide cube has a weight of 120 kg. Give the weight of the 2 m wide cube as a fraction of the total weight of the sculpture. Give your answer in its simplest form.

....

....

Notes

Mixed Practice 9

Yet more mixed practice questions to test which topics you've got to grips with. Enjoy.

1) The table shows the temperature in four ski resorts on January 1st.

Ylläs	Whistler	Vail	Chamonix
−19 °C	−4 °C	−14 °C	0 °C

   a) A pair of snow boots are designed to be used in a minimum temperature of −10 °C. Which ski resorts in the table would the boots have been suitable for on this day?

   ....

   b) The temperature in London on January 1st was 3 °C. What was the difference in temperature between London and Vail?

   ....

2) Jane has a 3.2 kg cuboid block of clay. Its width is 40 cm, depth is 10 cm and height is 5 cm.

   a) Calculate the surface area of the clay block.

   ....

   ....

   b) Calculate the volume of the clay block.

   ....

   c) Calculate the density of the clay in g/cm³.   *Convert the mass of the clay from kg to g first.*

   ....

   ....

   d) Jane divides the clay between her three children in the ratio of their ages. James is 5, Abeba is 7 and Sarah is 8. How many grams of clay does Abeba get?

   ....

   ....

Mixed Practice 9

3) A website has 8 T-shirts for sale at these prices: £7, £5.50, £9, £10, £7, £7, £7.50, £10

   a) Find the mode and median T-shirt price.

   Mode: ....

   Median: ....

   b) A T-shirt is selected at random for an advert.
   What is the probability that it costs more than £8? Give your answer as a decimal.

   ....

4) Work out the following. Give your answers as mixed numbers in their simplest form.

   a) $3\frac{2}{3} - 1\frac{1}{6}$

   b) $4\frac{6}{7} + 1\frac{2}{5}$

5) A bakery makes and decorates cakes.

   a) It takes 3 employees 18 minutes to decorate a batch of cakes.
   How long would this take 2 employees? Assume the employees all work at the same rate.

   ....

   b) A bottle contains 425 ml of syrup. 12 cakes need 300 ml of syrup.
   How many cakes will a whole bottle be enough for?

   ....

   c) A recipe requires 16 fluid ounces (fl oz) of syrup. Is there enough in the bottle of syrup for this recipe? Explain your answer. 1 fl oz ≈ 28.4 ml

   ....

Notes

Mixed Practice 10

Good job, you've made it to the final set of questions. Now show what you can do.

1) Chris sets up a moth trap each night in July.
The table below shows the number of moths trapped each night.

You only get whole moths, so this group is for 3, 4, 5, 6 or 7 moths.

No. of moths (m)	Frequency	Midpoint	Frequency × Midpoint
3 ≤ m ≤ 7	10	....	....
8 ≤ m ≤ 12	13	....	....
13 ≤ m ≤ 17	6	....	....
18 ≤ m ≤ 22	2	....	....
Total	....		....

a) In June, Chris caught an average of 9 moths a night. Does the data suggest that he caught more moths on average in July than in June? Support your answer with a calculation.

....

....

b) Chris's scale drawing of one of the moths he traps is shown on the right. He uses a scale of 1 : 3. Calculate the real-life width of the moth.

....

2) Three corners of a parallelogram ABCD are plotted on the axes below.

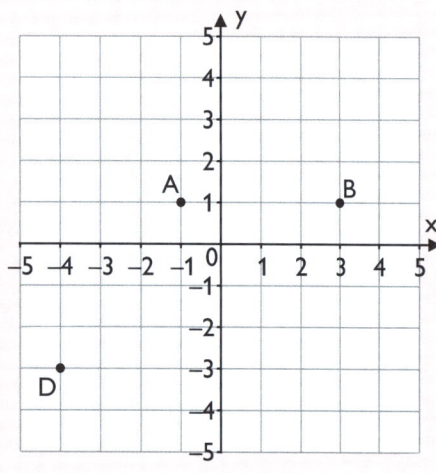

a) Give the coordinates of corner C. ....

b) One of the angles in the parallelogram is 53°. Find the other 3 angles.

....

....

....

Mixed Practice 10

3) The times, in seconds, for five competitors in a 100-metre wheelchair race are given below.

   20.27, 18.91, 18.72, 20.5, 18.07

   a) Order these times from shortest to longest.

   ....

   b) A sixth competitor records their time as 19.455 s. Round this time to 2 decimal places.

   ....

   c) Calculate the average speed of the fastest competitor in metres per second.
   Give your answer to 1 decimal place.

   ....

4) Work out the following.

   a) $3 + 2 \times 4^2 + 1$

   ....

   b) $40 - \dfrac{2 \times 15}{3^2 - 4}$

   ....

5) Kailash is on an island and wants to visit the coast with the lowest chance of rain.
   A weather forecast gives the probability of rain on each coast:

   North: 0.27   **East:** $\dfrac{8}{25}$ **South:** 32.5%   **West:** $\dfrac{1}{4}$

   Which coast should he visit? Show your working.

   ....

   ....

   ....

Notes

Gaps and Revision Tracker

You or your teacher can use the space below to make a note of any topics you need to brush up on. Come back here often for a reminder of what you need to work on and to keep track of your progress.

Topics to Work on	😐	🙂	😉
	☐	☐	☐
	☐	☐	☐
	☐	☐	☐
	☐	☐	☐
	☐	☐	☐
	☐	☐	☐
	☐	☐	☐
	☐	☐	☐
	☐	☐	☐
	☐	☐	☐
	☐	☐	☐
	☐	☐	☐
	☐	☐	☐
	☐	☐	☐
	☐	☐	☐
	☐	☐	☐

Gaps and Revision Tracker

Topics to Work on	😐	🙂	😉
	☐	☐	☐
	☐	☐	☐
	☐	☐	☐
	☐	☐	☐
	☐	☐	☐
	☐	☐	☐
	☐	☐	☐
	☐	☐	☐
	☐	☐	☐
	☐	☐	☐
	☐	☐	☐
	☐	☐	☐
	☐	☐	☐
	☐	☐	☐
	☐	☐	☐
	☐	☐	☐

CGP

www.cgpbooks.co.uk